Texas Signs On

Number Seventy-five:
*The Centennial Series of the Association of
Former Students,
Texas A&M University*

TEXAS
SIGNS ON

The Early Days of Radio and Television

Richard Schroeder

Texas A&M University Press
College Station

Library of Congress Cataloging-in-Publication Data

Schroeder, Richard (Morton Richard)

Texas signs on ; the early days of radio and television / Richard
Schroeder. — 1st ed.

P.   cm. — (Centennial series of the Association of Former
Students, Texas A&M University ; no. 75)

Includes bibliographical references and index.

ISBN 0-89096-813-6 (alk. paper)

1. Broadcasting—Texas—History.   I. Title.   II. Series.

PN1990.6U5S36   1998

384.54'09764—dc21   97-46657

CIP

To my mother
Doris Elizabeth Stallard Schroeder

Contents

Illustrations

Preface

In 1915 teenager Alfred P. Daniel saw a radio tower being built across Buffalo Bayou in Houston. He rode his bicycle to the site, watched, and asked workers every question he could. Daniel went home and started constructing his own radio. Within a few years, he founded WCAK, the first radio station in Houston, and later radio station KPRC.

Daniel's illustrious career began in his childhood; this book was born in mine. One morning in 1949 at Sanger Elementary School in Waco, my fourth-grade class was taken into a room used for projecting movies. We saw a ten-minute film concerning a subject about which none of us had heard: television. After the film, my mind would not think of anything else; I was enthralled.

A few months later my family drove to Dallas for the weekend. At an aunt's house in the corner of the den was a strangely shaped cabinet. It was a television receiving set. I asked that it be turned on but was informed that WBAP-TV, the only station on the air, did not start broadcasting until five or six o'clock in the evening. After much begging and pleading, Mother and Dad agreed to stay until I saw something on that screen. What I actually saw was unimportant.

At that time I was only a "looker-in," the name the Federal Radio Commission gave to television watchers in the 1930s. That was until a Saturday in 1953, when the Waco newspaper announced that radio station WACO was going to have an open house and demonstrate "television." I jumped on my bike, pedaled eight blocks to the station, and just stayed. Lee Glasgow, manager of WACO, had bought television equipment confident that he would soon be granted a construction permit for the first station in Waco. The equipment was assembled in a radio studio. Two cameras and a switcher fed images to monitors. I stood in the corner all afternoon, watching. The station's staff was polite; they showed me the cameras and how they worked. I even touched one, but they finally made me leave. They needed to lock the doors.

The next summer Aunt Mina and Uncle Earl took me to WBAP-TV in Fort Worth. The staff had us sit on studio seats in front of the control room windows. There was an old "shoot-'em-up-bang-bang" on the monitor; everything was dimly lit and quiet. After a few minutes, four men came through a door. Lights were turned on, two men stood behind cameras, and one stood between. Johnny Hay took his place behind a small counter with two or three food items before him. Then, before I could comprehend what was happening, the movie on the monitor faded. Hay's image faded in, the man between the cameras pointed his finger, and Hay delivered a sixty-second commercial. For months I "replayed" that in my mind.

After KANG-TV and KWTX-TV started operations in Waco, I hung around every dark corner. I watched the stations televise the news, a farm program, a talent contest, a cooking show, a program for women, and *Uncle Elihu and P. J. Possum*. At home I attempted to construct a look-alike television camera on the back of my wagon. I continued visitations of WBAP-TV during college. One evening I even got in the way of Frank Mills while watching cameramen operate those monstrous TK-40A color cameras for *Teenage Downbeat* and the six o'clock news—and was barred from the station.

During my college studies and throughout my teaching career, stories, events, and observations about historical happenings in Texas broadcasting heightened my interest and curiosity. I listened to stories of Dr. Brinkley on his Mexican border station talking to the continent. I read about KUHT-TV in Houston first using television to educate. I missed school and watched the Harry Washburn murder trial, knowing then that it was making history. I heard remarkable accounts of Gordon McLendon's fantastic "recreations." I visited announcer Johnny Kay in the KRLD radio studios. I learned about "pirate" radio stations in the Lone Star State from a professor. I looked over the shoulder of an engineer at WBAP-TV who toiled one hour aligning the first color cameras in Texas. I stood next to a video engineer at KRLD-TV playing taped commercials on that station's first Ampex 1000 videotape recorders.

The realization of the number and importance of historic events in Texas broadcasting answered many questions—and begged others. What factors indigenous to Texas culture, its environment, its society, and its broadcasting personnel, staffs, and administrators inspired and drove the profession to produce such an inordinate number of industry firsts; attracted numerous social, medical, and religious outcasts to border stations across the Rio Grande; and made early broadcasters believe they could operate pirate radio stations and get away with it? This project is not a sociopsychological analysis of the human spirit striving to be first, rebelling against authority, trying what has never been attempted, etc. Nevertheless, these pages may offer an inquisitive reader some insight.

Texas broadcast history has been prolific, unique, revolutionary, colorful, interesting, and "cutting edge." It has made substantial contributions to the industry nationwide. Much has been written concerning this subject. There are dissertations on McLendon and Jim Byron and *The Texas News*, two master's theses on the Texas State Network, books on Mexican border stations and Bob Wills, individual and station histories, and many other works. Absent was the one single collection encompassing all historic events related to broadcasting in Texas. Before preparing my dissertation, I found graduate school papers a stilted collection of historical facts. For my dissertation I interviewed the professionals in WBAP-TV's history—those who lived it. Their recollections, stories, and anecdotes were fascinating, informative, and, in their own words, a history of the station. I learned to appreciate and write historical preservation text composed of basic facts clarified, demonstrated, exemplified, and strengthened by the insights of working professionals.

Texas Signs On is a documentation of historical facts fortified with personal histories, recollections, and experiences. In industry terms, it is a spin-off of my dissertation. Preparation for the book entailed investigating the holdings of all known historical society collections; newspaper clip files; station historical files; and university, city, and county special collections and archives. Personal recollections came from interviews of seventy-one individuals whose careers were in Texas broadcasting. Some important limitations existed. Predictably, large amounts of information, especially station files, have simply been thrown away. Many professionals had died. Information known to exist was inaccessible. Certain newspapers did not allow access to morgues and clip files. Nevertheless, sufficient information exists.

It was necessary to accept another obvious limitation, that no one study can find or use every historical fact about every broadcast station in Texas, so this project concentrated on the major events, the earliest or first events, the unique or unusual events, the events which exemplify all manner and size of stations, and personal experiences. There was never any intention or desire to write a dictionary of every radio and television station in the state. Within these self-imposed guidelines, all pertinent materials were used.

It is believed this preservation was successful. It presents an accurate and realistic account of the first fifty years of Texas broadcasting. It allows the reader to form an image of this industry during that formative, evolutionary period. It is a factual work, a tribute to the people who made it work. *Texas Signs On* is a continuation of my observation of Texas broadcasting history. For me it is the best alternative to not having been there and personally participated.

Acknowledgments

I must thank the many people who helped produce this book. They include Alex Burton and Paul Porter, who helped initiate it; the people who assisted me at libraries, archives, and special collections; those who wrote to me and sent materials or leads; and especially the seventy-one individuals who were willing to sit down with me and talk for hours—some for five and six—about their lives and experiences in Texas broadcasting.

Morton Richard Schroeder
Greenville, Texas

Texas Signs On

Pre-Regulation Broadcasting

The Beginnings to 1927

In the winter of 1921–22, several seemingly unimportant and unrelated events happened in the state of Texas that were to help shape the state and its people for decades to come. In fact, the effects are still evident. This is a history of these and other related events.

- R. M. Lane, a writer for the *(Dallas) News,* was invited to the "executive chamber" and introduced to the executives of the publications. He was given an easy chair and a good cigar. The group's spokesman asked, "Tell us something about this thing—radio. What is there to it, and how long do you think it will last?"[1]
- One evening in Houston, Alfred P. Daniel, a longtime radio enthusiast, spoke into "a set rigged up in a Quaker Oats box." Daniel broadcast the request "Anyone hearing this telephone me!"[2]
- On Thanksgiving Day, William P. Clarke of Waco was seated before a crystal radio receiver with its headphones on his ears listening to a series of dots and dashes. Clarke then took off the headphones, walked over to a window, and with a megaphone yelled out the window, "Texas forward pass; eight-yard loss."[3]
- Amon G. Carter, owner and publisher of the *Fort Worth Star-Telegram,* had been warned by friends that a little black box would kill newspapers. He asked his circulation manager, Harold Hough, what he knew about radio.

  "Hardly anything at all," admitted Hough.

  Carter told Hough, "If this radio thing is going to be a menace to newspapers, maybe we had better own the 'menace.'"[4]

These events and these people, with their lack of knowledge of and experience in broadcasting, were soon to have a great influence on the development of radio, or "wireless," in Texas. Hough and Carter started WBAP in Forth Worth. Lane and the *News* officials began WFAA in Dallas. Daniel built WCAK in Houston. Clarke wrote one of the first newspaper columns on radio in the state and started WWAC in Waco.

On which date an individual in the state first put together a crude crystal receiver and listened to a signal from a distant place is not known. The earliest mention of "wireless" is in newspaper clip notes of Louise Kelly of Wichita Falls. Kelly, a public schoolteacher on her own fruition, helped preserve the history of the city and the surrounding area for decades by clipping articles from local newspapers. She indicated that on July 12, 1910, a "wireless station may be established here."[5]

The first documented use of "wireless" was in 1911 at the Agriculture and Mechanical College of Texas at College Station. From that year until 1921, wireless was "experimented with" by amateurs in their homes, at armed forces bases, in radio clubs, at educational institutions, in businesses, etc.

After the first license for a broadcasting station was granted on August 4, 1921, to WRR in Dallas, additional stations were quickly established. From 1921 to 1927, when the U.S. government passed legislation regulating the industry, dozens of radio stations were established by individuals on their back porches, newspapers wanting to increase circulation, universities as experiments in classes, churches to spread their messages, electronic and department stores to sell receivers and give buyers something to which to listen, hotels for publicity, entertainment parks and movie theaters for publicity, and many others, including, interestingly enough, automobile repair shops. Many of these early stations at one period or another were unlicensed by the U.S. Department of Commerce. Many began and ended before Washington and most local people knew. Some of these stations left a record of their existence; many did not.

The years between 1921 and 1927 were the initial period of growth for radio stations and listening audiences, when the fledgling industry determined what it was to be, what it could and would program, and what role it could play in the lives of Texans. It was during this period that certain stations established themselves as the dominant force in the industry for decades to follow. This put them in a position to dominate the development of television many years later.

The Development of "Wireless"

"Wireless" has been known for more than a hundred years. Around 1850 Michael Faraday of England discovered a "field of force" theory in studying the relationship between electricity and magnetism. James Henry in the United States found that electrical experiments conducted in one part of his house affected instruments in a distant room. On April 30, 1872, William Henry Ward of Auburn, New York, received a patent for a telegraphic tower. The patent read: "Different towers may be erected on the different continents; and if they are all what is technically called hooked on—that is to say, connected to the earth—a signal given at one tower will be repeated at all the towers, they being connected with each other by the aerial current." Nathan B. Stubblefield transmitted voice as early as 1892 in Murray, Kentucky. Reginald Aubrey Fessenden, who earlier had worked for Thomas Edison, was employed by the U.S. Department of Agriculture to test the idea of disseminating weather information by wireless. He is credited with superimposing voice and music on a high-frequency "carrier" using a continuous wave generator in Brant Rock, Massachusetts, on Christmas Eve, 1906.[6]

In 1899 in Detroit, Michigan, Thomas E. Clark put an antenna on top of his Banner Laundry building and began broadcasting to lake steamers under the name Clark Wireless. Clark soon began voice transmission and assisted William E. Scripps in establishing a wireless station for the *Detroit News,* which was later to become WWJ. In 1906 Lee de Forest transmitted a voice across his laboratory room to a receiver employing a vacuum tube detector. In San Jose, California, Charles "Doc" Herrold's first antenna was knocked down during the San Francisco earthquake of 1906. In 1909 his radio was the main attraction of his university engineering classes. His experiments in voice transmission grew into weekly programs—each Wednesday evening with news bulletins and phonograph records. His station became KQW, and later KCBS in San Francisco, California.

As more amateurs experimented in wireless and interference grew, government involvement was inevitable. The Wireless Ship Act of 1910 required oceangoing steamers leaving a U.S. port to have on board an efficient apparatus for radio communication in good working order and a skilled operator. The Radio Act of 1912 was the first radio-licensing law passed by the U.S. Congress. It required a transmitting station to have a license from the Secretary of Commerce and Labor, the operator to have a license and to be a U.S. citizen, amateurs to broadcast at 200 meters or above, and the Secretary of Commerce to assign wavelengths and time limits. This was the basis of radio law until the Radio Act of 1927.[7]

David Sarnoff, contract manager for American Marconi, wrote a memorandum dated September 30, 1915, describing a "Radio Music Box." This apparatus would have amplifying tubes and a loudspeaking telephone mounted in one box that could be placed in the parlor or living room. This box, or "household utility," was to bring music into the home by wireless.[8]

On April 6, 1917, with a state of war existing with Germany, all amateur radio apparatuses in the United States were ordered "shut, dismantled, and sealed." Almost all of radio was taken over by the navy and army. Except for a few specially licensed stations, amateur radio stopped. The ban lasted until mid 1919.

In the early 1920s radio grew rapidly. Parts and receivers became available: first crystal sets, then sets with tubes. Public buying increased steadily. In 1921 the Department of Commerce adopted a "broadcasting" class of radio station. In January of 1922 there were eight broadcasting stations in the United States. By July there were seventy-six. All broadcasting stations were assigned to transmit on two frequencies. A wavelength of 360 meters (833.3 kilocycles) was allocated to "news, lectures, and entertainment." A wavelength of 485 meters (618.6 kilocycles) was reserved for "government functions" like crop and weather reports. The two frequencies received their placement because of maritime radio service. Because 500 kilocycles was the frequency for the optimum average length of a ship's antenna, that was selected as the international distress frequency. When broadcasting began, the frequencies below 500 kilocycles were in use, so the frequency band of 550 kilocycles and up was selected.

In the early 1920s radio listeners quickly developed a desire to hear stations from distant places. In many cities, one night a week was declared "silent night." After Dallas's broadcasting stations began operations, "silent night" in that city was Wednesday after 3:00 P.M., or after a local baseball game ended. At one period, all stations in Texas and, possibly, the United States were "silent" on Wednesday nights because "DX" listeners (a term for people who like to listen to distant radio stations) wanted to try to hear radio from Europe or abroad. "Silent night" was observed until 1927.

As the number of stations grew, having all stations on 360 meters was untenable. Some stations escaped interference by operating slightly above or below the assigned frequency. Other operators would "dial around" the frequencies until they found a "clear spot." Herbert Hoover, secretary of the Department of Commerce, was unsure of his powers under the Radio Act of 1912. The law did not give him any discretion in the issuing of licenses. He could not refuse to issue a license, regulate station power, or make regulations.

In the spring of 1922, the Department of Commerce ran out of three-letter combinations for station call letters and started assigning four-letter combinations. In addition to 360 meters, 400 meters was made available. Any station using that frequency was a Class "B" station, which could operate with 500 to 1,000 watts but could not use phonograph records. This rule tended to create an elite class of well-financed stations. Poor station owners had to stay on the heavily congested 360 meters. Early in 1923 Hoover changed the allocation rules. High-power stations with 500–1,000 watts would be allotted various channels between 300 and 545 meters. Some time-sharing of frequencies was necessary. Stations not over 500 watts would operate between 222 and 300 meters. All low-power stations remained on 360 meters.

On January 12, 1922, the American Telephone and Telegraph Company got involved in broadcasting. AT&T started "public radiotelephone broadcasting." WBAY in New York City was first to try "toll broadcasting." Because of transmission problems, a different transmitter with different call letters was used. On August 16, 1922, WEAF became the first station to sell commercials.[9]

The Beginnings of Texas Radio

In March of 1911, J. B. Dickinson, manager of the Texas Fiscal Agency at San Antonio, informed F. C. Bolton, a professor of engineering at the Agriculture and Mechanical College of Texas in College Station that a "wireless system was expected to reach the college in a few days." 5AC was installed by F. E. Duchareme. The wireless system was to link the college with Texas University in Austin. It was also meant to instruct students at both schools in radio transmissions. "I had in mind to place the institution in wireless communication with a number of cities in the state," said Dickinson. "The company has now decided to erect a station in Austin in close proximity to the state university in order to connect the two greatest schools in the South by wireless." Finished on May 17, 1911, the station was, according to Dickinson, "the greatest and most complete wireless station possessed by any institution of learning in the world."[10]

In 1912 the Physics Department at Texas University in Austin used the donated equipment to maintain a ham transmitter. In 1915 Dr. S. Leroy Brown, professor of physics, licensed 5JA for experimentation in his high-frequency laboratory. The station used Morse code to broadcast crop and weather reports and "kindred subjects." 5JA was situated in a shed attached to "Y" Hall, the physics shack. Brown broadcast from 1915 until the federal government suspended broadcasting during World War I. Then Brown received a special permit to operate. The station temporarily closed when Brown was transferred to supervise armed forces ground work.[11]

Alfred P. Daniel, who established radio in Houston in the 1920s, became interested in wireless before World War I. Daniel was seventeen in the summer of 1915. He climbed into his tree house one day and saw a radio tower being built across Buffalo Bayou. "I pedaled my bike as fast as I could over to see that tower," Daniel said. "I asked the DeForest people, who were building it, all about radio. Then I went home and started rigging up my own sets." During World War I he enlisted as a radio specialist. The army sent Daniel to Texas University in Austin, the country's first military school for radio technicians.[12]

Jack McGrew, KPRC general manager in Houston, remembered Daniel and his experiments: "Alfred P. Daniel . . . built a little radio station in his garage. He had no call letters; this was before call letters. Alfred put his station on the air, and his programs consisted of playing a phonograph in front of a microphone.

There were dozens of people around the country doing the same thing. They were all amateurs having fun listening to each other because there wasn't anyone else to listen. . . . When the Department of Commerce clamped down, that shut him down."[13]

In 1918 a gypsy fortune-teller at a party at Ellington Field in Houston told Daniel, "Get into radio work and stay there." In 1919 Daniel, who was licensed for amateur station 5ZX, was a member of the Houston Radio Club. The club conducted schools to teach beginners how to make radio receivers. James L. Autry, Jr., one of the first amateur radio operators in Houston, was president. In 1916 he was licensed for 5ED, located at #5 Courtlandt Place. Clifford Vick, another club member, had a license for 5ZO. Hurlburt Still was licensed for 5DL, located at his business, Hurlburt-Still Electric Company, at 1101 Capitol Avenue. In 1920 Daniel was also licensed for 5AO, located in his home at 2704 Brazos Street.[14]

William Penn Clarke of Waco had set up 5ZAF and 5FB in his home at 728 North 13th Street before World War I. Clarke "lived, slept, and ate radio," said Frank Baldwin, editor of the *Waco Tribune-Herald*. "Back in 1917, a short, hesitant, but pleasing, half-pint of human nature came up the stairway to ask us would we be interested in radio." Baldwin hired Clarke to write a column on radio.[15]

In 1916 Henry "Dad" Garrett, an electrical engineer at the Dallas Fire Department, conducted experiments in wireless. He was interested in transmitting information to fire trucks while they were fighting fires. A problem occurred at a fire at the Buell Lumber Company in south Dallas in 1912. Every fire truck in Dallas was dispatched, and when a second fire was reported in north Dallas, it was impossible to contact the south Dallas firefighters because telephone lines had been destroyed. Fire equipment could not be transferred to north Dallas. Garrett equipped his car with a small homemade receiver and began experimenting with receiving messages. He tried an antenna made of fine wire wrapped around two small poles inserted in the running boards of his car. Soon Garrett received weak voice transmissions at White Rock Lake in northeast Dallas transmitted from the central fire station five miles away.

Bennett Emerson, a Western Union employee, was interested in wireless. His radiophone equipment, 5DU, which could send and receive, was located in his home on Wendelkin Street in Dallas. Frank M. Corlett, another Western Union employee, built a small amateur transmitter in his home at 1101 East Eighth Street. By 1920 Corlett and Emerson were broadcasting messages for the fire department. On election night, April 5, 1921, Mayor Sawnie R. Aldridge broadcast a "Thank-You" speech from Emerson's home. Aldridge thanked thousands of Dallas voters for their support during his election campaign.[16]

The 1921 Department of Commerce *Radio Service* listed Corlett with two licenses. Station 5XG used varied wavelengths, and 5ZC was licensed on 200 and

425 meters. Emerson held the license for 5ZG, transmitting on 200 and 375 meters. The Agriculture and Mechanical College of Texas had 5XB, transmitted on 300, 500, and 600 meters; and 5YF transmitted on wavelengths 200 and 375 meters. Other 1922 Texas radio stations were:

5YI   Rice Institute, Houston, on 200 and 375 meters.

5ZX   Alfred P. Daniel, Houston, on 200 and 375 meters.

5ZAF   William P. Clarke, licensed on 200 and 375 meters, and 5FB, 728 North 13th Street, Waco.

5CY   Howard Hughes, Jr., 3921 Yoakum Boulevard, Houston, with 500 watts.

5DW   Dave Ablowich, Jr., 2109 Park Street, Greenville, with 500 watts.

5ES   M. L. Goldstein, 1225 Washington Street, Waco, with 750 watts.

5GM   Morton H. Sanger, 1806 Washington Street, Waco, with 500 watts.

5IR   C. B. Baxter, Grafton Street, Dublin, with 500 watts.

5NY   Charles Henry Garrett, 2000 Prairie Avenue, Dallas, with 500 watts.

5PL   Herbert E. Gebhardt, 1506 Buena Vista Street, San Antonio, with 500 watts.

5VR   William E. Branch, 2609 Clarence Street, Dallas.

5ZH   J. Laurance Martin, 605 East 4th Street, Amarillo.[17]

WRR: Dallas

In July of 1921 Emerson sold his equipment to the city of Dallas for $250.00, establishing the first municipally owned radio station. Transmission under the direction of Police and Fire Signal Superintendent Garrett was from the second floor of the Central Fire Station at 2012 Main Street. On August 4, 1921, a provisional license for a Land Radio Station, Limited Commercial Class, was issued to the city of Dallas for WRR (Where Radio Radiates; some people thought the call letters stood for We Reach Rockwall) by the Department of Commerce, Bureau of Navigation, with 100 watts transmitting power. *It was the first broadcasting station in the state of Texas,* the fifth or sixth station in the United States.

Fire dispatchers, bored by long periods of inactivity, began to tell jokes, read from the newspaper, comment on the weather, and play records. This assured fire personnel that the primitive equipment was working properly. They grew to like the music and entertainment—and so did the public. A regular audience began to develop. Requests for entertainment were received. Soon, specific hours were dedicated to various musical programs. John Marley and other local musicians were asked to broadcast. The comedy team of "Honey Boy and Sassafras" performed. Dr. George W. Truitt of the First Baptist Church broadcast his Sunday sermons.[18] A representative station's schedule for two days in 1925 was:

Sunday, October 11, 1925

6:00–8:00 P.M.	Jack Gardner's Orchestra
8:00–9:00 P.M.	Mrs. Ralph Porter and Assisting Musicians
9:00–10:00 P.M.	Jack A. Davis, Pianist. James Wood, Tenor

Monday, October 12th, 1925

12:00–1:00 P.M.	Weather, Early Markets, Music by Hartwell Jones, Pianist
3:00–3:30 P.M.	Markets, Cotton, Sports
5:00–5:30 P.M.	Police Reports, Markets
6:00–6:30 P.M.	Bedtime Stories. Silent until November 1st
6:30–7:30 P.M.	Adolphus Hotel Orchestra from main Dining Hall
8:00–9:00 P.M.	Lee Walling, Baritone, and Assisting Musicians
9:00–10:00 P.M.	Magnolia Band.[19]

One of the earliest listeners was J. Frank Thompson of Cleburne. Thompson began tinkering in radio in 1920, building crystal receiving sets that allowed him to listen to WRR when it started broadcasting in 1921. Because of the demand from local people, he was soon building twenty crystal radios a day. The receivers were sold at Cash Zimmerman's auto parts store in Cleburne. In 1922, after studying radio for two years, Thompson and his friend Horace Graham started designing and building on the second floor of Zimmerman's store a battery-powered receiver with a loudtalker. They wanted a radio that could be heard by all persons in a room, not just the one using the headset. The unit was the first radio of its type in the state. Zimmerman told Thompson that if he would display the radio in the store, thousands of people would come to listen to and see it. Shortly, RCA and Westinghouse started building similar battery-driven radios that sold for fifteen dollars. During the depression years, that was too expensive for many Cleburne residents. Consequently, residents continued to gather at Zimmerman's store to listen to Thompson's radios.[20]

In 1925 the city of Dallas discovered that the transmitter for WRR would no longer meet new frequency requirements of the Department of Commerce. The

The people of Cleburne gathered at Cash Zimmerman's auto parts store as early as 1921 to listen to WRR on J. Frank Thompson's radios, built on the second floor above the business. Courtesy Layland Museum, Cleburne, Texas

city could not fund the $12,000 needed to keep the station on the air and decided to abandon WRR. Public protest changed that decision. Within ten days a petition with 5,000 signatures asked Police Commissioner L. S. Turley to continue operating the station. A committee was formed to raise money. It was headed by Edwin J. Kiest, owner of the *Dallas Times Herald,* and George B. Dealey, president of the *Dallas Morning News.* The newspapers operated KRLD and WFAA. The funds were raised, and on October 5, 1925, WRR was granted a new license to operate on 246 meters with 500 watts. In 1931 the police and fire departments started operating 5AZQ specifically to transmit police and fire calls and information. The call letters were later changed to KVP.[21]

The Department of Commerce's *Radio Service* edition of June 30, 1922, lists for the first time a classification for "Stations Broadcasting Market or Weather Reports (485 Meters) and Music, Concerts, Lectures, Etc. (360 Meters)." Sixteen stations were licensed in the state:

WDAG	J. Laurance Martin; 605 East Fourth Street, Amarillo, Texas	360m
WCM	University of Texas; Austin, Texas	360m, 485m

WRR	City of Dallas, Police and Fire Signal Department; Dallas, Texas	360m, 485m
WDAO	Automotive Electric Co.; Ervay and Corsicana Streets, Dallas, Texas	360m
WFAA	A. H. Belo and Co.; Dallas, Texas	360m, 485m
WPA	*Fort Worth Record*; Fifth and Throckmorton Streets, Fort Worth, Texas	360m, 485m
WBAP	Wortham-Carter Publishing Co. (*Star-Telegram*); Fort Worth, Texas	360m, 485m
WHAB	Clark W. Thompson (Fellman's Dry Goods Co.); Galveston, Texas	360m, 485m
WCAK	Alfred P. Daniel; 2504 Bagby Street, Houston, Texas	360m
WEAY	Will Horwitz, Jr.; 612 Travis Street, Houston, Texas	360m
WEV	Hurlburt-Still Electric Co.; McKinney Avenue and San Jacinto Street, Houston, Texas	360m, 485m
WFAL	*Houston Chronicle* Publishing Co.; Houston, Texas	360m, 485m
WGAB	Q R V Radio Co.; 1213 Prairie Avenue, Houston, Texas	360m
WTK	Paris Radio Electric Co.; 42 South Main Street, Paris, Texas	360m
WFAH	Electric Supply Co.; Port Arthur, Texas	360m
WCSR	Alamo Radio Electric Co.; 608 West Evergreen, San Antonio, Texas	360m[22]

Early Radio Stations

The establishment of WRR helped precipitate the building of broadcasting stations throughout the state. By the end of 1922, many towns and cities had one, two, three, even five stations—some with licenses, some without. As the decade progressed, stations generally evolved toward establishing themselves as a powerful faction of the state, or toward extinction. Many self-financed stations operated by individuals struggled and eventually stopped broadcasting. They could not keep up with larger stations with transmitters of ever-increasing power and wider varieties of available talent and programming. Without the backing of some business, small stations could not compete. The following stations began broadcasting in the 1920s but did not exist as of National Frequency Reallocation Day:

3 A.M., November 11, 1928. For some of these stations, the only record of their existence is the station's call letters and town.

Abilene	WQAQ, 1923, *Abilene Daily Reporter*
Austin	WNAS, 1923, Texas Radio Corp.
	KFQM, 1924
Beaumont	WMAM, 1923, Beaumont Radio Equipment
Beeville	KFRB, 1925, Hall Brothers Rialto Theater
Dallas	KFFZ, 1923, Al. G. Barnes Amusement
Denison	KFPQ, 1924
	KFQT, 1924
El Paso	WPAT, 1923, St. Patrick's Cathedral
Fort Stockton	KGFL, 1927
Galveston	WIAC, 1923
	KFOQ, 1924
	KFUL, 1925, Thomas Goggan & Brothers Music
Houston	KFYJ, 1925, Houston Chronicle Publishing
Laredo	WWAX, 1923, Wormser Brother
Orange	KFGX, 1923, First Presbyterian Church
Plainview	WSAT, 1923, Plainview Electric Company
Port Arthur	WPA, 1924, Gulf Refining Company
San Benito	KFLU, 1925
Stanford	WOAZ, 1923
Tyler	WOAP 1923, Tyler Commercial College
Wichita Falls	WKAF 1923, U. S. Radio Supply[23]

Large stations like WBAP in Fort Worth, WFAA in Dallas, WOAI in San Antonio, and KPRC in Houston started a steady evolution to power and dominance. These stations, which started at low power, sometimes 5 watts, soon increased that power to 50 watts, then perhaps 250 watts, then 500 watts, until, by the end of the decade, most transmitted with 50,000 watts. Additionally, as a station increased power, the Department of Commerce allowed it to change to a different frequency sufficiently lowering its chances of interference from other stations' signals. All small, lower-powered stations continued to broadcast on one extremely congested frequency.

Fortunately, sufficient but fragmented information exists about some radio stations that were established in the 1920s. All these fragmented histories taken as a whole portray how stations began, evolved, and dominated. They show the type of individuals who formed stations, what they considered to be the value of this new industry, the kind of programming that was developed (and how), the problems faced by owners and personnel, the talent used, the conditions endured by the performers, what adjustments stations made to survive and eventually start making money, and listener reactions. Unfortunately, no single station left a comprehensive history; most did not leave any.

Amarillo

Three stations were operating in Amarillo in the early 1920s. WDAG, which started in 1922, was owned by J. Laurance Martin and the National Cycle Company, located at 605 East 4th Street. Martin had earlier operated 5ZH. In 1923 he also operated WRAU, licensed by the *Amarillo Daily News*. In the mid 1920s WRAU was absorbed by WDAG. Martin believed in using the two stations as a promotional arm of the city of Amarillo and the West Texas panhandle area. He believed that "every city of any importance in the United States has broadcasting stations." He suggested that "every evening in the fall and winter that the temperatures here be given out so that the world may know that Amarillo has a temperate rather than frigid climate." "We are looking forward to inquiries from every Chamber of Commerce and many civic organizations that are desirous to get their communities before the country at large."[24]

WQAC (Where Quality Always Counts) in 1923 was owned by E. R. Gish of Gish Radio Supply, located at 108 East 8th. Gish soon started KGRS (Gish Radio Supply). For a time the station was located on the second floor of a service station owned by Gish. His mode of operation was very casual. If he were broadcasting when a customer drove into the service station, Gish would say, "I've got to sell five gallons of gas." He would go downstairs, leaving nothing being transmitted: dead air.[25] Stan McKenzie, who was born in West Texas, heard about Gish:

> This guy in Amarillo ran a service station, and he lived above the service station. He would get up there and turn on his apparatus, and he would broadcast; and I don't know what he did. It was a one-man show in the twenties. He would be broadcasting, and then he would tell his audience, "Oh, I see I have a customer downstairs. I'm going to sign off now, and I'll be back on in a few minutes." He would go down, sell gas to the fellow and get his money, go back upstairs, and turn his station back on again.[26]

Gish tried to scoop the local newspaper. He would get an early edition of the newspaper, rush to the service station, turn on the transmitter, and read the newspaper to his audience.

On National Frequency Reallocation Day in 1928, WDAG and KGRS began sharing 1410 kilocycles transmitted from two different localities with 1,000 watts.

The stations were supposed to share time by mutual agreement. Problems arose when both wished to broadcast the same event. This happened in the early 1930s when both broadcast the same football game with two different transmitters on the same frequency at the same time. Both announcers were in the same press box, sitting next to each other. The interference for listeners was terrible. There were so many complaints that the personnel of both stations were arrested by the sheriff for trespassing. In the mid 1930s, both stations merged to form KGNC.[27]

Austin

"Mary, I know Catalina is the cat's meow, but you must get back to Los Angeles and prepare your trousseau." This was the first radio voice message at Texas University. After World War I had closed it, 5JA was again licensed in 1921 by George R. Endress, resident architect. "We were giving a dinner party the night George Edwin (a university student) picked up the message," recalled Mrs. Endress. "When he came into the house and told us, one of the men at the party said in astonishment, 'You mean you actually heard those voices?'" The station was located at 711 West 23rd Street in Austin. It was rebuilt with newer equipment from the physics department storeroom. The antenna was now a tower atop "Y" Hall. "One of the station's services," stated Mrs. Endress, "was to air the university's football games. My husband and George Edwin used to sit up till all hours listening to it."[28]

Dr. Brown, upon returning to the university from service in the war, spent $1,000 to build and license WCM on March 22, 1922; it became Austin's first broadcasting station. It was licensed "in order that it might disseminate market reports and transmit student messages." WCM originally broadcast with 500 watts on 833 kilocycles (360 meters). In 1922 Endress also received a Special Land Station license for 5ZAG at the same address. On September 30, 1922, the station owned "two KW De Forest Radio and Telegraph instruments and a one-half KW Navy Simons spark transmitter. It also has a CR 7 and CR 6 receiving set with loudspeaker."[29]

In 1924 WCM was assigned 1120 kilocycles with a reduced power of 250 watts. At the same time, the station was taken over by the Texas Markets and Warehouse Department in Austin. On October 27, 1925, WCM was relicensed back to the university and became KUT, broadcasting on 1300 kilocycles with 300 watts. A new transmitter was built by Robert Shelby and a new studio was constructed by Paul Boner, both university employees. Shelby later became chief engineer for the National Broadcasting Company and developed that network's system of compatible color television. Boner would be a consultant to many broadcasting stations constructing new facilities.

KUT broadcast three nights a week from 8:00 to 10:00. Evening programs were discussions by university faculty, state officials, and agricultural experts. The station broadcast concerts featuring musical organizations from Austin and the university. There were no sponsored programs or commercials. On Sunday mornings KUT broadcast the St. David's Episcopal Church services. During football season the station broadcast the university's home games. Orland Murphy was KUT's sole announcer. In early 1927 while temporarily off the air, KUT was assigned 1290 kilocycles. On November 11, 1928, National Frequency Reallocation Day, KUT was assigned 1120 kilocycles. KUT's transmitter was now atop the Driskill Hotel in downtown Austin.[30]

In 1927 Congress had enacted a law that required radio stations to use crystal control to stay on frequency. Crystal control cost five hundred dollars. The university decided that radio was becoming too expensive and sold KUT to two Houston businessmen, the English brothers, on February 19, 1929. The transmitter had moved from the Driskill Hotel to an eight-by-ten-foot abandoned office on a golf course on Georgetown-Fiskville Road. The brothers sold KUT to the Rice Hotel in Houston on December 9, 1929. Later that year KUT merged with KGDR of San Antonio. KUT was operating on 1500 kilocycles with 100 watts. The Rice Hotel sold the station to Hearst Publications in 1932. The call letters were changed to KNOW.[31]

Beaumont

"This is station KFDM, the Magnolia Petroleum Company, Beaumont, Texas, radiocasting its first concert." The announcer was J. W. Newton, known as "Magnolene Mike." It was Wednesday, October 1, 1924, opening night for KFDM (Kall for Dependable Magnolene). There was a prayer by Rev. Frank Rhea and a dedication speech by Mayor J. Aurton Barnes. He praised the refinery for its public spiritedness. Then the announcer turned the program over to the "Oil Right Doctor," Dr. Harry Cloud, and the Magnolia Band. The program also had the Magnolia "Scrap Iron Quartet"; Mrs. Refuge Raye Loving, who sang; and Joe Landry and the "Saxophone Sextet."[32]

Broadcasting by the band of the Magnolia Petroleum Company Refinery started earlier on November 13, 1923. The band transmitted a program over 391 miles of the company's private telephone line to the Magnolia Building in Dallas from where it was relayed to WFAA. A similar concert was broadcast on March 1, 1924. The program consisted of several classical numbers, marches, fox trots, and waltzes and finished with "Magnolia Blossom," composed by Cloud. The station also promoted the city of Beaumont. Its name was spelled several times to preclude letters addressed to "Vromont," "Vormont," and "Bomont" as from the November 13 concert. Special announcements emphasized Beaumont's "thirty-foot channel to the sea."[33]

Refinery manager E. E. Plumly started the station and the band as a goodwill

The smaller of the three studios used by KFDM, Beaumont, in the 1920s. Courtesy Tyrrell Historical Society Library, Beaumont, Texas

measure. The transmitter and studio of KFDM were in the penthouse atop the Main Office building. The transmitter was a Western Electric No. 101-B, 500-watt set operating on a wavelength of 360 meters. A large studio, the whole second floor, was "just a box" with no sound treatment and a few windows overlooking the refinery. A small studio was in the refinery's commissary building, and another studio, announcer's booth, and control room were in a corner of the "roof garden" of the Hotel Beaumont. The commissary studio was draped with burlap for sound absorption. The downtown roof garden studio had floor-to-ceiling windows overlooking the street. To reduce noise and reverberation, the windows were draped with full-length velvet curtains. None of the studios was air conditioned.[34]

The station manager was also the refinery safety officer. The station's engineer was Clyde Trevey, who also operated WOD, the company's ship communication station. Since both stations used the same antenna, Trevey had to schedule the public station's broadcasts between ships. G. E. Zimmerman, the radio technician, came to the station from WFAA in Dallas. The band members, for payroll purposes, were listed as employees of the refinery's paint department. Their job was to paint tank cars. The station broadcast Tuesday and Friday at noon and at nights. The band provided the bulk of the entertainment. KFDM did not carry advertising, only institutional announcements for Magnolia.[35] Jack McGrew, one of two announcers at KFDM in the late 1920s, recalled:

> KFDM broadcast no commercials. We occasionally reminded our listeners that KFDM stood for "Kall For Dependable Magnolene," the trade name of the gasoline marketed by Magnolia Petroleum Company, but that was it—no hard sell, no tigers in tanks. In fact, the first initiative toward honest-to-goodness commercial advertising on KFDM came from an outsider, the owner of Beaumont's leading dry goods merchant, the White House Department Store, who called the station manager one day and asked if he might be interested in selling a few "advertisements" calling attention to a sale. After conferring with his superiors, the manager agreed to sell a few "advertisements." What the rates and other conditions were—I have no idea—I only know that Gailey and I were given short announcements to read at certain intervals.
>
> The copy was certainly mild enough—in fact, as the practice of selling advertising time became more widespread, both stations and networks imposed pretty severe restrictions on what might be said. Usually, what resulted in most cases was what might be called today, somewhat condescendingly, institutional advertising—no elaborate product description, no disparagement of competitors, no prices of merchandise, and, most certainly, no mention of products or services of questionable taste. Instead, sponsors' names became part of program titles: a popular dance orchestra became the "Cliquot Club Eskimos" ("Cliquot Club" being the name of ginger ale) and the singing duo Billy Jones and Ernie Hare became "The Interwoven Pair" ("Interwoven" was a brand of men's socks). My own favorite was "The Palmolive Hour." The featured singers were "Paul Oliver" and "Olive Palmer."[36]

KFDM presented news and sometimes election returns. McGrew relates how those returns were "acquired" on one occasion:

> The Texas Election Bureau, a cooperative enterprise of major Texas newspapers, had a virtual lock on the election reporting process in the state and was not about to share its monopoly with upstart competitors. *The Beaumont Enterprise* and *Beaumont Journal* enjoyed close relations with county and city offices where the votes were counted. I had a hand in "pirating" the local returns. *The Enterprise-Journal* plant was on a downtown street across from the

Central Fire Station, and it was the newspaper's custom to project local and state returns from a "magic lantern" type projector mounted in a second story window to a large screen hung on the fire station wall for the benefit of those citizens interested enough in the election to come downtown and watch. There was a drugstore halfway down the street with a pay telephone and a clear view of the screen. On election night, I commandeered the telephone and relayed the returns to the station as rapidly as they were posted. After that, the newspapers abandoned the practice.[37]

On October 2, 1925, KFDM presented a birthday celebration. The program started at 7:00 P.M. and ran until 2:12 A.M. One of the most popular sections of the show was the trip by the "Famous KFDM Special." This musical segment followed a mythical railway to Cuero, Texas, where it was received by the citizenry of the city. Then it cheered its way to Lampasas, Texas, where the mayor gave the "Special" a hearty welcome. The train then traveled to Sulphur, Oklahoma; Punta Gorda, Florida; and many other cities before returning to Beaumont. The entire musical trip took forty-five minutes. The "Special" originated from "Castor Oil Clarence's" harmonica imitating a locomotive. This was the third trip for the Special. This trip carried 6,500 "radiophans" who wrote and asked for reservations.[38]

While KFDM ran a very tight ship, McGrew discovered that many other stations ran a more low-key operation. While doing a sports remote in Galveston, McGrew went to the local station to hire an engineer, and met Roy G. Clough. It was a Sunday, and Clough was the owner, operator, engineer, and staff. While McGrew was talking to him, Clough was also playing records over the air. If the record came to an end, without saying anything to the listeners, Clough would pick up the tone arm, turn the record over, put it back down on the revolving turntable, and drop the arm onto the record. All this was done "on the air." "Sometimes he turned the same record back and forth, two or three times," remembered McGrew. This was the only radio station in town, and "it was pretty loose . . . strictly informal," stated McGrew.[39]

College Station

5YA, which had been operated since 1911, had become 5XB in 1921. (The *Y* had designated an educational institution; the *X* in the new name designated an experimental radio station.) On Thanksgiving Day, Texas University traveled to College Station to play the Agriculture and Mechanical College of Texas. The football game had been a rivalry for many years. There was heightened interest in College Station and Austin to "keep up" with the game because the Aggies were undefeated. Earlier in 1921 several colleges in the Southwest Conference began exchanging weekly reports of sporting events by amateur radio for school publication. Tulane University in New Orleans, Rice University in Houston, and Oklahoma University in Norman participated with the Agriculture and Mechanical College of Texas and Texas University. For that Thanksgiving game, W. A. Tolson, chief operator of 5XB at the university in College Station, along with Harry Saunders and Franklin K. Matejka, as well as George E. Endress, Charles C. Clark, W. Eugene Gray, and J. Gordon Gray at 5XU at Texas University, decided to transmit a play-by-play report from Kyle Field.[40]

To broadcast reports in Morse Code from the stadium to Austin, a twisted-pair wire was strung between the electrical engineering building on the campus to the football stadium. A telegraph key was installed in the press box. Even though the key was approximately three quarters of a mile from the "Rock Crusher" transmitter, "keying" it at the stadium activated the rotary spark gap transmitter at the station, which operated on "about 375 meters." The operator at the stadium listened to the transmutations on another circuit. A second twisted-pair wire was run from the home of a professor and amateur radio operator who lived next to the stadium. The operator/reporter could hear his transmission and was available to receive "breaks" or inquiries from the receiving station in Austin. The operator was Harry Saunders, a Morse operator with Western Union. Tolson, the instigator of the broadcast, did not work it because he was a member of the Aggie Band. He did, however, have to leave the band and race to the electrical engineering building just before halftime to replace a blown fuse in the motor turning the spark gap transmitter.[41]

Because telegraphed code could not keep up with the action on the field, a set of abbreviations was created for the game with the help of Aggie coach D. X. Bible. A broadcast of "TB A 45Y" meant "Texas Ball on the Aggie's 45-yard line." "T FP 8Y L" was interpreted in Austin, and in many other places, as "Texas forward pass; 8-yard loss." What started as a "point-to-point" description of the game became a broadcast to many amateur stations within a 300- to 400-mile radius. Known to be listening were NKB in Galveston, which "broke in" during halftime wanting the score because the operator had been busy with maritime traffic and had lost track; 5NI in Greenville; 5RS in Cladwell; 5JA/5ZAG and 5QY in Austin; and 5ZAF in Waco, operated by William P. Clarke. Clarke installed his receiver at a local newspaper. The reports Clarke received were announced by megaphone to a crowd of interested sports fans who gathered at the newspaper office.[42]

William A. Tolson, who was instrumental in planning the broadcast, helped establish WTAW (Watch The Aggies Win). It was reported that the call letters came from the Department of Commerce, which affixed the first letter, W (as it did all broadcast stations in the early 1920s), and then reversed Tolson's initials for the remaining letters. After graduation Tolson worked in television research

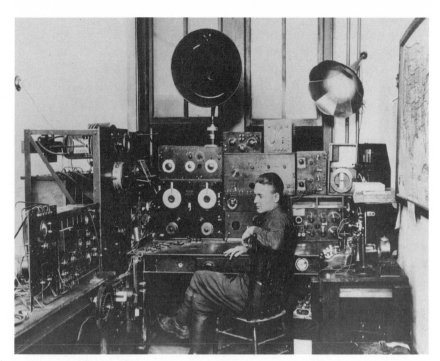

W. A. Tolson, chief operator of 5XB at the Agriculture and Mechanical College of Texas at College Station, with equipment used to transmit the first play-by-play broadcast of a sporting event in Texas. The football game between A&M and Texas University was broadcast direct from Kyle Field in College Station on November 24, 1921. The switch in front of Tolson's knee was remotely controlled by a key at Kyle Field. Courtesy Special Collections, Manuscripts & Archives, Sterling C. Evans Library, Texas A&M University, College Station, Texas

for RCA in Camden, New Jersey. In 1940 Tolson was named a "Modern Pioneer of American Industry" by the National Association of Manufacturers.[43]

Mac Weldon Jeffus worked for WTAW in the late 1920s while he attended the Agriculture and Mechanical College of Texas: "WTAW was on the second floor of the electrical engineering building, so we could use their generators. . . . I was a member of the radio club and I lived in Millner Hall, and the station was in one of those army shacks right down under my window between there and the mess hall." Jeffus saw the remote equipment for WCM in Austin at the inauguration of Governor Sterling. The Aggie band played in the parade and then attended a dance that evening:

They were broadcasting on their little station over there; and the guy had a microphone down on the stage where the orchestra was, and then he had an

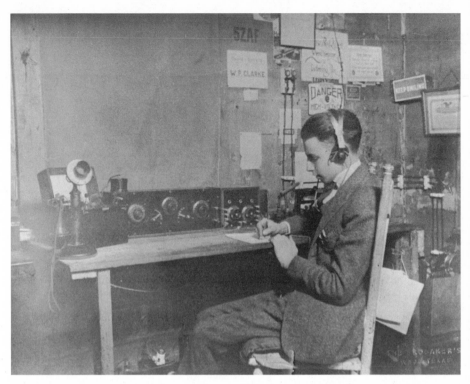

*William P. Clarke, operator of amateur "wireless" station 5ZAF, Waco, receiving the
"coded" account of the first play-by-play transmission of a sporting event in Texas,
November 24, 1921. Courtesy Special Collections, Manuscripts & Archives, Sterling C.
Evans Library, Texas A&M University, College Station, Texas*

announcer's microphone upstairs . . . and every time the orchestra would quit,
he would take these two wires, untie them, and twist the two wires on from the
announcer microphone. Then he'd untie them and twist the orchestra microphone back on when the orchestra started playing again. I went back and told
the chief engineer, "We're a whole lot more up-to-date than that bunch is over
at Texas. We've got a switch in our microphones."[44]

Dallas

WRR had been broadcasting since August of 1921. WDAO, licensed to the Automotive Electric Company, situated at 915 South Ervay, started broadcasting between August of 1921 and June of 1922. It was the second station in Dallas. WFAA
(Working For All Alike), the radio service of the *Dallas News and Journal,* started
on June 26, 1922, as the third station in Dallas.

R. M. Lane, a writer for the *News,* received a telephone call in November of 1921: "Is this the radio man?"

Lane answered, "Yes, what there is left of him."

Lane was summoned to the roof of the *News* building by a person he did not know. Lane was told by the stranger, "Just take a slant at that smokestack and tell me whether or not I could hang a wireless aerial to it."

Lane was led into the "executive chamber" of the *News and Journal* and introduced to the executives of the two publications. He was given an easy chair and a good cigar. The group's spokesman then asked, "Tell us something about this thing—radio. What is there to it? How long do you think it will last?"[45]

WFAA arose from the efforts of Walter Dealey. As a boy he had toyed with telephones made of taut string between tin cans and learned heliographic transmission with small mirrors. He liked to code with pencil tapping. Radio became his hobby. Dealey joined the *News* in 1920 after college. He helped persuade his father in 1922 to invest "in a strange new proposition called radio."[46]

Dealey made friends with Henry "Dad" Garrett, chief electrician for WRR. Dealey was a member of the commission that controlled that station. He persuaded his colleagues to establish WFAA. Garrett loaned the *News* L. B. Henson, who took a tangled mass of wires, generators, condensers, transformers, and other pieces of equipment and built a transmitter that could be a 50-, 100-, or 150-watt station. The transmitter was installed in a nine-by-nine-foot shack on top of the old *News* building. The original antenna stretched from a water tower across the block to a twenty-foot mast on the twelve-story Texas Bank Building. The main antenna was an eight-wire cage, 124 feet long, seven-by-eighteen woven silicon bronze wire. Getting to the roof studio was not easy:

> Visitors and staff alike journeyed three floors by elevator, then climbed a half-floor to the composing room level. They threaded their way through Intertypes, make-up banks, and haughty printers to a steep, narrow steel stair which ultimately reached the proof gallery.
>
> There was usually a rest here to gain breath and fight down the feeling that all should be roped together Alpine-wise before tackling the last stage, another steeper and narrower steel stair which got onto the roof by way of a treacherous step-down. Final progress across the roof was complicated only by the necessity of avoiding clusters of ventilators, skylights, antenna guys, and minor structures housing machinery of either the newspaper or the station. Studio and engineering staff lived in such close proximity that listeners were never in doubt as to the source of mechanical difficulties. Its unpainted wooden table holding the transmitter panel with its five white-faced meters and matching row of little black knobs did not quite bridge the gap between matter and the myster-

ies of sound snatched from the air. The small motor generator hummed outside so shyly that it escaped more than casual notice.[47]

As a youngster, Mac Weldon Jeffus, later an engineer for WFAA, got to tour the station a few months after it started:

I got to go over there and go through the station when they were up on top of the *Dallas News* building on Commerce Street right after they went on the air, and I got pretty well acquainted with Mr. Calhoun. He was the first announcer, and he later won the announcer award for the whole United States. When I got to [Texas] A&M, he sent me a letter about announcing and how to get started.

I went there (WFAA) because I had heard they were on the air. He was a reporter that did announcing on the side. He was down on the first floor. . . . I just went over there one day and asked for Mr. Calhoun, and he came out to see me, shook hands with me, and took me back to the big studio he had which was a curtain . . . hung around the news library—and one carbon microphone on a stand.

Right up above it, in a little wooden building, was a 250-watt transmitter with four tubes in it, and a motor generator under a little box outside the engineering building—and they had a microphone up there where they signed off—and met the two guys, the two engineers, . . . Russie Hall. They did not have any telephone lines up there that I remember; and when they got ready to sign off, Mr. Calhoun would say, "Shut 'er down, Russie" or "Shut 'er down, Eddie." They would kick that generator off and down they would go.

The antenna was up on the old Texas Bank Building and the old MKT building. It was a six- or eight-wire antenna across there; and when they changed their frequency, they had to put up a new antenna. They got the fire department to "bring down" their longest aerial ladder.[48]

The studio trembled and shook from the vibration of the heavy presses. Traffic noise came through the windows. Wooden walls draped with cotton fabric reverberated. The carbon microphone with its ordinary telephone mouthpiece was hooded in a heavily padded box.

Victor H. Schoffelmayer, agricultural editor of the *News,* played the piano one day when a speaker was delayed. He added, "I mustn't be recognized. What do you suppose my farmers would think if they caught me playing the piano?" Count Rubinoffsky played for WFAA for several years and developed a faithful public of admirers. Rubinoffsky traveled to many stations in Texas and would play both on-air and off-air concerts for young audiences.

The original transmitter of WFAA, Dallas, in 1922, located on the roof of the Dallas News and Journal *building. Courtesy Texas/Dallas History and Archives Division, Dallas Public Library, Dallas, Texas*

The station was two weeks old when it broadcast its first prize fight. Benny Leonard successfully defended his lightweight crown against Rocky Kansas at Michigan City, Indiana. Rounds were summarized as they came in off the wire. One listener responded, "You could hear the 'plump' of the gloves, the shuffle of feet on the canvas." More mail was received after one announcer stated, "A beautiful sight. Eddie must have used his antenna polish. Reception should be better now that the rust has been taken off." Writers wanted to know where "antenna polish" could be purchased.

One day a woman climbed to the rooftop studio and asked to see the announcer.

"I am the announcer," stated the man at the microphone. "Did you wish to see me?"

"I did," replied the woman, "but perhaps I had better stick to my imagination."[49]

WFAA broadcast on a frequency of 360 meters, as did all five stations in the Dallas–Fort Worth area. By July 1, 1922, all five agreed on a schedule to divide time. The Dallas stations' (not including WPA's and WBAP's in Fort Worth) schedule on 360 and 485 meters for Friday, June 28, 1922, was:

12:00–12:30 P.M.	WRR	Weather bulletin on 485 meters, followed by music on 360 meters
12:30–12:45 P.M.	WFAA	Weather bulletin on 485 meters
12:45–1:10 P.M.	WFAA	Music on 360 meters
1:10–1:40 P.M.	WFAA	Markets, including noon quotations on cotton and quotations on poultry and produce
2:00–3:00 P.M.	WFAA	First baseball bulletins, spot cotton and other market reports, and news bulletins
3:00–3:30 P.M.	WRR	News bulletins, baseball scores, and music
3:30–4:00 P.M.	WDAO	Musical program
6:00–6:30 P.M.	WRR	
6:30–6:40 P.M.	WFAA	Government market report on 485 meters
6:40–7:00 P.M.	WFAA	Baseball scores and news bulletins on 360 meters
7:00–7:30 P.M.	WRR	Police bulletins
7:30–8:00 P.M.	WDAO	Musical program
8:00–8:30 P.M.	WFAA	Musical program
8:30–9:00 P.M.	WRR	Musical program
9:00–9:30 P.M.	WDAO	Musical program
9:30–10:00 P.M.	WFAA	Bedtime story for children, followed by West Texas and Texas-Oklahoma baseball scores and news bulletins[50]

The radio schedule for June 29, 1922, listed "Wedding Ceremony" at 8:30 P.M. On that day, John Henry Stone and Mable Brady were married by Reverend Thomas H. Harper. The bride was at the studio of WDAO, the groom at WRR, and the minister at WFAA. The wedding march was broadcast from WFAA and Reverend Harper read the vows; then, each in turn answered. Hundreds of automobiles filled Ervay and Corsicana Streets near WDAO's location while the ceremony was in progress. A large crowd gathered at Sanger Brothers and several other listening places. The groom claimed his bride in the transmitter room of WDAO.[51]

On July 1, 1922, WFAA moved its studio into the library on the second floor of the *News*. In the library a tent was pitched to kill echoes. Other sound absorption methods had failed. Leaving the glass doors of bookshelves open so the volumes could deaden sound did not work. The tent worked, but it was not perfect. One evening the Bel Canto quartet was singing religious numbers. During the performance the tent came down. The group finished with each of the four men and their accompanist holding one arm up.[52]

Prior to and after WFAA's sign-on date, the newspaper ran articles discussing radio-building techniques. The paper offered a free print of specifications for building a simple radio. The most popular receiver was the "Shut'er Down, Eddie" set. Parts for the receiver cost $7.50. In early radio days, there was little formality between station and listener. That was how the "Shut'er Down, Eddie" set got its name. As Jeffus remembered, that was the order for transmitter engineer Eddie Zimmerman to discontinue broadcasting or "cut the switch." It was the "Star Spangled Banner" of 1922.

Broadcast talent was of varied quality. One businessperson with a flair for music devised a fiddle out of a broomstick, cigar box, bridge, and a long gut string. One citizen came to perform as a one-man band. A young merchant imitated wild creatures like toad frogs, honey bees, mosquitoes, and horseflies. There was a barnyard imitator; he insisted that listeners should be able to identify different breeds of dogs by their barks. One volunteer even aired the sounds of traffic. He challenged the radio audience to follow him through different makes of automobiles and to tell whether trolleys were running empty or loaded by his interpretation of motor hum and wheel clatter. A dependable programming subject was the *Dallas News* presses. They were frequently called upon when programming became dull. A microphone was dangled through the window of the ground-floor press room. Listeners loved it and phoned asking for more. At times, a traveling microphone took a tour of the newspaper plant. Listeners heard the beat of telegraph printers, the clatter of typewriters, the clinking rhythm of Intertype machines, and an occasional description of their operation by department heads.

WFAA went to a higher power, 500 watts in 1929, after Walter Dealey took a vacation with a receiving set and attempted to receive WFAA from different locations in California. He could not. He wired Dallas, "Run all night Friday." Dealey finally received his station, but quickly telegraphed A. Frank Hamm of Western Electric, "Rush 500-watt transmitter by express." On September 29, 1922, WFAA became a Class B station. It was assigned a wavelength of 400 meters. WFAA was now one of the most powerful stations in the country.

By late 1922 the station had moved to its third studio, occupying space formerly used by three editorial offices. All studio surfaces were covered with one-inch felt, held in place by copper wire. A thick carpet deadened the floor. Other surfaces were hung with yellow silk. The carpet was so thick that planks had to be laid when the piano was moved. A trip down the length of the studio generated static electricity charges. A telephone in an alcove permitted the announcer to converse with the operator. Response was by telewriter, scrawled in the control room and reproduced facsimile in the studio.[53]

Robert Z. "Bob" Glass had operated 5MJ in Dallas when he was at Forest Avenue High School. In 1924 he built a 50-watt station, KFOP. A year later he was hired by an organization called "Dallas Radio Laboratories" to build a 500-watt station. The call letters were to be KDRL (Dallas Radio Laboratories). Upon checking the listing, it was discovered that those call letters were already being used. The letters were rearranged and became KRLD (Radio Laboratories of Dallas). The station began operations February 14, 1926. The studios were on the second floor of the Adolphus Hotel, and the transmitter and antenna were on the top floor. Power for the oscillator and modulator was furnished by auto storage batteries located with the transmitter. In 1926 Glass was the only employee of the station except for the telephone operator. He was announcer, engineer, administrator, etc. The station was acquired by Edwin J. Kiest, publisher of the *Dallas Times-Herald*, shortly after it started broadcasting.[54]

The original "bread-board" 50-watt transmitter of KRLD, Dallas, built and operated by Robert Z. Glass in 1926 and located on the top floor of the Adolphus Hotel. Courtesy Texas/Dallas History and Archives Division, Dallas Public Library, Dallas, Texas

El Paso

Radio in El Paso started in the winter of 1921 as an experimental station by Leroy Hill and Associates at the Mine and Smelter Supply Company on San Francisco Street. The studio was a small storeroom at the back of the second floor. One of its first talents was sixteen-year-old Karl Otto Wyler and his four-piece band, "The Merrymakers." "I remember that they wanted some music," said Wyler, "and asked us to play." Wyler discovered that "[s]ome people simply did not believe that sound could travel hundreds of miles to be picked up by receivers and heard by individuals. 'There was something eerie about it.' He recalled that when the first crystal sets came out, he took one to his grandmother, set her down, put on the earphones and let her listen. 'She took off the earphones and handed them back to me. Her only comment was "I don't believe it." And she never did.'"[55]

In 1923 WDAH was sold to the Trinity Methodist Church and was operated only on Sundays. A year later another station started broadcasting "now and then" at Five Points. KFXH transmitted at 50 watts with homemade equipment built by W. S. Bledsoe. Wyler started singing for free. He became known as "The Happiness Boy" because he rattled off humorous anecdotes between songs like "The Bootlegger's Daughter" and "Who's Gonna Wash Your Laundry When the Chinamen Go to War." "I wasn't very good," remembered Wyler. "In fact, I was pure corn. But I was loud and that's what mattered." Wyler remembers that the microphone was about the size of a dinner plate. "You had to hold them close to your mouth and fairly yell to be heard."[56]

El Paso's first full-time, permanent station was licensed as KGKE on July 1, 1929, by Bledsoe and W. T. Blackwell, operator of Tri-State Music Company. The station was to transmit on 1310 kilocycles with 100 watts and share time with WDAH. KGKE was given permission by the Federal Radio Commission to start broadcasting on August 2, 1929. Before transmissions started the call letters were changed to KTSM (Tri-State Music). Bledsoe was the first manager, and Wyler, again unpaid, was the announcer who opened the station. Wyler was now "Karl the Kowhand." "I'll never forget opening night, August 22, 1929," Wyler recalled. "The studios were in a basement at 103 South El Paso Street. I walked before the mike with my ukulele and began to sing." He was hired a month later.[57]

"Karl the Kowhand" played his uke and banjo and thumped away on the piano while talking or telling stories with his sidekick, the Admiral. His act was still "pure corn":

> *"How do you like Kipling?"*
> *"I don't know. How do you Kipple?"*

"Where are the envelopes?"
"They're stationery."

Wyler read the Sunday "funnies" to children on one of the station's programs. *Night Court* was a comic skit show; Mrs. Calvin Hatchett was *Old Meg,* and *Cecil and Sally* and *Eb and Zeb* were also locally created shows. Also featured on KTSM were *Pat Burke and His Tone Pictures,* a musical request show; *Betty the Shopper,* a program for "Women Only"; *The Story Book Man,* airing songs and stories; *The Physician's Club,* a show about health; and the musical group *The Harmony Girls.*[58]

Fort Worth

The first broadcasting station in Fort Worth was WPA. It was founded in March of 1922 by Leonard Withington, owner and editor of the *Fort Worth Record,* and John R. Granger, the mechanical superintendent of the newspaper. WPA was located in a shack on top of the *Record* building. It was a one-man operation, with W. H. (Bill) Pitkin, known as "Sparks," as the sole staff member. Pitkin manipulated the transmitter, announced, read the news and weather reports, and played phonograph records. He also answered telephone calls reporting the reception good "as far away as Poly." Some of the entertainers on WPA were Mrs. Madeira Manchester, soprano; Mrs. William Cullen Bryant, contralto; Miss Anna Mae Hopkins, accompanist; and Mrs. Leonard Withington, announcer. Mrs. Bryant, who sang the first solo broadcast, remembered:

> I had been to Dallas with Mrs. Withington for a Harmony Club meeting; and when we returned to Fort Worth, we drove to the *Record* to pick up Mr. Withington. He was busy in his office, so to pass the time waiting for him, Mrs. Withington suggested that we go up on the roof of the building to see the new radio transmitter. After I had been introduced to the operator, Mr. Pitkin, he learned that I was a singer.
>
> "How about doing a number?" said Pitkin.
>
> There was no piano for accompaniment, but I agreed. He placed me before the microphone, and I well remember that my song was "Carry Me Back to Old Virginny." I also recall that I was so thrilled by this unusual experience that I floundered a bit during the song, mixing up some of the words. It was, indeed, something new for me in those days.[59]

Another performer was Jack Webster Harkrider. Years later he was scenic designer and producer of the "Ziegfeld Follies" at the New Amsterdam Theater in New York City.

Pitkin wrote a column in the paper called "Radio Record." In one column he commented, "It is not expected that our present temporary radiophone set will reach much beyond 10 miles, although it has been heard at Weatherford; but the new permanent set is being installed and will be able to 'put it over.'" On April 17, 1922, a new 100-watt transmitter was first used. Headlines read, "Far Parts of the State of Texas Report *Record*'s Radio Programs Clearly Received." In late April a studio for live programs was built in the office of the society editor on the second floor. Mr. and Mrs. Withington announced from the studio. WPA's studio microphone was set into a wooden kitchen mixing bowl. The "mike" was suspended from the arm of a common hat rack. The wooden bowl served as an eliminator of echoes and other interfering noises.

In September of 1922, WPA broadcast the opening game of the Dixie Baseball Series from Fort Worth. It was a play-by-play broadcast direct from the ballpark. In 1923 WPA was abandoned when William Randolph Hearst bought the *Record*. In 1924 the Rev. J. Frank Norris bought the transmitter for the First Baptist Church in Fort Worth, and WPA became KFQB.[60]

KFQB began broadcasting in June, 1924. It was operated by the *Search-Light* Publishing Company, the monthly periodical of the First Baptist Church. H. B. Greene, nicknamed "Colonel," installed KFQB's transmitter on the roof of the church. The station broadcast the church services. On October 25, 1926, the church sold the station to J. M. Gilliam, the business manager of *Search-Light*. He built studios in the basement of the Westbrook Hotel, located at Fourth and Houston Streets in Fort Worth. The transmitter remained on top of the church. Featured entertainers on KFQB were "Zack and Glenn"—Glenn Hewitt and Zack Hurt, who years later became popular as a sportscaster. Zack and Glenn played the ukulele, sang songs, and cracked jokes.

Gilliam sold KFQB to W. B. Fishburn, owner of a cleaner and dyer, on December 12, 1927, for $8,500.00. The studios remained in the Westbrook basement and the transmitter on the roof of the church. Soon after, control of the radio equipment returned to the First Baptist Church. Then a studio was built adjacent to the transmitting equipment. The studio and transmitter were lost on January 12, 1929, when a fire destroyed the church. KFQB's frequency was acquired by Texas Air Transport Broadcast Company, a division of Southern Air Transport on August 8, 1930, and became KSAT. Owner A. P. Barrett soon changed the call letters to KTAT. Years later KTAT contributed to the formation of the Texas State Network.[61]

WBAP was the second station in Fort Worth. The call letters came from a future President of the United States. When Harold Hough, circulation manager of the *Fort Worth Star-Telegram,* applied to the Department of Commerce in 1922 for a license, Herbert Hoover, secretary of commerce, personally assigned the call letters WBAP. He told Hough that the call letters should stand for "We Bring a

Program." (Some of the staff thought: "We Bore All People." During Prohibition, "We Bring a Pint.")[62]

The license made legal the station which had been operating for months. In late 1921 Amon G. Carter, owner and publisher of the *Fort Worth Star-Telegram*, was warned by friends that this little black box would kill newspapers. Carter asked his circulation manager, Harold Hough, what he knew about radio.

"Hardly anything at all," admitted Hough.

"How much?"

"Nothing."

Carter told Hough, "If this radio thing is going to be a menace to newspapers, maybe we had better own the 'menace.'"

One of the first things Hough had to learn was what role the company could play in the business—listener or broadcaster. Hough asked a friend who operated an electrical supply firm for a radio.

"How far do you want to listen?" the friend asked.

Hough replied, "Listen! I don't want to listen. Amon wants to talk."

"How much will it cost?" Carter cautiously asked when Hough reported back.

"Well, we can get the transmitter for $200.00, and it shouldn't cost more than $50.00 to set it up," Hough replied.

"All right," said Carter. "We'll put $300.00 in this radio thing, and when that's gone, we're out of the radio business."

Hough found a home-built transmitter in Dallas which had been constructed as a hobby in the kitchen of William E. Branch. Hough bought the equipment, which was then packed in an old tomato box and moved it to the *Star-Telegram*. He hired Branch to install it in the office of Louis J. Wortham, Carter's co-owner and co-publisher of the newspaper. The first studio was his office because he happened to be out of town at the time. On May 2, 1922, WBAP was licensed to broadcast with a power of 10 watts on a wavelength of 360 meters. The antenna was strung across Seventh Street to the Fort Worth Club building opposite the *Star-Telegram*. By the 1930s, when the station started to make money, it was $500,000.00 in debt.[63]

One of the most popular talents in the early days of WBAP was an announcer calling himself the "Hired Hand." Harold Hough told stories and rang a cowbell. In those days the custom was for announcers to sign off programs with just their initials. Full names were never given. Hough signed off one of the first nights with the letters "HH." When letters poured in asking who "HH" was, the reply was just "the Hired Hand up from the boiler room." The pseudonym "Hired Hand" was adopted, and one of the most famous personalities of early Texas radio was born. This was ironic; most of the earlier times when Hough was on the air, he was annoyed at being forced to perform when another announcer or *Star-Tele-*

*The transmitter of WBAP, Fort Worth, in 1922, located in the Star-Telegram building.
Courtesy Fort Worth Star-Telegram Photograph Collection, Special Collections
Division, University of Texas at Arlington Libraries, Arlington, Texas*

gram reporter did not show up or a speaker or singer would not arrive on time.
Hough would rather manage the station than be an announcer. "In the beginning of radio, I used to hang around the mike some," stated Hough. "But radio
soon grew up, and it was time to begin selling soap. This was a slick job, requiring
smooth gab, so the boys with lace on their tonsils moved in and crowded me off
the air."[64]

In the 1920s the staff had a nickname for WBAP. It began with a preacher who
had been approached by the station's staff to talk on the air. The preacher asked,
"Them radio waves—they go a fur piece, don't they?" The staff answered that
they did—that they covered the earth. The preacher said that he must decline
because it was written in the Bible that when the gospel spread throughout the
world, judgment day would come: the world would come to an end. Afterwards,
the staff referred to WBAP as "Fur Piece Radio."[65]

Carter walked in one of the first nights while Hough was announcing. Hough
said, "Why don't you make a speech, Mr. Carter?" Carter made a speech. The

The studio of WBAP, Fort Worth, in the early 1920s, located in the Star-Telegram *building.* Courtesy Fort Worth Star-Telegram *Photograph Collection, Special Collections Division, University of Texas at Arlington Libraries, Arlington, Texas*

next day the station received a postcard from a woman in Mineral Wells who wrote, "Your speech came in fine." From then on, radio received preferential treatment with Carter and Carter Publications. WBAP increased power from 10 watts to 500 watts on October 13, 1922, and changed frequencies to 400 meters and 485 meters for weather reports. On May 12, 1923, the power increased to 1,500 watts on 630 kilocycles. WBAP's studios moved from a corner of an office to three rooms on the second floor of the *Star-Telegram* building. By 1928 WBAP occupied half of the second floor.[66]

Winston O. Sparks of Fort Worth recalled his brother Earl, who was disabled with heart problems, was one of the earliest radio listeners:

My grandmother was living with us at that time, and she kept telling my mother, "Why do you let Earl spend all his time doing that? There is no way he could hear anything."

Being handicapped, he could not run and play with the other boys. He just sat there for hours listening. My mother said that the most amusing part about it was that my grandmother sneaked in his room one day and put those [headphones] on and listened. My brother was at school. She listened and she listened and she listened. She could not believe it. She would slip back in there and listen. My grandmother thought that that was such a waste of time, and then she was so embarrassed when she finally found out that here was a miracle of sound coming through those wires.[67]

From the beginning, WBAP tried many innovations in programming. During the first years, it broadcast regular reports from livestock, grain, and cotton exchanges, using privately leased telephone lines. Regular church services; national, state, and local newscasts; and weather forecasts became standard.[68] Programming included musical request shows; music by local trios, orchestras, church choirs, and neighborhood bands; bedtime stories for children; and, on some occasions, even fire calls. At that time WBAP did not carry commercials.

In the early days Hough also instigated one of the most well-known sounds in Texas broadcasting. While having his photograph made for listeners, Hough posed in overalls, a checked shirt, and a long-billed railroad cap while holding a broom and a cowbell. The sound of the cowbell became the station's identification for decades to come.[69]

Hough would get on the radio and talk about anything that came to mind. When he got tired, he would say, "Well, shut 'er down!" Then the station would go off the air. One program was *The Truth Society*. The purpose was to find the "most truthful man in the country." Memberships were mailed to everyone who submitted a "tall tale." The winner was decided on George Washington's birthday. One of the most popular "whoppers" was about the mule in the corn field: the sun was so hot the corn started popping, and the mule froze to death thinking it was snowing.[70]

Less than four months after WBAP went on the air, it broadcast an on-the-scene description of a sporting event. The Texas League baseball series was being played between the Fort Worth Panthers and the Wichita Falls Spudders. The five-game series was at Panther Park, across North Main Street from the future site of LaGrave Field. At that time, announcers did not describe games as they were being played. Nevertheless, WBAP decided to broadcast a play-by-play description of the series. One man was stationed at Panther Park and another in the studios. The two were in telephone contact. The person at the ballpark would describe each event of the game over the telephone, and the announcer would describe it to the radio listeners. WBAP broadcast the first and second games using this arrangement. The first game broadcast was on Wednesday afternoon, August 30, 1922, the second game on Thursday afternoon. According to Bud Sherman, a sportscaster at WBAP years later:

> The reaction of radio fans was very favorable. It encouraged WBAP to send an announcer to the ballpark for the third game. On Friday afternoon, September 1, 1922, the announcer described the game directly from the ballpark. Harold Hough stated years later, "I must have been the one who did the mike work." The announcer did not work from the press box. "In those days, I just grabbed an old orange crate or any other make-shift seat available," stated Hough, "took off for the ballpark, and planted myself wherever I could find a place to plant."
> A *Fort Worth Star-Telegram* article described this historic broadcast:
> The play-by-play broadcast was sent into an ordinary telephone transmitter and carried over more than 8,000 feet of iron telephone wire to the set at the *Star-Telegram* building. In order to cut out the noise of the fans as much as possible when plays were being announced, a cardboard tube was fitted over the phone, and a small megaphone was inverted on this tube. A handkerchief was stuffed into the megaphone to prevent distortion of the voice by resonance.[71]

WBAP did not broadcast the 1922 Dixie Championship Series. WBAP was silent while the 10-watt transmitter was being replaced by a new 500-watt transmitter. The station resumed broadcasting the Dixie League games in 1923, but there was no set schedule. "Whenever the spirit moved me and my cohorts," recalls Hough, "we would grab a microphone and spend an afternoon at the ballpark." Later that year, the station received a new supersensitive microphone that it used to broadcast these games. On the microphone was inscribed: "Used by President Harding in St. Louis, June 21, 1923." That speech was one of the first attempts in the nation to form a "chain" of broadcasting stations. WFAA in Dallas was part of that historic event. By 1925 WBAP's staff consisted of an engineer, an announcer, a control operator, the "Hired Hand," and Eileen Flake, who at times did everything around the station, including announcing.[72]

J. R. Curtis received a license for a station in Fort Worth when he was a student at Texas Christian University in the 1920s. Curtis had become interested in radio through the Boy Scouts during World War I. He was assigned the call letters KFRO (Keep Forever Rolling On). When he graduated from college in 1927, he did not have the money to start his station; the telephone company wanted a transmitter fee. Curtis let his license lapse. Later, in February 1935, Curtis would start KFRO in Longview.[73]

KFJZ originally was a 50-watt government transmitter used in World War I at Camp Bowie in Fort Worth's Arlington Heights district. W. E. Branch acquired the equipment from the government after the war and moved it to his home on Avenue L in Fort Worth's Polytechnic district. He constructed a small building in his backyard to house the transmitter; his living room was the studio.[74] Dave Naugle, who later worked at KFJZ, remembered how that station started: "Branch had it in his garage . . . in Poly. He would sign on when someone came by and wanted to do something—play the piano, or sing, or talk. He would go out and turn the thing on; they would appear; and they would leave; and he would turn it off. A lot of radio stations did that sort of thing in those days."[75]

In the middle 1920s, Branch sold KFJZ to the Southwestern Baptist Theological Seminary in Fort Worth. Seminary officials operated the station for a brief period and then decided the station was "not worth the effort" and told Branch to "come and get it." Branch moved KFJZ to the basement of the Northern Texas Traction Company Building at Third and Main Streets. The transmitter remained in Branch's backyard. Branch did not make KFJZ commercial until 1926. On January 12, 1928, Branch sold KFJZ to H. C. Allison, who moved it to the Moore building at Tenth and Main Streets. There was no control room. The station broadcast for two hours daily—from 8:00 to 10:00 P.M. Truett Kimzey, chief engineer, moved the transmitter to the Sunny Hill Dairy Farm near the I&GN Lake. Allison operated KFJZ for six months. In the summer of 1928, he leased it to The Texas Hour, a group headed by George Gleeson, a Fort Worth attorney. Control returned to Allison in 1929, and he sold it to H. C. Meacham, who moved the station to Meacham's Department Store at Twelfth and Main Streets. It was from the store studios that one of the most famous radio groups began their career: the Light Crust Doughboys. In 1932 Ralph S. Bishop bought KFJZ and moved the studio into the Hotel Texas in quarters abandoned by KTAT.[76]

Greenville

Dave Ablowich, Jr., had been broadcasting with a "homemade spark transmitter" since 1919. He had amateur radio license 5DW since 1920. In 1924 Ablowich was granted a license to operate KFPM in Greenville. The "homemade" transmitter and seventy-foot tower were located at his home at 2109 Park Street. KFPM broadcast with 10 watts and then 15 watts on a wavelength of 242 meters. The station was received in forty of the forty-eight states and in five provinces of Canada. The studio was located at The New Furniture Company in downtown Greenville. Programming included the latest Victor music, local sporting events, and many local country and western bands. The Kavanaugh Church was equipped to broadcast the Sunday services of the Reverend J. W. Fort.[77]

Leo Hackney of Greenville remembered seeing the KFPM studio: "This fellow's dad owned The Furniture Company. It was located on the top floor in a three-story building in downtown Greenville. Dave Ablowich was really interested in electronics so he built this station himself. He used rugs to create a room and sound absorption. I remember going up there when I was eight or nine years old. Like most radio operations back then, it was mostly local talent—just operated a few hours a day. Whenever someone came along and he thought they would be interesting to talk to, he put them on."[78]

Weldon Jeffus went to Greenville to see KFPM:

There was a 15-watt station—he had a 250-watt tube driving a little 15-watt tube for his transmitter—1932 or '33. The transmitter was out in the residential section and the studio was down in The New Furniture Store; and he had three rugs hung from the ceiling, and that was the studio. The microphone was one of these new condenser microphones that they had just come out with that you could buy in kit form, and he got it and put it in a tomato can: and that was his broadcast setup. I guess he had it on some kind of floor lamp. The *Paris News* was talking to me about putting a station in Paris. I went down to see that one and see how much he wanted for it.[79]

Years later Jeffus moved to 9th Street in the Oak Cliff section of Dallas. Living next door was Ablowich. "He had the whole station on the back porch—well, all the equipment," remembered Jeffus. Ablowich never broadcast from Dallas.[80]

Houston

By 1922 Houston had five licensed "broadcasting" stations:

WCAK Alfred P. Daniel, 2504 Bagby Street
WEAY Will Horwitz, 612 Travis Street
WEV Hurlburt-Still Electrical Co., McKinney Avenue and San Jacinto Street
WFAL *Houston Chronicle* Publishing Co.
WGAB Q R V Radio Co., 1213 Prairie Avenue[81]

In 1922, Alfred P. Daniel started WCAK using "a set rigged up in a Quaker Oats box." Daniel broadcast the request, "Anyone hearing this, telephone me!" A reply came from Rockport, near Houston. It was Houston's first "broadcasting" station. The station's first talent was Anna Clyde Plunkett:

It was in Alfred's home over on Bagby that the great experiment took place. Elizabeth Blaffer and I were to sing in a tightly-closed room upstairs with Louise Daniel at the piano, and several people waiting breathlessly downstairs to see if it would come through with all the doors shut. I sang my first number, Brahms' "Sapphic Ode," and Alfred bounded up the steps, burst into the studio, and shouted, "It works! We heard you just like you were in the same room with us."

Then Elizabeth sang "One Fine Day," and we closed with the duet from "Mme. Butterfly." That was Houston's first broadcast program, and Alfred Daniel's family and us made up our audience.[82]

WEV was operated by Hurlburt Still. The station broadcast from a garage at McKinney Avenue and San Jacinto Streets. WEV began in 1922 broadcasting music and impromptu speeches for three hundred receiving sets.

The *Houston Post* soon began regular daily concerts over WEV and WCAK. On the first program in May of 1922, Mrs. E. J. Flake, contralto, sang "Centrition" and "Perfect Day." Daniel permitted the use of his station for the first Saturday night and Sunday concerts. Thereafter, WCAK broadcast the concerts on Wednesdays, Saturdays, and Sundays. WEV broadcast the *Post's* concerts the other four days of the week. Both stations transmitted on 360 meters.[83]

WEAY began broadcasting on June 9, 1922. Gerald R. Chinski of 801 Francis Avenue was the operator. WEAY broadcast with 120 watts and could be "forced" to 150 watts. The station's tower was on the *Houston Post* building, with the antenna running across the street to the Iris Theater.[84]

Other stations in Houston broadcast for short periods. KFCV and WRAA were licensed in 1923. KFCV was operated by Fred Mahaffey, Jr. WRAA was licensed to the Rice Institute, broadcasting on 1170 kilocycles. In 1924 WSAV and WFO, the Iris Theater station, were licensed. At different times KFVI was operated by the Fifty-Sixth Cavalry Brigade Headquarters. KTUE started broadcasting in the early 1920s, licensed to the Uhalt Electric Company; it transmitted from the company shop. KTUE later became KXYZ.[85]

"Hello, folks everywhere," greeted Alfred P. Daniel. On Sunday, May 9, 1925, KPRC (Kotton Port Rail Center) opened as Daniel, program director, threw the switch and announced the call letters. W. P. Hobby, president of the *Houston Post-Dispatch,* had convinced Ross Sterling, principal owner of the newspaper, to get into radio. The *Post-Dispatch* acquired the equipment of WEAY from Will Horwitz. KPRC was licensed on 1010 kilocycles at 500 watts. The station was housed in four rooms on the roof of the *Post-Dispatch* building.[86]

Two years earlier Sterling had talked to Daniel about setting up a station. Sterling's son was a student of Daniel at a YMCA radio class. "When Mr. Sterling asked us how we'd like to have a real station, we said, 'Swell, We'll have some place to play our saxophones,'" stated Daniel. "So Mr. Sterling bought a 500-watt Westinghouse Electric transmitter, the kind I'd seen at the first convention of the American Radio Relay League in 1921 in Chicago. Ross, Jr., died that year, though," remembered Daniel, "and Mr. Sterling just put the transmitter into storage. Didn't even have it unpacked."

In 1925 the World Advertising Convention was in Houston. Herbert Hoover was scheduled to be a speaker. Daniel wanted to "put him on the air." Sterling consented, and a two-man staff unpacked the radio equipment and set up the station in three frenzied weeks. Hoover was the first "big name" on the station.[87] G. E. Zimmerman was the engineer at KPRC; Alfred P. Daniel, program director; Charles Baker, operator; and Grimes R. Walker in charge of remote control devices.[88]

The opening broadcast included comments by former Texas Governor Bill Hobby and Judd Mortimer Lewis, *Post-Dispatch* columnist and poet laureate of Texas. Music was provided by the Royal Scotch Highlanders from Florida, the First Garrison Band of Mexico, and the Humble Oil and Refining Company band. A 1925 broadcasting schedule for KPRC showed:

II A.M.	Official U.S. Weather Report
NOON	Official Agriogram from the Dept. of Agriculture.
1 P.M.–6 P.M.	Off the air.
6 P.M.	Studio Musical featuring Floyd Martin, tenor; William Gebhard, bass; Bill Maroney, saxophone; and Harry Hughes, piano.
8 P.M.	Southern Pacific Band, directed by W. Clark.[89]

During KPRC's first year it developed its own talent. Frank Tilton, a blind pianist, had a regular program with a large audience. Clauda A. Blanchard and his dance orchestra were weekly entertainers. "The Paramount Five" was a regular performing male quartet. Dr. A. H. Flickwir gave U.S. public health talks. Miss Harriet Dickson gave weekly book talks followed by road reports from the Motor League of South Texas. The McFarland Trio "walked right into the homes of music lovers." The Sylvan Beach Dance Orchestra dressed like sailors to play "on the radio." Judd Mortimer Lewis was *Uncle Judd,* the featured storyteller. J. Benson Carlisle, chief organist of the Texan Theater, played regular concerts. Reverend Charles Hard, the "Sky Pilot," originated a daily morning devotional and a Sunday religious program from his own studios in the M & M Building. "Sis and Otha" broadcast a daily studio program called *Tunefinders.*[90]

KPRC presented "prize nights" when the winners of various contests and promotions were announced. One radio contest winner received a gallon of Kill-KO insecticide. Another prize was a full case of Luxury Macaroni and Spaghetti. For a winning essay, another listener received a dozen bottles of Fly Flu Liquid Insecticide. One contest challenged listeners to "Write a Radiogram; Win a Prize." The contestants had to write a slogan using the letters "K," "P," and "R" and end with the name of the company, "Curtis." One winning entry was:

• • •

Keeping
People
Really satisfied is
Curtis Co.'s policy.[91]

San Antonio

The first radio broadcasters in San Antonio were the wireless operators at the armed forces bases. "They broadcast a lot of stuff which we could not copy," remembered Hoxie Mundine, later an engineer at WOAI. It was all coded until immediately after the war, when the stations started broadcasting voice and music. "The Army Signal Corps was the first to broadcast voice and music in this area," remembered Mundine. "They had a windup phonograph that they sat in front of the microphone, and they played phonograph records. They did not talk much. They identified who they were."[92]

The Sunday, September 25, 1922, edition of the *San Antonio Express* listed the radio schedule for all five stations for Tuesday, the 27th:

10:30, 12:15, 3:00, and 6 P.M., WOAI (485 meters), Southern Equipment, *Express,* official reports.
6:30 P.M., DM-7, Brooks Field, one hour of music.
7:30 P.M., AS-6, Camp Travis (480 meters), one hour of music.
8:30 P.M., WCAR, Alamo Radio Electric Co., one hour of music.
9:30 P.M., WJAE, *Express,* one hour of music.[93]

The five stations listed for San Antonio shared two frequencies. WJAE started broadcasting with 25 watts on August 5, 1922. It was the radio service of the *San Antonio Express.*[94] WJAE broadcast for only a few months. Mundine remembered why:

WJAE—that was on top of the old *Express* News building right across the river from the Nix Hospital. It was operated by the *Express* newspapers—mostly music and records. I think they did some local talent. They operated for approximately a month; and when WOAI went on the air, they went off the air. The *Express* Publishing Company had some kind of deal with WOAI that they would use the news from the paper. The *Express* would send them a rush edition in the morning, a proof or something so they would have the news, and they would give credit. Then, The *Express* took their station off the air.[95]

WCAR began broadcasting at 324 North Navarro Street in September of 1922; it was the second station in the city. The owner was Southern Radio Corporation of Texas. WCAR transmitted on 1140 kilocycles with 100 watts. In 1928 WCAR became KTSA (Kome to San Antonio).

At 10:30 A.M., Sunday, September 25, 1922, WOAI (World of Agriculture Information) began broadcasting as the third station in San Antonio. Mayor O. B. Black accepted the station for the city. G. A. C. Halff, president of the Southern Equipment Company, officially dedicated the station. Then, Madame Frida Stjerna, Swedish mezzo soprano, sang. The hour-and-a-half program was the first WOAI radio concert. The station officially started broadcasting the next morning with road reports, market reports, official weather reports, sports, and news bulletins. The first local commercial program on WOAI was *The Gebhardt Mexican Players,* sponsored by Gebhardt Chili. Beginning in 1924 and continuing into the 1940s, Rosita Fernández was "Rosita" for Gebhardt's singing Spanish commercials.[96]

According to Mundine, Southern Equipment became involved in radio because:

One of the vice-presidents went to New York City and came back with a whole carload of radios, so they had to put in a broadcasting station. That was the story I heard. They wanted to sell radios. Lots of local talent—ladies from local clubs. Dr. K. P. Hill was one of the area preachers from the First Presbyterian Church.

They did not play records. They had a few records for standby, but they were mostly classical music. Mr. Halff would not let you play just any old record. If you had to play a record, you had to play some high-class stuff. Even if an artist did not show up, and you played a record, it had to be good music.

Most people did not have a radio. A few people around the neighborhood started to get radios. If you had a radio, chances are most of the evenings after the homework was done, there would be a bunch over at your house listening to the radio. It was fun going around to the neighbors' houses.

The control room (WOAI) and the little transmitter—everything was in one very small room, and no air conditioning. The first studio was covered with monk's cloth over cotton batting to deaden it. In fact, it was too dead. The studio was separated from the control room by the ladies' room and the men's room.

In very early days they had no real controls for adjusting the volume, so they had this sign put up that said "softer," "louder," "nearer," "farther away"— something like that. It would light up on the panel. It was very crude mechanically. The guy in the back was watching the transmission meter; and when they got to jumping too far, then he would start flashing these lights. He did not have any way to look at a VU meter or audio meter—no way to adjust the volume—just tell him (talent) to move back and forward. . . . This system was probably confusing to the guy trying to perform.[97]

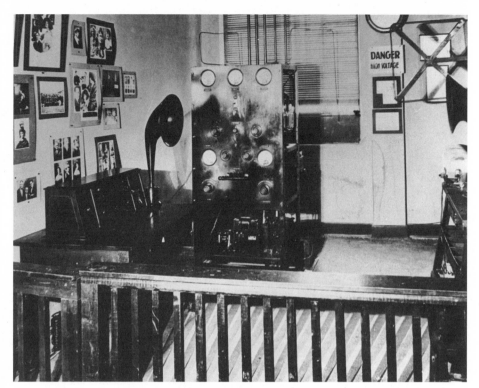

The original 500-watt transmitter of WOAI, San Antonio, September 25, 1922.
Courtesy Hoxie Mundine

KGRC (Kome to the Gene Roth Company) was located in the back of Roth's auto repair shop, the "66 Garage," near Main and San Pedro Streets. KGRC operated with 50 watts on 720 kilocycles, according to Eugene Roth:

My father was the real pioneer in this marketplace. He built a 50-watt transmitter from a book he borrowed from a library in 1925. This was a station he started on 720 kilocycles that eventually went to WGN (Chicago). His main business was the repair of automobiles. It was a hobby. He did not think much about . . . at that time. In fact, he did not have a license for KGRC for two years.

One day Dan Quayle, the postmaster for San Antonio, saw him on the streets downtown and said, "Gene, I've heard that there is a guy named Herbert Hoover in charge of the Department of Commerce, and he's started to keep track of radio stations."

Dad said, "What the hell for?"

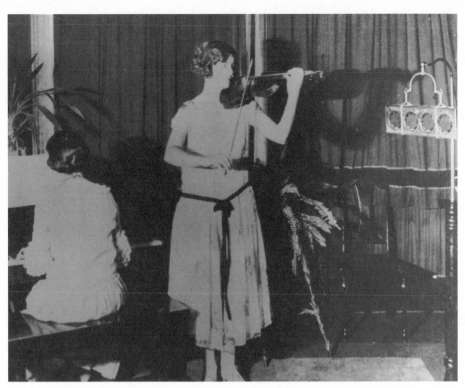

*Talent performing in the first studio of WOAI, San Antonio, in 1922.
Note the unusual microphone on the right with four "telephone" carbon elements
mounted into a metal frame. Courtesy Hoxie Mundine*

He sent a post card to Hoover and told him that he was on 720 kilocycles with 50 watts, and Hoover sent back a one-paragraph letter: "Thank you for the information. You are now licensed in San Antonio with the call letters of KGRC on 720 kilocycles." Dad owned it (the station) until his death.

There were a number of complaints about ten o'clock at night when *Amos 'n' Andy* was on WGN out of Chicago—to get off the air so they could hear them. He moved the frequency. He never asked anybody; he just did it, but he moved the frequency to the wrong end of the dial. I don't think that he studied about "reach"—the higher end of the dial. That's where all the "Class Four" are, and all the noise static, and interference from adjacent and co-channel stations. At that time he did not have an engineer because he would have advised him not to put it there. He could have put it anywhere. He could have put it at 550, 570, 590, 600 (kilocycles)—anywhere he wanted.[98]

At that time *Amos 'n' Andy* was the most popular show on radio. People would stay at home the night of its broadcast just because they did not want to miss it.

In San Antonio the motion picture at the Majestic Theater was stopped for thirty minutes so movie audiences could hear the program. Some movie houses put radios with "loud talkers," as some people called them in the 1920s, in the lobby. At the time of the broadcast, the projectionist would stop the film; the audience would go out to the lobby and listen to the show; and then after the show, the movie would resume. At some theaters, after equipment was installed for sound movies, the radio show was broadcast into the theater auditorium.[99]

Like many small-station owners, Eugene Roth was supporting the station with his business. According to his son, he did not sell advertising:

How did he pay the bills? He never thought of selling advertising; it was just a hobby with him. He would turn it on and off at will—just whenever he felt like messing with it. He played records; my mother played the piano.

One day a fellow walked in and introduced himself. His name was Charlie Shea. He said, "Mr. Roth, I've listened to your radio station, and I don't hear any advertising."

Dad said, "What are you talking about? What is that?"

A U.S. Army general speaking into a Western Electric Double Button microphone at WOAI, San Antonio, in 1923. The "command light board" on the wall was used by engineers three offices down the hall to move talent "nearer" or "away" or to get them to talk or sing "louder" or "softer." Courtesy Hoxie Mundine

Shea said, "That is how you make money and stay on the air with the radio station. It won't be a drain on your facilities."

Dad said, "Well, I don't know if there are enough people with radios to listen."

Charlie convinced him that he would sell if Dad would give him fifty percent. He would get half, and Dad would get half. Charlie was one hell of a salesman.

Dad had the physical facilities for a couple of years in the garage on Roman Plaza across from Sears. On the first floor were the mechanics, repairs, and body work. He was there for two years—antenna on top of the building—a horizontal wire.

Charlie came to dad not long after he came to work and said, "You know, Gene, if we started selling radios, we're going to do a lot better because you're right; every time I start talking to someone about advertising, they don't have a radio; and they don't know anybody who does."

So dad opened a retail radio sales organization in a hotel downtown called Paramount Radio Company. He sold Atwater Kents 'til the world looked level. He did so well that Mr. Joske of Joske's of Texas called dad in. Dad arranged to lease an area in the store to sell radios. It did an incredible amount of business, and the radio station got lost in the shuffle because he was making so much money with the sale of radios.[100]

After a couple of years, Roth changed the call letters to KONO. He moved the station to the St. Anthony Hotel. The studios were in the basement, and the transmitter, which now had a power of 100 watts on 1370 kilocycles, was on the fifth floor. Two sixty-five foot towers on the roof supported a "flat top" antenna. George Ing, engineer for KONO, recalled: "It was an ordinary hotel room. I rebuilt the transmitter almost as soon as I got there because the Federal Radio Commission (FRC) made a requirement that stations had to have crystal control for their frequency. Before then there was no crystal control; it was kind of haphazard. Stations could be way off their assigned frequency."[101]

One day Roth had a visitor at the station. "A man walked in and said he would like to see my dad," remembered the younger Roth. "My dad asked him into the office and asked, 'What can I do for you?'"

The visitor said, "Well, sir, I play the guitar, and I would like to play on your radio station."

Roth asked, "Well, you any good?"

He said, "I don't know."

He went out and got his guitar out of his car; he came back in and played for Roth, who said, "I think that you're pretty good. I think that we'll give you a show every week." The man was Ernest Tubb. He usually came to the show riding a bicycle.[102]

On December 7, 1926, Sam Liberto started KGCI in San Antonio. The station was licensed to Liberto Radio Sales, at 409 South Flores Street. KGCI was licensed on 1360 kilocycles with 15 watts. "Liberto's purpose was to sell radios," stated Hoxie Mundine.[103] KGCI later became KMAC.

Robert Bridge built KGCM in 1926. It broadcast with a 10-watt transmitter on 1140 kilocycles. The station was located on the back porch of Bridge's home at 2412 Main. In 1927 Bridge built station KTAP, another 10-watter on 1140 kilocycles. The frequency soon changed to 1310 kilocycles. KTAP later became KXYZ. Mundine visited KTAP: "Bridge and I were on his back porch when he operated it—just a small panel. It was just a 10-watter—didn't take much—sitting on top of a table with an antenna strung up in his backyard. He played phonograph records; he didn't talk much."[104]

KGDR was licensed in the spring of 1927 to Joe B. McShane. The station was located in the rear of 206 Laurel Heights Place. KGDR broadcast with 15 watts. Its frequency was 1250 kilocycles, then 1480 kilocycles, then 1450 kilocycles; and on National Frequency Reallocation Day, November 11, 1928, it was assigned 1500 kilocycles. On December 9, 1929, KGDR was acquired by KUT Broadcasting Company, owned by Houston's Rice Hotel. KGDR was moved to Austin, where it was consolidated and changed its call letters to KUT.[105]

Waco

By 1922 Waco had three broadcasting stations: WWAC, WLAJ, and WJAD. William P. Clarke, who in 1921 was one of the listeners and reporters of the Aggie-Longhorn football game, was responsible for WWAC in Waco: "WWAC was at Sanger Brothers (department store). I was the one who talked Mr. Sanger into letting me build a broadcasting station. I had gotten a license, Commercial Grade, on September 15, 1922, to operate it. It was in operation from September 25, 1922, until January 23, 1924, at which time I resigned. They no longer had anyone interested in the station, and it was abandoned."[106]

WLAJ was licensed to the Waco Electrical Supply Company, located at 618 Austin Avenue. The station was built and operated by Paul Deeley, amateur radio operator of 5AA.[107]

On July 22, 1922, WJAD was licensed to Jackson's Radio Engineering Laboratories, owned by Franklin Pierce Jackson. WJAD was located at 906 Austin Avenue. It operated three hours a day with 15 watts on 360 meters. The signal "didn't go farther than downtown Waco." By 1928, WJAD had increased power from 15 to 150 to 500 and finally to 1,000 watts.[108] William C. Tinus was a teenager who worked with Jackson:

I first knew Frank Jackson when I worked for him in his garage which specialized in repairing Cadillacs. My first transmitter was a Ford Model "T" spark coil, and the receiver was a crystal detector. Everything was homemade. There were two or three other "hams" in Waco. We saved our money and bought some of the earliest vacuum tubes—audiotrons—glass tubes with wires coming out both ends. . . . Frank was an ex-telephone man and was interested in radio. . . . We helped him build a good receiver, and he immediately got the bug to transmit as well as receive.

The first transmitting experiment was made in the garage about 1921. A tube intended to be an audio amplifier was rigged as a radio frequency oscillator, and a flashlight bulb was connected in series with the antenna lead-in to "tune-up" and see that we were putting some juice into the antenna; we had no ammeters, etc. I would guess the output was of the order of one-quarter watt. Then we put an old telephone microphone in series with the antenna; and when we talked into it, the bulb would flicker. We scrounged an old windup phonograph, and the music would make the bulb flicker. We "Hams" dashed home on our bikes and listened on our "Ham" receivers. Music was on the air, and we could hear Frank, too. What a thrill! This was the beginning of broadcasting in Central Texas.

Frank must have begun worrying about a license about the end of 1921. I do not know when he applied to the Department of Commerce for one, but he got it in July, 1922. When better tubes were obtainable, a better transmitter was built—an oscillator—amplifier with about twenty watts output; and, as I recall, WJAD operated from the garage with this in 1922. In the early days all of them (antennas) followed shipboard designs—two poles or towers—horizontal parallel wires with spreaders at both ends. . . . We soon learned that a single wire worked about as well for a receiver.

The Department of Commerce assigned all broadcasters to 360 meters, and a little later to 360 and 400. As more stations came on the air, the nighttime bedlam and squeals were terrific. Standard practice was to monitor (I did it at home.) and phone the transmitter to move over to a relatively clear spot on the dial. This interference mess was the prime reason for legislation leading to the FCC (FRC).[109]

Elfrieda Jackson, Frank's wife, remembered that he just decided one day in 1922, "Well, by golly, I'll just try building a broadcasting station." Frank would listen to WFAA and WBAP, and he went to see those stations. He then came home and built all the parts he had seen. He built a large oil vat in which he cooled his tubes. In 1923 Jackson sold the garage and opened a radio store. WJAD

The studio of WJAD, Waco, in the 1920s. Courtesy Robert E. Weathers, former owner, president, and general manager, WACO Radio Inc.

moved to the Hotel Raleigh. The transmitter, now rebuilt to 50 watts, was on the top floor, and the studio was on the second. About this time, WJAD started broadcasting "paid advertisements."[110]

Mary Holliday started helping at WJAD in the 1920s. She was an accomplished pianist and taught music. She could instantly sight-read any music. When musicians came to Waco or Baylor University, she would accompany them. She started accompanying musical guests at WJAD. At first she was not paid. Later, Holliday started working for the station and developed a talk and interview program concerning Waco and its people. In 1925 she took her young son to WJAD to perform. Jack Holliday sang one song:

> It was the kind of microphone that had the suspension wires on it. They lowered it to my height. I sang into the microphone, they thanked me, and that was it. In the next couple of weeks all these letters and telegrams came in telling the station how much they enjoyed my singing. Mother had a stack of these things and said, "Look." She read them to me. Remember, in those days people had all these dials, and they kept logs of how far away they could get and what they could get. They said, "We are pleased to report that on 'such

The original license for WJAD, Waco, issued to Jackson's Radio Engineering Laboratories on October 24, 1922. Courtesy Robert E. Weathers, former owner, president, and general manager, WACO Radio Inc.

A "Radio Applause Card," or "DX" card, sent to WJAD, Waco, in 1926. Courtesy Robert E. Weathers, former owner, president, and general manager, WACO Radio Inc.

and such' day at 'such and such' hour we heard little Jackie Holliday sing from your studio in Waco, Texas." They were from Canada, California. . . .[111]

WJAD's frequency changed many times. Starting on 360 meters, the station moved to 850 kilocycles in 1924. In 1926 it moved to 670 kilocycles, and in 1927 it was assigned 900 kilocycles. On National Frequency Reallocation Day, November 11, 1928, WJAD moved to 1240 kilocycles. Other frequency changes followed. In 1924 WJAD was a Class C station. It operated daily from 4:00 to 4:30 P.M. On Monday and Friday evenings it broadcast an hour-long concert starting at 8:00 P.M. WJAD was on the air for one hour at 11 A.M. on Sunday morning for church services. The studios moved from the Raleigh Hotel temporarily to the Central Christian Church at 1116 Washington Avenue. In March of 1929 WJAD moved to 801 Austin Avenue on the fourth floor of the Amicable Life Insurance Building. In December of 1929 the station was bought by the Central Texas Broadcasting Company. On April 1, 1930, WJAD changed call letters to WACO. These call letters were obtained from a shipboard station on the merchant vessel *Nebraskan*.[112]

Radio Receivers

In 1928, when stations were changing because of the newly formed Federal Radio Commission (FRC), receivers were also evolving. Sets with tubes that operated

Mary Holliday, Waco radio personality and one of the first women broadcasters, started helping at WJAD, Waco, in the 1920s. Courtesy Jack M. Holliday

on batteries had been available for years. Receivers that used alternating current (AC), and thus could be plugged into the wall of a house, were becoming available. Radios that used batteries continued to be needed in rural areas where electrification had not reached.

Crystal receivers, which used neither AC current nor batteries, had been used since the early part of the century. These simple radios remained attractive to radio enthusiasts because they were always a great item with which to experiment or "fiddle." They were working radios, and for decades they remained the only source of radio entertainment in areas of the state without electricity or easy access to town and batteries.

As children, many professionals became interested in broadcasting by building their own crystal sets. Alfred P. Daniel, owner of WCAK, Houston's first station, started before World War I with a crystal set. "But did you ever hear music from a crystal set?" asked Daniel. "That's the sweetest music ever broadcast."[113] "Those crystal receivers had perfect fidelity," recalled Ted Bender of KTSM in El Paso. "It was as good as your set of earphones if you had good earphones."[114]

Jack McGrew, of KPRC in Houston, started with a crystal set: "I built this crystal set in Galveston—1927 or '28. I built the receiver out of dime-store parts, like most kids in those days. I bought the parts at Kress's or Woolworth's. I wrapped a little crystal and a cat's whisker and hoped it worked. I learned it out of a Boy Scout Handbook."[115] Chem Terry, of WBAP in Fort Worth, also had a crystal set:

> I built a little crystal set when I was eight years old. I used the bed springs for an antenna. On the outside I used the water pipe. I wound my own coil, and at Woolworth I got a crystal and cat's whisker. I used to go to bed at night with my headphones on, and my mother would take them off when I was asleep. Everybody had a radio. People did not come to visit; they came to listen; and they would listen to programs that they were not interested in because it was so fascinating. They tried to get "far away" stations. The *Grand Ole Op'ry* became a staple with them.[116]

Hoxie Mundine of WOAI in San Antonio started using a crystal set around World War I:

> I wound my coils around an oatmeal box. You shellacked the box first—it firmed it up—then we would shellac the rest of it. Every once in a while we would bring one strand of the coil out, pull off a turn or two, and twist them together so we could hook them together later for taps.
>
> The galena (crystal) was mounted in a little cup called a "woods melt," which melts at a very low temperature. So they would bring that up to the melting point and lay that galena in there. Then, when it cooled, it was firm and made contact for the negative side of it. We used a cat's whisker, which was a little phosphorus bronze spring-wire on a little arm with a knot on the end of it. We would find a sensitive spot on it (galena) because everything was not sensitive. You found it by just trying and listening.
>
> This apparatus was so broadly tuned that if you were anywhere near a radio station, you could hear it. We used enameled wire for the coil. It was coated to be insulated from other turns because we did not space the turns. We did not get the true slide like in the commercial sets. We had to find some little con-

tacts with a flat head on them, drill the panel, put a bunch of them in there, then get a little slider, and go back and forth over those. That would vary the taps in the wavelength. If we could scrounge a variable condenser, we would hook it across there—which would give us some fine tuning.[117]

Roger Dickey, who was born in 1911, got interested in wireless in World War I. As a freshman at Grand Prairie High School, he read a *Radio Craft* magazine and learned about crystal sets. He saved his money and bought his first set at Kress's in Dallas:

After I got my crystal set, I got interested in what made it work. So I took the two ends off, and the thing came apart. The coil just collapsed. I thought, "Man alive! I've got trouble now." I looked around, and my grandmother had an old oatmeal box. I wound that coil back on that box carefully, and it worked just as good. Then I read in *Radio Craft* that you could take what they called a veri-coupler. It was a coil that worked one inside another. I tried that, and it worked pretty good. So then I read about using a vacuum tube; so I tore that all up, went over to Kress's, bought me a UV199, a one-and-a-half volt tube (probably didn't cost a dollar), and found a diagram—wound up with a regenerative receiver. It had a control for the regeneration. When I rigged that up— Boy!—I could get Pittsburgh.

I had a friend who had a crystal set who lived about a mile from us. He came in one day and said, "You can't believe that I got Pittsburgh on my crystal set."

It took me a while to figure out that when I was listening on mine, it was retransmitting that signal, and he was picking it up.[118]

Buddy Cruse, of KFJZ in Fort Worth, got parts out of old radios and built a crystal set. "We would listen to anything we could pick up. I didn't know the station's call letters and where they were from. If I found one, I listened to it."[119]

Claude Goode, who worked for the U.S. Weather Service, had a crystal set in the 1930s, long after other types of sets were available:

It required no electrical power. The crystal generated its own power . . . a crystal about the size of a quarter (about one-quarter inch thick) was mounted on the coil. A neat little holder mounted adjacent to the crystal was movable and held a whisker, or wire-like "tickler," which could be moved in a manner to tickle the surface of the crystal with the end. The "tickler" was moved until it made contact with a live spot on the crystal. Then a metal sleeve was moved along the copper tuning coil until the radio station was heard. It was necessary to use headphones, as there was not sufficient signal to activate a speaker.

I put up an antenna. I found the old copper coil off a Model T and unwound the copper wire. That made an excellent antenna. Using a hammer to drive a six-penny nail through the wall near where I planned to set the radio, I put the wires through the hole. One end of the wire was securely fastened to the aerial terminal, and about one hundred feet of the wire was run to a China-berry tree nearby. The other end of the wire was wrapped around an old tele-phone insulator, and the insulator was tied to a high limb of the tree. I found that by sitting up late at night, about 10:00 P.M., and moving the detector strip carefully along the copper-wire tuning coil, several distant radio stations could be found.

I found that by attaching copper wires to the earphone terminals, running the wires across the wood ceiling of the living and dining room, and then wrapping the ends of the wires around the headphone terminal, held in place by wooden clothes pins, my programs could be heard while eating. I also ran wires to my bed across the "breezeway." I went to sleep many nights—and would wake later with my ears hurting to find that the radio station I was listening to had gone off the air.

I was just interested in getting the program. We weren't interested in what channel. I was being an amateur radio operator at heart. I wanted to listen to the "farthest off" radio I could get with that little radio. Chicago just thrilled me to death. Anything that was "far off" was fascinating to a farm boy who had never been anywhere. We did not go on vacation like we do now. We didn't hear what was happening in other parts of the world unless we tuned in one of those newscasts on one of those radio stations.[120]

People who lived where electrification was not available and wanted a radio with a loudspeaker bought a receiver that used batteries.[121] Most had an "A" and a "B" battery, with some needing a "C." "They would last several months," re-membered Goode. "We didn't use them like you use television today; we didn't have time. We only listened for a short time at night—a couple of hours." The "A" battery was about six inches square. The "C" was like a motorcycle battery. The "C" battery made all the batteries last longer.[122]

Jack McGrew recalled his family's battery-driven radio:

My father had a receiver called "Amrad." It was manufactured by the same company that had manufactured for the Navy and Army during the first World War—receivers to be used in tanks and ships. It was battery operated. It had a big glass "A" storage battery. The case was made of glass so you could see the balls that jiggled up and down in the tube that ran just inside the case. It was six volts. That was to furnish the filament voltage. You could judge how near exhausted the battery was by the position of the little balls in the side of the case, so you could recharge it. We had a "B" and "C," but they were both dry charge. You recharged the A with just a regular charger.

Eventually the amplifier went out—one or more of them—the power transformer. So I put a potato peel across the terminals, and it worked just fine—or an apple peel. Beats me what it did. I'm not an engineer. Somebody told me, or I just fiddled around. I was a nut. I had to replace it periodically because if it dried out, it stopped working.[123]

Some individuals who had started with crystal sets later found themselves repairing the newer generation of receivers. Roger Dickey started repairing radios in the late 1920s:

I started a little radio repair shop. They were starting to get in some electric sets, but most were still battery sets. The "Majestic" was one of the first to make a big console set that was all electric—had five or six tubes in it. They were pretty good sets. They made their capacitors, put them in a metal can, and then put tar in there—covered them with tar. They would put maybe two or three capacitors in the same can and then just bring the wires out. Well, invariably one of those things would short out in that can, and the set was dead. I spent many hours with those sets in the shop melting that blamed tar out of there to get to those condensers so I could find the one that was shorted and replace it. Not many tubes went out.

The first set I got—I worked on it, and I could not find the trouble. I knew two boys who had been in the business for three or four years. They helped me find out what was wrong, and I followed their procedure. This particular set had a loud roar in it. You just took a capacitor that was the size for that set and bridged it across the different places; and when you hit the right one, the radio played all right, and the roar disappeared. From then on, I didn't have any trouble.[124]

George Ing repaired receivers when he returned to San Antonio after attending radio school. He mostly repaired "Atwater Kents." The major problem was the power supply. A capacitor would short out. "The bad thing was that the power supply was in a sealed box filled with tar," stated Ing. "Sometimes we would just put the component on the outside of the box."[125]

Hoxie Mundine was an engineer for WOAI in San Antonio. Before that, he repaired, sold, delivered, and installed radios:

They did not need scopes; they were so simple. We knew the diagrams by heart. It didn't make any difference if it was a Crosley or RCA. The "Crosley Showbox" and "Atwater Kents" went for about $35.00—a lot of money in those days.

My first job was repairing radios. There was a room full. I guess that there were five or six hundred there, mostly "Crosley Showboxes," that had not been repaired. The guys there did not know how to repair them. Some of them had been there for months. They had one little fault, and those guys did not know what it was. I had found out what the little fault was: a little coupling condenser. It was in a little metal can called a "bathtub." They developed a leak, and they allowed positive voltage to go through that leakage to the grid of the amplification tube. That automatically made it sound like the devil.

I was there for three or four days, and the boss came back to me and said, "What are you going to do about these radios?"

And I said, "Order me three or four hundred of those half-mic fast condensers."

He said, "Are you crazy?"

I took him back there and showed him what the problem was. So he called the factory, and in over a month, I had cleaned that all out.[126]

Roger Dickey worked on automobile radios beginning around 1930. Early cars did not have batteries. They had magnetos. The radios needed either two ninety- or forty-five-volt batteries to supply the current needed to light up the tube filaments. Philco sold an automobile radio that had the batteries under the front seat. Soon an automobile came out with a six-volt battery. One of the very first automobile radios had a flexible snake for tuning attached to a pod on the column below the steering wheel. The driver could reach behind the steering wheel and tune the radio. The flexible snake ran to the radio, which was down by the brake. Manufacturers tried to hide the antenna. One type of automobile radio had the antenna hidden under the running boards. This did not work because it was too close to the ground. Manufacturers also tried a mesh in the fabric top of the automobile.[127]

The years from 1911 to 1927 show a remarkable evolution for the radio industry in Texas. Wireless, a simple gadget that amateurs tinkered with, had evolved into radio broadcasting, a growing industry controlled by professionals. Many operators had given up, been pushed out, or been eliminated by the U.S. government. Radio was becoming big business—too big for many of the amateurs who had "tinkered" the industry into existence.

Large stations achieved dominance with their high-powered transmitters, and some with clear-channel frequencies. They had established, experimented with, and refined every major form of programming to be used by them and later by television. These stations developed strong schedules of entertainment and larger and larger areas of coverage, which attracted larger and larger numbers of loyal listeners. In 1926 national networking started providing these stations with an even larger variety of radio programming. The industry had established the characteristics and standards of radio broadcasting, thus determining which type of station had a chance to survive and which did not—consequently determining which stations would continue operating into the expanded growth period after 1927.

Regulations Come
to Broadcasting

1928 to 1939

Texas broadcasting in the 1930s was an industry in a long period of sustained growth influenced by several unique and interesting events. Many of these resulted from stations' actions taken because of rulings and regulations handed down by the newly formed Federal Radio Commission; others were actions taken by individuals and stations to circumvent that agency. Some of these events would have caused the following to be heard over radios in the 1930s:

> "Oh, we never do brag, we never do boast
> We sing our song from coast to coast.
> We're the Light Crust Doughboys from Burrus Mill."[1]

> "If this lady will take prescriptions number 50 and 61, see if there isn't a great big change taking place. Don't have an operation."[2]

> "You are listening to radio station 'Capital-X' in Austin."[3]

> "WBAP, the *Star-Telegram* station, Fort Worth," then the vociferous "clanging" of a cowbell, a second or two of silence, then "This is WFAA, 820, Dallas."

Each denotes an important and influential event in Texas radio history. The song of the Light Crust Dough Boys opened their radio broadcast. Their program was one of the main reasons for the establishment of another important event in Texas broadcasting in the 1930s, the grouping of stations into "chains." Dr. John R. Brinkley prescribed medicine by number for listeners who wrote letters describing their ailments. When the FRC revoked his broadcasting license in Kansas, he resurrected his over-the-air medical practice from studios in Del Rio and a powerful transmitter just south of the Rio Grande. His use of "Mexican stations with U.S. audiences" helped establish an entire radio industry unto itself: border radio.

In the early 1930s, many radio enthusiasts thought the FRC did not have the authority to regulate stations whose signal could not be heard outside the state's borders. "Capital-X" in Austin was one of at least ten Texas stations which challenged the FRC by broadcasting without a license. In the late 1920s the FRC assigned many stations to share a frequency. One in particular, between WBAP in Fort Worth and WFAA in Dallas, was unique, lasting for four decades. The announcement of the Fort Worth station's call letters, followed by the ringing of a cowbell, was one of the most remembered events in Texas broadcasting.

It was also during this period that the FRC issued rulings concerning technical standards necessitating the need for highly trained professional engineers. Now the "tinkerers" had to go to school in order to pass an engineering test required by the commission. Broadcasting was becoming a more complex and regulated industry, and stations and their personnel had to adjust.

United States Radio Broadcasting in the 1930s

Radio in the middle 1920s was essentially without controls or regulations. The Radio Act of 1912 did not give the Department of Commerce power to enforce its regulations on the developing industry. The Secretary of Commerce could not refuse to grant a radio license to any applicant on any grounds, still many stations operated without one. Stations started broadcasting, changed frequencies, and increased power at the whim of the operator.

In March 1927, there were 732 broadcasting stations in the United States; more were coming. A radio conference in 1924 had urged the elimination of 86 stations operating on 360 meters. Many operators were dissatisfied. Eugene F. McDonald, of Zenith in Chicago was. His station, WJAZ, could only broadcast two hours a week. McDonald decided to challenge the authority of the Department of Commerce which he considered "one-man control of radio with the Secretary of Commerce as supreme czar." Herbert Hoover, the secretary, had stated that he would welcome a test case of the department's authority. McDonald moved WJAZ to a different frequency without permission. The Department of Commerce filed suit. On April 16, 1926, the judge in the case of *United States v. Zenith* ruled that the Secretary of Commerce did not have the authority he had been exercising. The ruling only increased the bedlam which already existed. This caused Congress to reconvene on December 8, 1926, to pass legislation "to regain control of the situation."[4]

The Radio Act of 1927 was passed on February 23, 1927. It created the Federal Radio Commission (FRC), composed of five commissioners empowered to bring order to the industry. The commission was appointed for one year. After a year, power would revert back to the secretary of commerce. The commission was extended by congressional amendment for another year, then another year.

In the spring of 1927, the FRC started to "temporarily" extend radio licenses for sixty days. The commissioners realized that at least one hundred stations would eventually have to be abolished. A year later, the FRC issued General Order #32, which told 164 operators to "show cause" why they should not be abolished. Eighty-one stations satisfied the commission that they had "just cause" to continue broadcasting.[5] During this period, as the FRC experimented with allocations, many stations were ordered to change frequency, change power, and/or share a frequency with another station or stations. The FRC would assign or reassign a station and then "wait and see" if there were any complaints about interference. On November 11, 1928, National Frequency Reallocation Day, most Texas radio stations did one or more of the following: changed frequency; changed power; started, ended, or changed its time-sharing with another station or stations; or ceased operations.

At 3:00 A.M. on reallocation day, the *Report of the Federal Radio Commission* listed 32 broadcasting stations in Texas:

560 Kilocycles
    KFDM—Magnolia Petroleum Co., Beaumont; 500 watts
570 Kilocycles
    KGKO—Wichita Falls Broadcasting Co., Wichita Falls; 250 watts
800 Kilocycles
    WBAP—Carter Publications, Fort Worth, Texas, 50,000 watts
    (divided time with KTHS, Hot Springs, Arkansas)
920 Kilocycles
    KPRC—Houston Printing Co., Houston; 1,000 watts
1040 Kilocycles
    WFAA—*Dallas Morning News,* Dallas; 5,000 watts (construction permit issued for 50,000 watts)
    KRLD—KRLD Inc., Dallas; 10,000 watts
    (WFAA and KRLD divided time)
1120 Kilocycles
    WTAW—Agriculture and Mechanical College of Texas, College Station; 500 watts
    KUT—University of Texas, Austin; 500 watts
    (WTAW and KUT divided time)

1190 Kilocycles

WRR—City of Dallas; 5,000 watts

WOAI—Southern Equipment Co., San Antonio; 5,000 watts

(WRR and WOAI divided time)

1240 Kilocycles

KFQB—W. B. Fishburn, Fort Worth; 1,000 watts

WJAD—Frank P. Jackson, Waco; 1,000 watts

(KFQB and WJAD divided time)

1260 Kilocycles

KWWG—Chamber of Commerce, Brownsville; 500 watts

KRGV—Harlingen Music Co., Harlingen; 500 watts

(KWWG and KRGV divided time)

1290 Kilocycles

KTSA—Lone Star Broadcasting Co., San Antonio; 1,000 watts

KFUL—Will H. Ford, Galveston; 500 watts (daytime)

(KTSA and KFUL divided time)

1310 Kilocycles

KFPM—The New Furniture Co., Greenville; 15 watts

KGFI—San Angelo Broadcasting Co., San Angelo; 100 watts

KFPL—C. C. Baxter, Dublin; 15 watts

1370 Kilocycles

KFJZ—Henry Clay Allison, Fort Worth; 100 watts

KFLX—George Roy Clough, Galveston; 100 watts

KGKL—M. L. Cates, Georgetown; 100 watts

KGCI—Liberto Radio Sales, San Antonio; 100 watts

KGRC—Eugene J. Roth, San Antonio; 100 watts

(KGCI and KGRC divided time)

1410 Kilocycles

KGRS—Gish Radio Service, Amarillo; 1,000 watts

WDAG—J. Laurence Martin, Amarillo; 1,000 watts

(KGRS and WGAD divided time)

1420 Kilocycles

KTAP—Robert B. Bridge, San Antonio; 100 watts

KTUE—Uhalt Electric, Houston; 5 watts

KFYO—Kirksey Brothers Battery and Electric Co., Breckenridge; 100 watts

1500 Kilocycles

KGKB—Eagle Publishing Co., Goldthwaite; 100 watts

KGDR—Joe B. McShane, San Antonio; 100 watts

KGHX—Fort Bend County School Board, Richmond; 50 watts.[6]

Frequency Sharing

Radio stations' sharing time and frequency was unavoidable in early broadcasting. All stations shared two frequencies: 360 meters and 485 meters. Although some stations occasionally broadcast government reports on 485 meters, in 1922 virtually every station in Texas transmitted on 360 meters. Five stations in San Antonio and five in Dallas–Fort Worth shared time on that one wavelength. Later, 400 meters was added by the Department of Commerce for stations using higher power.

Even though the number of frequencies for broadcasting stations had increased dramatically by 1928, during frequency reallocation seventeen stations of the thirty-two in Texas were assigned to share time. Most sharing a frequency were in the same city; some were not. WTAW, licensed to the Agriculture and Mechanical College of Texas at College Station, shared time with KUT, licensed to Texas University in Austin. WFAA, owned by the *Dallas Morning News* shared time with KRLD, licensed to its competitor, the *Dallas Times-Herald*. This arrangement was ordered but never implemented. WBAP in Fort Worth shared time with KTHS in Hot Springs, Arkansas.[7]

WFAA-570/WFAA-820: WBAP-820/WBAP-570

WBAP, like many stations in Texas, had changed frequencies many times. It started on 360 and 485 meters then moved to 400 and 485 meters. On May 12, 1923, WBAP moved to 630 kilocycles. (About this time, reference to a station's frequency changed from meters to kilocycles and later to kilohertz.) In 1927 when the FRC changed WBAP's frequency to 600 kilocycles, the station was assigned to share time with WOAI in San Antonio. This was authorized but never implemented. On National Frequency Reallocation Day in 1928, WBAP moved to 800 kilocycles, which it shared with KTHS. In 1929 WBAP petitioned the FRC for permission to divide time with WFAA in Dallas. The FRC assigned the two stations clear channel 800 kilocycles with 50,000 watts. This arrangement became *the longest shared frequency in U.S. radio history.*[8]

"When Mr. Carter applied for radio," recalled Jim Byron, WBAP news director, "he always wanted the best—50,000 watts—clear channel. . . . But Fort Worth's population was not considered sufficient to warrant a full-time 50,000-watt clear channel station."[9]

Each year WBAP and WFAA agreed on the times each station would have the frequency. A partial schedule for 1931, signed by Harold Hough of WBAP and G. E. Chase of WFAA, was:

WFAA's Time
WBAP's Time
Daytime

6:00 A.M.—8:30 A.M.
8:30 A.M.—10:30 A.M.

10:30 A.M.—12:30 P.M.
12:30 P.M.—3:00 P.M.

3:00 P.M.—5:00 P.M.
5:00 P.M.—5:30 P.M.

5:30 P.M.—6:00 P.M.

Monday, Nighttime

6:00 P.M.—9:00 P.M.
9:00 P.M.—12:00 Midnight

The same evening schedule was followed on Wednesdays and Fridays. On Tuesdays, Thursdays, and Saturdays, the night times were reversed. Daytime schedules were the same Monday through Saturday. Sunday's times were entirely different.[10]

WFAA was not pleased at having to share a frequency and tried to solve that problem. In November of 1928, WFAA was consolidated with WRR, owned by the city of Dallas. WRR was full-time on 1280 kilocycles. Under the agreement, WFAA would erect and maintain studios and a transmitter for WRR and assume direction of that station's programming. This allowed WFAA to transmit NBC network programs over WRR's frequency when WBAP was using the shared frequency, 800 kilocycles. Program notes showed:

7:00–7:30 A.M., WRR for WFAA, Health Exercises
7:30–8 A.M., WRR for WFAA, Inspirational Hour

This arrangement did not last. The FRC did not allow WFAA to control the programming of another station. The inability of WFAA and WBAP to transmit programming when they wished led the two stations to share a second frequency in 1941.[11]

Amon Carter was not happy that his station shared a frequency with WFAA because this meant that WBAP was off the air approximately half the time. On occasions Carter took special guests to the station for a tour and interview, only to discover upon arriving that this was the time when WFAA had the frequency. Carter took Eddie Canter to the station one day and found that this was the case. This and other reasons prompted Carter Publications to purchase KGKO in Wichita Falls in 1935. Subsequently, when WBAP was not broadcasting on 800 kilocycles, KGKO was available so a guest might make a few "appropriate remarks."[12]

KGKO in Wichita Falls began broadcasting on September 9, 1926, and was licensed to the Wichita Falls Broadcasting Company. C. W. Snider was president, and Mayor R. E. Shepherd was the first commercial manager. It was later licensed to the Highland Heights Christian Church. The station transmitted on 1350 kilocycles with 250 watts. It soon changed to 1370 kilocycles with 100 watts. On September 8, 1928, the FRC changed KGKO to 250 watts on 570 kilocycles, the frequency which became known as the alternate frequency to 800 kilocycles. During the early 1930s, KGKO changed to 1240 kilocycles, and 570 kilocycles was licensed to KTAT in Fort Worth. Frequency 570 was assigned to KTAT until June 21, 1935, when that station and KGKO exchanged frequencies. For the second time, frequency 570 was assigned to KGKO in Wichita Falls, and KTAT in Fort Worth began broadcasting on 1240 kilocycles. The move was necessitated because of interference with WRR in Dallas. Thus, 570 kilocycles was assigned to KGKO when one year later Amon Carter and Carter Publications bought KGKO and moved the station and that frequency back to Fort Worth.[13]

Frank Mills started working at KGKO in the summer of 1936, just before the station moved. Mills had just graduated from college and was looking for a job with a 50,000-watt station. He had worked at WHO in Des Moines, Iowa, while he attended Drake University. Mills worked with, and sometimes substituted for, Ronald "Dutch" Reagan, who was the station's sports announcer. Mills remembers Reagan as an excellent sports reporter who used very few notes and whose style was so unique that no one could emulate him.[14] Bob Hicks, from Midland, remembers that Reagan was one of the speakers at the first convention of the Texas Association of Broadcasters held in San Antonio.[15]

Mills came to Texas with a student who lived in Wichita Falls and went to Dallas and Fort Worth to see the Texas Centennial celebration. While in Dallas he attempted to audition for WFAA but was told there were no openings:

We go back to Wichita Falls, and the girl said, "If you want to stay down here, why don't you audition at KGKO in Wichita Falls?"
   I said, "Who is that?"

"Local station."

I said, "How big is it?"

"I think that it is 5,000 watts."

I said, "I wanted a 50,000 watter."

She said, "The only reason it is still here is that Mr. Carter bought it, and he is about to move it to Fort Worth."

The *Wichita Falls Times-Record News* up there had the thing in court litigation up there. There was only one station. It left Wichita Falls without a radio station. . . .[16]

Mills started working for KGKO during the summer of 1936. "We were on the second floor of the Kemp (Hotel). Two studios, three offices—down at the end of the corridor—during the oil boom. Holy Toledo! I tried to get into the hotel to get up to the studios, and these guys would be standing up there on this balcony . . . hanging over these rails trying to sell oil leases. When I would come in from the outside, they would be hanging on telephone poles waving these oil leases . . . wild!"[17]

Carter Publications received permission from the Federal Communications Commission (FCC) on September 24, 1935, to move KGKO to Fort Worth. (The Federal Radio Commission had been replaced by the Federal Communications Commission with the passage of the *Communications Act of 1934* on June 19, 1934.) A month later, the commission suspended permission until a hearing could be held. The hearings started on Monday, January 27, 1936, in Wichita Falls. Opposition to the move was raised from people in the Texas cities of Wichita Falls, Burkburnett, Iowa Park, and Childress and the Oklahoma cities of Walters, Lawton, and Snyder. Citizens feared that the loss of their local station would leave them without any service. KTAT in Fort Worth claimed that the move would hurt them financially.

In the Fort Worth hearings, Harold Hough, general manager of WBAP, and G. A. Kahn, business manager of KGKO, testified that Carter Publications was ready to spend $50,000 for a new station plant; promised programming from Texas Wesleyan College in Fort Worth, North Texas State Teacher's College in Denton, North Texas Agriculture College in Arlington, Fort Worth Public Schools, and Tarrant County Medical Society; would create studios and programs at Texas Christian University; and would establish a remote transmission wire to Wichita Falls.[18] "We brought witnesses all the way from Oklahoma City down to Fort Worth to testify in that case," stated Abe Herman.[19]

On Wednesday, July 15, 1936, the chief examiner for the FCC, David G. Arnold, recommended that KGKO be allowed to move to Fort Worth. On December 31, 1937, a year and a half later, the FCC approved. KGKO's new transmitter was to be located halfway between Fort Worth and Dallas, with studios in the Medical Arts Building in downtown Fort Worth. KGKO/570, Fort Worth, began broadcasting on May 1, 1938.[20]

"I signed them on the air down here," recalled Mills. "I came down a few days before that. I remember that morning just as well: eight o'clock, standing there—Bong!—I signed us on the air."[21]

"That gave Carter Publications a station and a half," remembered Jim Byron. "We had half of 820 and all of 570. So, eventually, because of economics, half of 570 was sold to the Belo Corporation. That gave them two halves of two stations and gave us two halves of two stations."[22]

On May 18, 1938, KGKO presented a thirty-minute "Opening Celebration" coast-to-coast on the NBC-Blue network. *Cowhand Jamboree* was a variety and old-time minstrel show. The master of ceremonies was Don McNeill of NBC's *Breakfast Club*. The program originated from the Fort Worth Municipal Auditorium. At that time, it was the largest network program ever originated in Texas. It was carried on KGO, San Francisco; WBZ, Boston; WJZ, New York; KDKA, Pittsburgh; CFCF, Montreal, Canada; plus approximately twenty other stations around the country.[23]

WFAA and the Belo Corporation purchased half interest in KGKO from Carter Publications on July 26, 1940, in order that WFAA could have an alternate frequency. The price was $250,000. Carter wanted the Belo Corporation to pay him the cost of purchasing the station and moving it to Fort Worth. He also wanted it clear of any federal income taxes.[24]

Switching from one station to another was complicated when WFAA and WBAP were sharing one frequency, 800 kilocycles. After WFAA bought half of 570 kilocycles, switching one station off a frequency and on to the other, with the other station switching the opposite direction, created unusual problems. Each station had its transitional sound for when it changed frequencies. At WFAA the change was signaled by a chime. At WBAP it was announced by the vociferous clanging of a cowbell. The cowbell had been the symbol of WBAP since its inception in 1922 by Harold Hough, "The Hired Hand up from the boiler room."

"The old cowbell was the signal to make the switch," stated Chem Terry, announcer for WBAP. Then the announcer would say, "WBAP, *The Star-Telegram* station, Fort Worth."[25] "Our deal was one chime, a 440 cycle middle "A," stated Clarence Bruyere, staff engineer for WFAA. "At times an announcer would forget the chime, and so he would say, "WFAA, 820, Dallas, bong!" He would say it and try to get an 'A.'"[26]

Dave Naugle made many changeovers for WFAA: "I didn't know when they (WBAP) finished over there, but the engineer would have his finger up; and when it was time for me to say, 'This is WFAA, 570, Dallas,' he would point his finger.

I never heard WBAP say anything. I looked at the clock, but I still didn't do it by the clock; I did it by the finger. I would say, 'This is WFAA, 570, Dallas'—hit the dinger. They (WBAP) only rang the cowbell when they were giving up the frequency. They didn't ring the cowbell when they were receiving the frequency."[27]

Alex Burton, of WBAP, described sharing two frequencies:

Some of the time you were on ABC and some of the time you were on NBC. And ABC sometimes had their news at five minutes to the hour, and NBC had their news from the hour to five minutes past the hour. . . . You would read a local newscast into the ABC; then you would have five minutes of national news; then they would ring the damn cowbell; then you would go into NBC and you would get five minutes of national news; and then you would read the same damn five minutes of local news coming out of NBC. And it changed everyday; one thing on Monday and something different on Tuesday.[28]

Chem Terry worked Saturday afternoons at WBAP:

We had the Texaco Opera . . . because Mr. Carter owned 51 percent of KGKO and WFAA owned 49 percent . . . WBAP got 51 percent of the broadcast time of KGKO. Frequency 820 (descendant of 800) was split fifty/fifty—except Saturday afternoons when I was running both of them. We were on both frequencies.

The engineer would listen to WBAP, and I would listen to KGKO. We were running fifty-five [thousand] watts of power [fifty thousand watts on 820 and five thousand on 570]—the only time I have ever heard of that. WFAA was off the air completely.

I had two microphone stands there. If he gave me a signal to "break," I knew what break to make on his [frequency]; and if I gave him the signal that I was going to make a break, I would cut mine [microphone] on and make my break in there. We never made a break on both frequencies at the same time; they were staggered. . . . NBC would always give the chimes, "This is NBC, the National Broadcasting Company: Bong! Bong! Bong!"

I had two microphones there . . . in the same studio. Keep in mind: we had WBAP/820; we had KGKO/570; we had TQN, the Texas Quality Network; we had LSC, the Lone Star Chain; we had NBC, the National Broadcasting Company; and we had ABC, the American Broadcasting Company. That is six different things you had to keep in your mind all the time—where you were and what you were doing. I don't know how I kept track of things.[29]

WFAA had its problems. At times a changeover occurred in the middle of a speech or sporting event. Even if the president was talking, the FCC required the stations to identify themselves as they changed. WFAA personnel would whisper the call letters as softly as possible when they did not want to interrupt the program. Of course, just after they whispered so they would not interrupt the program, that program disappeared. According to Denson Walker, past manager of WFAA, WBAP always rang the cowbell, whatever the event. During one football game, the changeover occurred as a player with the ball was running toward the goal. The audience heard the description of the player running, then nothing. In later years, the stations agreed not to switch frequencies in the middle of events.[30]

The U.S. government signed the Havana Treaty on December 13, 1937. The treaty set down which frequencies would be reserved for priority use by Mexico and the United States. Consequently, 795 of the 883 radio stations in the United States had to change frequency. WBAP and WFAA had to move because 800 kilocycles became a Mexican clear channel. WBAP/WFAA moved to 820 kilocycles on March 29, 1941, at 8:00 G.M.T. (2 A.M., Texas time), National Frequency Change Day.[31]

This unusual arrangement of frequencies and ownership again became a problem in the early 1940s. The FCC adopted its "Chain Broadcasting Regulations" in 1941. The "duopoly" part of this regulation was aimed at preventing a network from owning two stations in the same area. It was primarily aimed at breaking up the National Broadcasting Company, which owned two networks: NBC-Red and NBC-Blue. Consequently, the NBC-Blue Network was sold to Edward J. Noble, "The Lifesaver King," and became the American Broadcasting Company (ABC). Some interested people thought the arrangement of WFAA, WBAP, and KGKO with two frequencies and mixed facilities violated this rule. In 1944 the two stations asked for a ruling by the FCC that they were not in violation.[32]

While in Washington, D.C., in 1941, Abe Herman had a friend who worked at the FCC tell him that Carter Publications would soon be given an order to dispose of one of its two frequencies. Herman telephoned Harold Hough in Fort Worth. Herman was advised to go see Sam Rayburn, speaker of the U.S. House of Representatives. At the meeting with Rayburn, Herman explained that WBAP did not own two stations and two frequencies. He contended that "two halves make one." Rayburn asked Herman to put his argument in a memorandum. Herman did. The next morning, Herman saw Rayburn and James Fly, chairman of the FCC, talking in the dining room of the House of Representatives. Herman's memorandum was in front of them.

On February 14, 1947, the FCC ruled that the two stations could continue operating on two frequencies.[33] "I am the only attorney in the FCC Bar," stated Herman, "who was able to persuade this commission that two halves don't make but one."[34] With the ruling, the FCC set strict rules. The two stations could not have joint sale of time and rate cards; could not have joint contracts or networks; could not have joint use of artists or talent; must maintain separate executive and studio staffs; must have no common expense fund; must not pool revenues; must eliminate joint advertising representation; must never allow one station to operate simultaneously on both frequencies; must make prescribed changes in the operation of both transmitter plants.[35]

On April 27, 1947, the commission granted the request that WBAP and WFAA be granted a one-half interest in both the assets and broadcast license of KGKO; those call letters were deleted. The two stations would then be known as WFAA-570/WFAA-820 and WBAP-820/WBAP-570. The sharing of frequencies that started in the late 1920s ended in 1970. Carter Publications, owner of WBAP, paid the Belo Corporation, owner of WFAA, $3.5 million for its one-half interest in clear-channel 820 kilocycles and relinquished its one-half interest in 570 kilocycles.[36]

Broadcast Schooling

In 1929 the FRC began to tighten up the engineering standards for the industry. Radio operators were required to hold a second-class telegraph license. The person who "tinkered" with the station's equipment was quickly becoming outmoded. Engineers had to go to school or achieve higher levels of technical competency through self-study.

Frank Parrish, an engineer at WBAP, received his license in Tyler:

The guy who ran the radio part did not know much about it. These schools were very common. They ran ads in local newspapers: cotton marketing, bookkeeping, telegraph operators . . . later they started one in Fort Worth: Draughn's Business College.

There were sixteen in my class. We had to take rapid calculations— figure out different things in your head. That had nothing to do with the curriculum. Typing—had to have typing. Most of the guys who left there were going aboard ships as ship operators. You hadn't ever heard about broadcasting at that time. You were supposed to learn Ohm's Law—all the electrical terms—diagrams and what not. I guarantee, you didn't know anything when you got out of there, but I got my first job from there. I got a second-class telegraph. That gives you eligibility to work at a broadcasting station. The difference between first phone and second phone was code speed—how fast you could receive and send it. . . . You had to take at least twenty words a minute for the second; first class was thirty.[37]

Parrish started working for WBAP in 1929 taking meter readings at the transmitter every thirty minutes for the FRC's engineering log. He went to the studio only "to pick up my check." WBAP kept three studio staff members in the studio at any given time: one operator and two announcers from the staff, which consisted of Herb Southern, Dave Dogular, Dave Burns, Merl Tucker, and Bud Sherman. The office staff was the manager, George Cranston, and a secretary.[38]

Johnny Smith, of KFJZ in Fort Worth, attended the Port Arthur Radio School to get his first-class license. "You first had to start learning Morse code," said Smith. "I never did thoroughly learn it cause I could care less about Morse code."[39]

George Ing, of KONO in San Antonio, had to go out-of-state. "I subscribed to many magazines like *QST*. I wanted to get into broadcasting, but you had to have a second-class telegraph license, and there was not one (school) in San Antonio. So I went to New Orleans and attended the Gulf Radio School to get my code speed up because that was one of the most important things on the test in 1928. You had to draw a diagram of a spark transmitter or a tube transmitter. The whole exam had nothing to do with broadcasting."[40]

Station Engineering

When Ing first came to San Antonio, the predecessor of KABC was a small station with its transmitter in the owner's residence on Mulberry Street. The transmitter was built in the "bread-board" style, where components were laid out on a table. Ing started working for KONO. Its transmitter was "composite," or homemade. "The FRC did not require modulation monitors, so the only way to judge modulation was to watch the rise and fall of the antenna current meter pointer," said Ing. "The Commission did not require frequency monitors, but a station had to stay on its assigned frequency." Radio inspectors would periodically come from New Orleans to check the station's frequency with a small wooden box containing a wave meter. Later, the FRC had "roving mobile outfits" and a monitor station in Oklahoma.[41]

Chem Terry was responsible for running a test at KBST in Big Springs:

> They used to give me the chore of doing a frequency check once a month. I had to go in at two o'clock in the morning—from 2:00 to 2:15—I'd run records and give a station break every two minutes. They could monitor it in St. Louis. . . . They listened up there, and you would get a report. All stations had to do the frequency check; it was an FCC rule. If you were off your frequency just the least bit, you had to correct that baby and do it again. Every two minutes I would fade down the music and say, "You are listening to KBST in Big Springs, regular frequency check," give the frequency, and bring it (music) back up again. You got a notification from the FCC telling you when they would be listening.[42]

• • •

KONO in San Antonio had a transmitter in a regular guest room on the fifth floor of the St. Anthony Hotel. The motor-generator that supplied power for the transmitter was in the bathroom. The antenna was a flat-top "T" supported by two sixty-five-foot steel towers on the roof. These antennas were not very efficient. They directed the radiation upward instead of toward the horizon.

KONO and KMAC shared time on 1370 kilocycles. KONO would broadcast for two hours and then go off so KMAC could broadcast for two hours. The two stations alternated all day. Occasionally an operator would fail to turn off the transmitter at the scheduled time. The two transmitters would have slight differences in their frequency, resulting in a terrible "heterodyne" effect. The listener heard a loud whistle.

To save money, Gene Roth, owner of KONO, had the early-morning engineer do double duty as announcer. KONO put a microphone and turntable in the transmitter room. This combination engineer and announcer was called a "combo" man. This was a common practice in small stations.[43]

Buddy Cruse visited KFJZ's early transmitter:

[Truett] Kimzey used to teach electronics out at the old Shady Oaks farm to anybody who wanted to come out at night. It was a dairy where KFJZ had their first transmitter. It was an inverted "L" horizontal antenna. Inverted "L" will radiate vertically. Your signal will go out moving up and down and come around back to the ground—depending upon the wavelength. The old horizontal they would put up a telephone pole. . . . When they started going vertical, they started going to quarter waves. A lot depended upon the amount of ground you had to put in, because your ground system has to be so big—and it ought to be good soil—good conductivity—not too much rock and very little clay. That is why KFJZ moved their antenna from the dairy to an area below the dam of the power plant just south of LaGrave Field because the Trinity River went through there, and they felt they could get a lot more moisture in the ground from the river.[44]

Many unusual engineering techniques were used to "get things done." Paul Huhndorff used his own technique when working on a new transmitter in Houston. Huhndorff installed an REL (Radio Engineering Laboratory) transmitter with "open" transmission lines. To tune the transmitter, "we put a fluorescent light on the transmission line and a thermometer on the final of the transmitting tube," said Huhndorff. "When the temperature went down and the light got bright, we knew we had it 'tuned up' to the antenna."[45]

Stan McKenzie developed a new engineering technique when his station in

Seguin was scheduled to broadcast a bi-district high school baseball game from a neighboring city. When he and his crew arrived at the ballpark, they discovered that the telephone company had failed to install a line for their broadcast. McKenzie made a deal with the local radio station. He ran a phone line from the press box to a barbed-wire fence behind the stadium and "hooked-up." They "scratched" the barbed wire so they could get a good contact. The fence ran a mile down a road to a point near the local station. McKenzie then ran a line from the barbed-wire fence into the station and used one of the station's phone lines to broadcast the game back to Seguin. "It was terrible quality, but it worked," said McKenzie.[46]

Buddy Cruse was a transmitter engineer for KFJZ. Some of his shifts were at night when there was a baseball game at LaGrave Field nearby. He would climb the tower and watch the game. A person could touch an amplitude modulation broadcasting tower, depending on the type. "If it were a shunt feed with the bottom grounded, there was no danger. You wouldn't walk up to a tower for a station with 50,000 watts and do that," said Cruse, "but all the stations in those days were 250 watts up to one thousand. You would see some of the tower men jump from the ground to the tower—if it was the right type."[47]

KAND (Can of chili) in Corsicana was operated by a Mr. West, owner of Wolf Brand Chili. Its transmitter was located in a house north of town. The transmitter was in the living room. The chief engineer had the option of living at the transmitter, since some engineer had to always be near the transmitter. Meter readings were taken every thirty minutes.[48]

WFAA in Dallas and WBAP in Fort Worth had their transmitters at Lake Worth. At first the two stations had separate transmitters for 800 kilocycles. In the early 1930s, the two stations started sharing a transmitter. The first RCA 50,000-watt transmitter for 800 kilocycles was serial number "3." Studios were separate. WBAP's studios were on the twenty-second floor of the Blackstone Hotel. The station had one main studio and one small studio that together occupied the whole floor. There was a hall where people could come and watch the production of a program. There were two offices and a musician's lounge. In the 1930s the studios for WFAA were the "Penthouse Studios" on top of the Santa Fe Building.[49]

Smaller stations usually had one studio. The control room might have an engineering board with two turntables. The studio would have one or two microphones, with possibly one microphone in the control room or an announcer's booth. In the 1930s the studio of any radio station *always* contained a piano. The control room at KAND had two turntables and two microphones in the studio. The control board had a network line and a remote line. These lines were raw lines— straight lines except that the phone company took out the batteries. They were just straight wires.[50]

Batteries were used for equipment in the studios of WBAP. There were wet batteries for all the tube filaments and dry cells for the plates. They usually lasted a month. WBAP used batteries until 1932, when Frank Parrish got tired of worrying with them and built the station a rectifier to replace them.[51]

One of the earliest microphones used was the Western Electric Double Button carbon microphone. George Ing used one at KONO:

These microphones were like your telephone, only there were two of them back to back. It was called Double Button. Each button was two metallic diaphragms, and the space between them was filled with carbon granules. The voice compressed and decompressed the carbon granules, and that varied the electrical current. The fidelity was pretty good, but there was always a very soft hiss in the background, caused by the current going through the carbon granules. Also, the carbon granules tended to pack. The announcer would frequently signal the engineer to turn the mike current off so that he could rotate the mike and unpack the granules. We would do it sometimes every fifteen minutes. The engineer would then check to see if the current through each button was the same.[52]

Announcers had to work fairly close to carbon microphones. Talking into the microphone caused "lip-rush." (To blow into a microphone causing a deep bass and "rumbling" sound.)[53] At many stations in the late 1920s, the RCA 4-A-1 replaced the Double Button. In the 1930s, better microphones came into use: the "Salt Shaker," the Western Electric A316, and the RCA 44BX. Bill Bradford of KSST in Sulfur Springs used a 44BX:

If you were really uptown—a new microphone called the cardioid, which was a combination ribbon and dynamic element—then there were ribbons—RCA 44BX. If you "close talked" a ribbon microphone, you got a deep, deep voice—actually it just got muddy. It was just a corrugated piece of tin foil—aluminum foil—a little ribbon of aluminum that would flex, and there was a magnet on both sides of it. This was the moving element—very low impedance thing that you ran up to 500 Ohms. Blow in it and all you had was a long piece of aluminum; it was gone. Knowing that this was going to happen—and that was the nice thing about the engineer of that era—he did not simply plug in circuits. The engineer at that time was a repair man and a scrounger—and swapped ideas. Fortunately, the Hershey Bar of that time was wrapped in very thin aluminum foil, which everybody called "tin foil." The good engineer kept a razor blade and his own set of gears; and when some idiot announcer, whom he would scald alive, blew into the ribbon microphone, it took about three

An original Western Electric Double Button carbon microphone first used at WJAD, Waco, in the early 1920s. Courtesy Robert E. Weathers, former owner, president, and general manager, WACO Radio Inc.

An original RCA Model 4-A-1 condenser microphone installed at WOAI, San Antonio, in December, 1929. Courtesy Hoxie Mundine

hours to repair it. You took your razor blade and cut a thin strip of aluminum, which you then fed between these two gears, these two meshing gears. That corrugated the aluminum. Then you had to take this piece and somehow clamped it between these two very narrow magnets. The width had to be just right, and you were back in business. Nobody could afford to send one back to the factory.

This Western Electric A316 microphone was really state of the art at that time. It was more flexible than the ribbon. If you wanted, you could simply make it a dynamic microphone, or you could make it a full ribbon; or you could combine the two and make a cardioid package. You did it with a switch. It even combined backwards. You could control the positive and negative, and you could get this very unique dead back. If you had an announcer who liked to sound like [H. V.] Kaltenborn, you could switch it to ribbon; and if he "closed talked" it, it was a real "Boom, Boom, Boom." The dynamic was sharper and cleaner.

The cardioid gave you that dead backside, which meant that if you were in a small booth, you would put the back side to the glass, and it reduced that "bathroom" sound. You would have one of those mainly for your control room. You would have a couple of "salt shakers." Before World War II, there were some carbon microphones. They were very good, but they still "hissed."[54]

A common practice of small stations during the Depression years was the "trade out." The station traded on-air advertising in return for goods and services. This was usually given to the staff as part of their salaries. George Ing of KONO in San Antonio got his clothes by trade outs. Ice and milk were delivered to his home every day. The staff at KAND in Corsicana were paid so much a week, plus "chili." Jack McGrew of KFDM in Beaumont received some of his pay in meal tickets. They were cards with a number of stars printed around the edges; he could present these to the cashier at Fuller's cafe each time he ate there.[55]

One very common trade out was between stations and hotels that furnished space for studios and offices, and sometimes even for transmitters. Ves Box worked for a station that paid its rent in trade outs. "KRLD [Dallas] was on the mezzanine floor of the Adolphus Hotel. The station would include the name of the hotel in the station breaks, and that would pay the rent . . . for example, 'KRLD, Voice of the Great Southwest in Dallas, Fort Worth, located in the Adolphus Hotel' and 'KTSA in the Governor Hotel, center of everything in San Antonio.'"[56]

Electrical Transcriptions (ET)

Starting in the 1920s, one of the most reliable sources of radio programming was the electrical transcription, or ET. During the 1930s and '40s, long before magnetic audio recording was developed, the ET was the only method available to preserve a radio program. This was basically a sixteen-inch disc of vinyl, like the 33 1/3 rpm record that became popular in the 1950s. When placed on a broadcast lathe, an ET blank could be "cut" and audio programming recorded.

Most ETs came from transcription services; most stations subscribed to at least one. There were many available: World, Associated, Lange Worth, McGragor, Columbia, Standard, NBC Thesaurus (perhaps ten in all). Programming included entire shows, individual songs, musical numbers from known bands, sound effects, and a special type of programming as described by Alex Burton:

It was sixteen inches across. There would be five or six songs on one side; and you would turn it over, and there would be five or six songs on the other side. You would have the key "going in" and the key "going out," and how long it was—and there was a little arrow on the label so you could cue it up without hearing it.

The label of an electrical transcription (ET) of Lanny Ross music from the World Program Service. Note the arrow on the bottom used to help cue the record. From the author's collection

If you took the transcription services, they would send out a script for—*The Lanny Ross Show.* You could go from music to music . . . and you would know exactly how long the introduction was. You could start the music, fade it under, read the script, crank it up, and there was the song; it was all timed and everything. It was part of the service.

You would get these scripts every month—a big bundle of scripts. . . . If you chose to run the program . . . it sounded like it was being produced right there in the studio; it was all done on albums. . . .[57]

Hoxie Mundine used ETs for decades at WOAI in San Antonio:

World ETs were vertical cuts (the needle moved up and down). Standard was horizontal (the needle moved from side to side). You had to have both horizontal and vertical (tone or pick-up) arms. I don't know—it [Standard] just had a different sound to it. Standard had the best bands.

We had to return everything; they reused it. That is why we lost so much stuff—all the episodes of *Little Orphan Annie, Judy and Jane,* and *The Lone*

Ranger. There were two episodes on it—one on one side and one on the other. The first equipment we had was for playing 33 1/3; that equipment was the same equipment they used for the first talking pictures.[58]

The Standard Transcription Service in 1936 provided a subscribing station with a library of approximately 800 selections. Artists included Gene Austin, song stylist; Jascha Borowshy, gypsy orchestra; Cleo Brown, pianist and singer; The Brownies, novelty trio; Larry Cotton, tenor; Tom Doring, swing band; the Farr Brothers, novelty trio; Alfred Garr, tenor; Aaron González, tango rumba orchestra; Hal Grayson, dance orchestra; and Red Harper, novelty singer.[59]

Wendell Mayes's father subscribed to a service that allowed the station to keep the material until its contract ran out; then all material had to be returned. ETs were shipped to his station by Railway Express. There was a delivery of four or five once a week. The station paid a monthly fee of approximately one hundred dollars. The Mayeses' station also received ETs from the U.S. Treasury Department. The station did not have to return these. A man in a Cadillac would come to the station and buy the old ETs for the vinyl. "We would save all this stuff up until he would show up," said Mayes. "He would throw them in the back of his car, and he must have had a ton of that stuff. . . ."[60]

During World War II, because of the shortage of vinyl, the base of many ETs was glass and easily broken. On some ETs that had two, three, or even four sides to a program, the first side usually played from the outside edge inward like a regular record. The second side might play from the inside out. This eliminated a noticeable change in sound quality as the program switched from one side to another.

Many stations did not have a cue channel for records and ETs. (A cue channel was an off-air sound system that allowed engineers and disc jockeys to "cue" a record—find the beginning of the sound. One method of cueing a record was: the needle was placed at the beginning of the record's groove and then the record was turned by hand until the very first sounds were heard in the control room over the cue channel. Then, the record or ET was backed-up a quarter or half turn. Some engineers did not turn the record by hand; rather, they started the turntable, let the record turn, and when the first sounds were heard, they stopped the record with their hand or a finger, backed it up, and then turned off the turntable. The record was then cued—ready to be used on the air. When needed, the engineer or disc jockey put a finger on the record and turned the turntable on while keeping the record still. As the last sounds of the preceding speech or record were heard, the engineer or disc jockey lifted his finger, and the record "hit," or started, about one or two seconds later. Later turntables could get up to speed quickly, and disc jockeys only had to turn the turntable on and the show started.

Certain types of ETs could not be backed up or the station did not have a cue

Two Western Electric vertical and lateral turntables installed at WOAI, San Antonio, in December, 1930. They played and "cut," or recorded, radio programs to make electrical transcriptions (ETs). Years earlier these two machines had been the turntables that furnished sound for the first talking motion pictures. Courtesy Hoxie Mundine

channel, so records or ETs had to be cued differently. "We worked many years without a cue channel," said Mundine. "The verticals—we could spin them and listen. We would have to put our ear down close to them . . . run it to a certain point, count the turns, and then pick it (tone arm) up. We could not back up because the needle might . . . dig-in."[61]

Burton remembered another method of working without a cue channel: "One station I worked at—they used steel needles. They (engineers) would tear off a piece of paper about an inch or so square, put it on the record, put the needle through the paper, and turn the record by hand on the turntable until they heard a sound—that was what the paper did; it picked it up. Then you put your finger on the tone arm, pulled away the paper, and threw it on the floor, and then moved the [needle] back one groove. Then you flicked on the turntable and there was the music."[62]

At KONO in the late 1920s, the operators changed the steel needle after each record. During World War II, because of shortages, some stations used cactus needles. Starting in the late 1920s, to keep the public from being fooled into thinking that the orchestra playing the music was really in the studios of the station "right then," the FRC required stations to announce before each record or ET: "This is a phonograph record." At other times announcers would say, "The following program is recorded," "The preceding program was recorded," or "The preceding program has come to you by electrical transcription."[63]

Even with the development of magnetic recording after World War II, ETs continued to be used. Ted Bender at KTSM in El Paso used ETs into the 1960s, particularly one program:

> The first time records were played on a network was Bing Crosby for Philco. Those discs came to El Paso—in the 1950s. Bing Crosby came in on disc. The good part of the acetate was not in the beginning or at the end. The instruction and the timing on it, and the cueing on it, were so elaborate. You didn't touch it with your fingers. The things were sixteen inches in diameter, and you could not use the first few inches and the last few inches.
>
> We were very late getting tape here. Wire never entered the picture here. I had a wire recorder, a Webster, but it wasn't any good for broadcast work.
>
> Disc recording we could make. Disc recording we could play. When did we go to tape? I guess it was with the Magacorder. . . . You had to play back on the same machine that you recorded on. They all had idiosyncracies. If you recorded on machine A, you wanted to play back on machine A; you did not want to take it to machine B. Magacorder were the first tape machine we had. Now it's a name nobody even thinks about.
>
> We were never the first to have anything, and we hung onto the old a lot longer than other places. We always used to tell the story that "one of these years El Paso is going to be dragged, kicking and screaming into the twentieth century, and they had better hurry up cause we are about to go to the twenty-first."[64]

Mexican (Texas) Stations with U.S. Audiences

One of the most unusual and remembered events in Texas broadcasting during the 1930s was the advent of powerful radio stations located just south of the Rio Grande and transmitting to audiences in the United States. Although locations other than across from Texas were used, it seems that those stations within sight of Texas soil are best remembered. One in particular, XER, later XERA, owned by Dr. John R. Brinkley, attracted the most attention and is still remembered by more people. XER's transmitter was located just south of the river. The studios were located north of the border in the city of Del Rio. Its audience was enormous, and listeners heard the station from incredible distances.

"I loved to DX," stated Harold Romey of Concordia, Kansas. He put up a special antenna on the roof and listened to stations "from coast to coast." Romey had an old eight-tube "Airline." He started to listen to some of the clear channel stations in Texas and Dr. Brinkley after he left Kansas in 1931. "Especially on Sunday nights," Romey remembered, "old Dr. Brinkley was always on with duets, trios, and banjo picking, which I really liked to listen to."[65]

XED/XEAW, Reynosa, Tamaulipas, Mexico

XED was the first border station. It began one year before Brinkley built his "border blaster." XED, "The Voice of Two Republics," began in 1930, transmitting with 10,000 watts. The station was owned and operated by four Texans from McAllen and Hidalgo and one Mexican citizen. The partnership hired W. E. Branch to plan and construct XED. In the 1920s Branch had started KFJZ in his Fort Worth backyard and sold Harold Hough the first transmitter for WBAP in Fort Worth.

The transmitter for XED was located in Reynosa. The studios were across the Rio Grande in the Hotel McAllen. The inaugural program was a one hundred–hour spectacular. In September of 1931, the station's controlling interest was bought by Will Horwitz from Houston. Horwitz had operated WEAY in Houston, one of the first stations in that city, for a short period in 1922.[66]

Horwitz started having trouble with the U.S. and Mexican governments. The Mexican government objected to XED advertising the Tamaulipas lottery and receiving "baskets full of money." In April of 1932, Horwitz was arrested by U.S. postal inspectors for mail fraud. While the owner was in jail, Mexican tax agents closed the station. Before the end of the year, the station's original owners again started broadcasting as XEAW, "The Voice of International Service." In 1935 XEAW was purchased by Brinkley, who in 1939 sold it to Carr Collins, an insurance agent from Dallas.

Carr Collins and his brother Hal marketed Crazy Water Crystals. The Collins brothers took the natural mineral water from a spring in Mineral Wells, boiled it down to a crystal, and sold it in small packages. Customers took a spoonful of crystals, stirred them into a glass of water, and drank it. The water was advertised as being for anyone suffering from a condition "caused or being made worse by a sluggish system." Crazy Water Crystals were originally advertised on stations in the United States. The product was very popular and profitable. The Collins brothers bought the Mexican station when the U.S. government started disapproving of some of their claims about Crazy Water's healing powers.

In the early 1940s, XEAW was suddenly and unexpectedly closed when the Mexican government gave its frequency to another station in Monterrey, Mexico. The Collins brothers moved their equipment from Mexico to Corpus Christi. In September of 1944, the FCC granted a license to the Collins brothers and their

W. E. Branch built the original 10-watt transmitter for WBAP in Fort Worth, built and operated KFJZ from his home in Fort Worth, and engineered and built many Mexican stations, like XER for Dr. John R. Brinkley, that broadcast to the United States from south of the Rio Grande. Courtesy Fort Worth Star-Telegram *Photograph Collection, Special Collections Division, University of Texas at Arlington Libraries, Arlington, Texas*

new partner, Baylor University, for KWBU, broadcasting with 50,000 watts. The station continued to make money for the Collins brothers, and subsequently the university. In 1956 the station was donated to Baylor.[67]

Bob Hicks, president of KBAT and KQIP in Midland, was born in China Springs. He became interested in radio while attending Baylor University. Part of the broadcasting courses was to produce programming for KWBU. He and other students produced shows that dramatized the news and current events. The programs were sent to Corpus Christi by phone line or electrical transcription.[68]

XER, Ciudad Acuña, Coahuila, Mexico

John Richard Brinkley, M.D., Ph.D., M.C., LL.D., D.P.H., Sc.D., Lieut. U.S.N.R., was probably the best-known doctor in early U.S. broadcasting. Brinkley, the son of a country doctor, tried to attend Johns Hopkins Medical School. When his application was refused, he attended Bennett Eclectic Medical School in Chicago and then the Eclectic Medical University in Kansas City. He earned his medical degree in less than a month. Brinkley's degree, which focused on herbal healing, homeopathy, and naturopathy, was recognized in eight states; one was Texas.[69]

Brinkley located his medical practice in Milford, Kansas, in October of 1917. He opened an office and a drugstore that stocked patent medicines. People in Kansas knew him as the doctor who thought he could rejuvenate the sexual drives of elderly men by transplanting goat glands into them. The idea of using goats had originated earlier when Brinkley had worked for Swift and Company, meat packers. It came to his attention that the goat was the healthiest animal slaughtered. In fact, some veterinarians told Brinkley that they never remembered seeing one sick.[70]

One day in his clinic, Brinkley was talking to a patient who wished to be sexually potent again. "I'm all in," complained the patient. "No pep—a flat tire."

Brinkley remembered the goats and told the man he "wouldn't have any trouble if you had a pair of those buck glands in you."

The patient begged for an operation. "Why don't you go ahead and put a pair of goat glands in me? Transplant 'em. Graft 'em on."[71]

After much pleading and some outright threats, Brinkley secretly performed the transplant. The man claimed the operation was a tremendous success. Word rapidly spread, and Brinkley was forced to continue the procedure. He finally accepted the idea as practical, worthwhile, money-making, and medically sound. The operation consisted of transplanting the thyroid, pituitary, and pineal glands from a goat kid into humans. An advertising consultant, hired by Brinkley to help publicize his practice, told him, "Dr. Brinkley, you've got a million dollars in your hands and you don't even realize it!"[72]

The operation became well known across the nation. At one time there was talk of operating on Woodrow Wilson, but certain people wanted it kept secret; Brinkley wanted the publicity. He claimed the ailing president would be better in thirty-six hours.[73]

Brinkley learned about radio on a trip to California in 1922. On returning to Kansas, he built KFKB (Kansas First, Kansas Best, or Kansas Folks Know Best), broadcasting on 1050 kilocycles with 1,000 watts. The station quickly gained the reputation as the most popular station in the United States: "The Sunshine Station in the Heart of the Nation." It was from here that Brinkley started his career of prescribing medicine, sight unseen, over the air to listeners who wrote him describing their ailments. His theme was, "Don't let your doctor two-dollar you to death." He used code numbers for prescribing medicine that were understood by drugstore personnel who "went along" with him. Brinkley received a kickback for every bottle of medicine sold by the 1,500 pharmacists who belonged to the Brinkley Pharmaceutical Association.[74]

His nightly medical show, *Medical Question Box,* gave "free" medical advice: If this lady will take numbers 50 and 61, and that good old standby of mine, number 67, for about three months, and see if there isn't a great big change taking place. Don't have an operation.

I suggest that you have your husband sterilized, and then you will be safe from having more children, providing, you don't get out in anybody else's cow pasture and get in with some other bull.[75]

This over-the-air medical practice prompted the Federal Radio Commission in 1931 to refuse renewal of the station's license. Grounds for denial stated that Brinkley was practicing "point-to-point" communication. The state of Kansas revoked Brinkley's medical license. On his last broadcast, on February 21, 1931, he announced that he was building a new station in Mexico.[76]

In the spring of 1931, Brinkley started constructing a $30,000 building and $175,000 transmitter across the river from Del Rio. Money seemed to be no problem. While visiting the manufacturer of transmitter power tubes, Brinkley was told they would cost $36,000. He reached into his pocket and counted off thirty-six $1,000 bills. To that date, those tubes were said to be the most powerful ever made. One engineer who helped plan and construct the station was W. E. Branch of Fort Worth.

XER, "The Sunshine Station Between the Nations," began broadcasting on October 21, 1931, on 735 kilocycles, between WGN in Chicago on 720 kilocycles and WSB in Atlanta on 740 kilocycles. At first Brinkley tried to keep his studios in Milford, sending the programming to the transmitter by phone line. This allowed him to stay with his hospital in Kansas, but the line cost $10,000 a month.[77]

Brinkley started flying to Mexico. L. D. Yates, brother of Darrell E. Yates, who still owns KRBA in Lufkin, flew Brinkley back and forth from Kansas to Mexico. Yates remembered Brinkley in the 1930s: "It was speech and yelling."[78]

Claude Goode of Greenville listened to Brinkley: "He was a high-pressure salesman and very convincing . . . about his hospital—his medicine—how great it was. He made people believe it. If you had any kind of disease, he would mention it at one time or another—that they had medicine that would cure that. If you would come down to his hospital, you would come back feeling like a two-year-old. My folks did not believe this. He really oversold it as far as we were concerned. We listened just to see what he would say."[79]

The station's transmitter was clearly visible from the Texas side of the Rio Grande. Later, Brinkley's studios and hospital were moved to Del Rio. Most every night Brinkley sold the continent on the virtues of his "compound operation," which claimed to relieve prostate trouble, sexual debility, sterility, dementia praecox, hardened arteries, high blood pressure, diabetes, neurasthenia, epilepsy, and various stomach, kidney, bowel, and nervous ailments.[80]

XER started broadcasting with 50,000 watts. Soon it increased its power to 75,000 watts. Trouble with the Mexican government put XER off the air temporarily. During his absence from Mexican radio, Brinkley bought time on stations in the United States. On Sunday, November 17, 1935, Brinkley returned to the air with XERA. At one time the station claimed to be "the world's most powerful broadcasting station." XERA broadcast with 500,000 watts; but Brinkley was quoted as saying that with its directional antenna, it was the same as one million watts being aimed at the United States. (Except for experiments in the 1930s by WLW in Cincinnati, Ohio, AM radio stations in the United States have never broadcast with more than 50,000 watts.) Every night when the air cooled and the atmospheric bounce increased the reach of amplitude modulation (AM) stations, XERA's coverage and audience multiplied with regular listeners in Brazil, Peru, Hawaii, Alaska, and many other distant places.[81]

The station's most famous personality in the decades following Brinkley was Wolfman Jack. He started listening to XERF (which followed XERA) as a kid in New York. In 1960, after working at local stations, Wolfman drove to Del Rio and walked into the middle of a small war over the possession of the station. For a time after he was hired, Wolfman wore a gun on his hip while at work. With his unusual radio personality, voice, and delivery, Wolfman and his program helped save the station.

Every evening until 4 A.M., when the station's powerful sky waves skipped off the ionosphere layer of the atmosphere, Wolfman broadcast to North America. He became famous for his unique style of growling and howling:

"Well AAWWWRRIIGHT Baaayyyybee . . . We gonna feeel it to-nite . . . OOOOOOWWWWWWOooooooooooooooo . . . This is Wolfman Jack down here with the donkeys . . . Wherever ya are, and whatever ya doin', I wancha to lay ya hands on da raydeeooo, lay back wid me, and squeeeze ma knobs . . . I mean this next record gonna knock you right on da flo-wa."[82]

XENT, Nuevo Laredo, Mexico

Norman Baker, the lavender-shirted, cancer-cure wizard, was a "spellbinder." He had the ability to speak extemporaneously and hold an audience. In 1924 Baker received a license to operate KTNT (Know the Naked Truth), a 500-watt station in Muscatine, Iowa. He wanted to "shake up" the entrenched social order and "watch out" for the rights of the masses. On June 5, 1931, the FRC refused to re-new Baker's license on grounds that KTNT was operated "to subordinate the interests of the listening audience for those of the licensee."[83]

Baker hired W. E. Branch to build him a 150,000-watt station across the Rio Grande from Laredo. XENT started operating early in 1934. The station's pro-gramming was "homey," featuring old songs, marches, Hawaiian medleys, children's shows, and stirring talks by Baker. W. Lee O'Daniel (late of the Light Crust Doughboys), along with his band, the Hillbilly Boys, who played and ad-vertised Hillbilly Flour, used the station to campaign for governor of Texas.

Broadcasting on XENT started at 6:00 P.M., when nightfall greatly increased the station coverage. Baker spoke every ninety minutes. Soon he opened a hospi-tal in Laredo using the slogan "Cancer Is Curable." Baker stayed in Mexico at his station because an arrest warrant had been issued for him in the state of Iowa.[84] He was eventually arrested, tried, and sentenced for mail fraud stemming from his hospital operations in Eureka Springs, Arkansas. While Baker was in prison at Leavenworth, Kansas, in the early 1940s, XENT ceased operations.

After his release, Baker filed a petition with the Federal Communications Com-mission claiming that that agency had allowed Alamo Broadcasting of San Anto-nio, operators of KABC, to "steal" XENT's transmitter while he was in prison. The petition claimed that in 1936 the FCC had instigated indictments charging Baker with making and transporting across the border into Mexico, without permission from the FCC, a phonograph record that was broadcast on XENT. The record dealt with a method Baker claimed cured external cancer. He believed the FCC, and other U.S. government agencies, had used this opportunity to put his station off the air.

Baker also claimed that in April of 1945, Alamo Broadcasting "went to Nuevo Laredo and loaded four large trucks with said transmitter and other radio equip-ment, preparatory to crossing the bridge under cover of night." Since the FCC "froze" all improvements in broadcasting stations in the United States during World War II, Baker requested that the FCC revoke Alamo Broadcasting's con-struction permit and forbid its use of any equipment obtained from XENT. The petition was denied, and Baker never returned to Mexican broadcasting.[85]

XEPN, Piedras Negras, Mexico

Jack McGrew worked at KFDM in Beaumont in the early 1930s. A broadcaster named Gillium had leased the station from the Magnolia Oil Company. During those Depression years, Gillium sold time on the station to anyone who could pay. McGrew remembers one person who bought time:

> He would literally come into town every six months and buy time on the air. His routine was very simple. He would offer to tell your fortune if you would send him a dollar—and he did this on the air—and, boy, the money poured in. It was fantastic the amount of money he would get in a thirty-minute program. He could go five days a week for three or four weeks until it began to "peter out." Then he would move on to some other place. He would come back about every year or so. Rajah Rayboid . . . he kept his act within the state. He didn't have to go very far because there are chumps everywhere. In the Depression days, we would sit there and watch him count his money; it was insane. They would send in the money before he would tell the fortune. They would send in a letter, "Tell me so and so." He finally wound up on one of the outlaw stations in Mexico.[86]

Rayboid, Marjah, Reverend Ethel Duncan, astrologer Dad Rango, and other charlatans moved to Mexico to broadcast on XEPN (Eagle Pass–Piedras Negras). The station was constructed because the city of Eagle Pass boosters wanted "a little old border blaster of their own." The business people and citizens of Eagle Pass and Piedras Negras contributed to a radio fund. Landowners across the river competed for the honor of donating the land for the station's transmitter. Construction started in the spring of 1932. The transmitter was located nine miles northwest of Piedras Negras. The studios were in the Yolanda Hotel in Eagle Pass. The station's supporters persuaded W. E. Branch to build the station and become part owner.

The station attracted a wide variety of talent, including jazz orchestras, comedians Ma and Pa Smithers, blues singer Ora Starnes, Uncle Buster and his International Hot-Timers, a six-piece fiddlers' band, and singer Peg Moreland from WFAA in Dallas. Talent came from Hollywood. Country and western entertainers arrived from everywhere. The most popular country singer was Cowboy Slim Rinehart, sometimes called "The King of Border Radio." W. Lee O'Daniel and the Hillbilly Boys announced they were planning to live in the border town and play regularly over XEPN.

Before XEPN started broadcasting, radio astrologers and psychologists performed on stations in the United States. When they were banned by the FCC, they moved to the border. The first astrologer to arrive at XEPN was Dr. Edward

Owen, alias "Abra," from Fort Worth. Dr. Korda Ramaine (real name—Bob Nelson) was considered the leader of the spook industry. Rajah Rayboid moved his fortune-telling to the station. The psychic with one of the largest followings was Dr. Ralph Richards, M.D., Ps.D.

Eventually the Mexican government "outlawed" seers and astrologers on border stations. The psychics were replaced by "voices of temperance" speakers and preachers. Prohibition was law in the United States, and border stations were used to voice opinions concerning it. Most speakers spoke against the movement to repeal it. Preaching against the "horrors of liquor" continued even after prohibition had been repealed. Branch brought to the station the Rev. Sam Morris from Stanford, Texas. One of his most famous speeches was entitled "The Ravages of Rum." He condemned young women who used whiskey or gin as becoming "social outcasts, unmarried mothers, gangster molls, and pistol-packin' mamas." He preached on XEPN for most of the station's history. Decades later, he operated KDRY in San Antonio. Rev. J. Frank Norris, known as the "Texas Cyclone," spoke on XEPN and XER against the use of "devil water." In the 1930s Norris was the owner of, and a regular performer on, KFJZ in Fort Worth.[87] In 1936 a Dr. Spann used XEPN to advertise his Dallas cancer clinic.

In the late 1930s, a war developed at XEPN. Branch and his partner, C. M. Bres, had strong disagreements about how the station was being operated. Branch and a small army forcibly took possession of the transmitter and held it for three weeks. Just when Branch thought everything was secure, the transmitter was mysteriously destroyed in a powerful blast. Branch announced that he would rebuild the station, but never did. Later he gained control of XELO in Tijuana and moved it to Juárez, across the border from El Paso. Branch died in the early 1950s in an "accident" while working on the transmitter of XELO. Some believe he committed suicide.[88]

XEG, Monterrey, Nuevo León, Mexico

"XEG, Fort Worth 11, Texas" was one of the best-known mailing addresses in broadcasting in the 1950s. With 150,000 watts of power, XEG called itself "The Voice of North America." The station, as with many border stations, sold anything by mail order, especially religious articles. One religious advertisement promised listeners that if they mailed in a prescribed amount of money, they would receive "a genuine, autographed picture of Jesus Christ."

The station programmed a large amount of preaching, a main staple and money maker on most border stations. XEG's theme proclaimed, "From early evening till late at night, the gospel voice to help you think right. Stay tuned to ten-fifty on your dial to ease the burden of life's many trials. XEG, ten-fifty."[89]

• • •

Outlaw Stations

In the early 1920s, it was not unusual for radio stations in Texas to broadcast without a license. WBAP in Fort Worth started transmitting in 1922 before Harold Hough received a license. KGRC in San Antonio broadcast two years without one. Many considered the stations south of the Texas-Mexico border as unlicensed U.S. stations. They had transmitters in Mexico but studios in Texas.

Broadcasting in the United States without an official license from the U.S. government supposedly ended with the creation of the Federal Radio Commission in 1927. The FRC was empowered to grant licenses, and stations were obligated to obtain one. Some operators in Texas did not believe that federal law controlled broadcasting activities contained solely within the state's border. "Unlicensed," "outlaw," "bootleg," or "pirate" stations were not rare in Texas.

Clarence Bruyere built and operated an unlicensed station, in a sense, when he was a teenager: "Our radio was an old Philco . . . and I had a Philco record player that had an oscillator in it . . . and I stuck a long piece of wire on it and ran it outside . . . my dad would drive around the block and you could hear me playing music. So from that standpoint, I had an outlaw radio station . . . 1938 . . . in the Morning Side addition of Fort Worth. It probably only went a block, if that far. Frequency—it was down on the low end of the band . . . around 530 or something."[90]

Weldon Jeffus visited the operator of an "outlaw" station in Paris, Texas, in the early 1930s. He recalled:

It was a "bootleg" station laid out on top of a bench in a garage in the north part of town . . . and he was arguing that the FCC could not shut him down. Ted Williams was the guy who put it all together. It was not any company involved except that this guy was a genius in radio stuff. He wound the transformers and everything and put that thing on the air; and it sounded good. It was on North Main Street . . . in his garage. He had the parts strung out on a bench and the antenna stuck up in the air. It was just records; he announced records—an hour or two a day—no set schedule . . . broadcast when he wanted to—when it hit him. I went out and watched him. Anybody called up: and if he had the record, he would play it for them. He could be picked up in Hugo [Oklahoma] seventeen miles away. He could not have been on for more than two or three months—FCC just came over and shut him down.[91]

L. D. Yates, who once flew Brinkley from Kansas to Mexico, operated an outlaw station in Sweetwater. "He built his own radio station in Sweetwater and was just broadcasting up a storm," said Darrell Yates, L. D.'s brother. "He just put it together and went on the air—I don't even know if he had call letters. The town of Sweetwater was very upset that they [FRC or FCC] took him off the air. He broadcast speech, and he never had a turntable."[92]

"There was a 'pirate' radio station in Brownwood in the 1930s," remembered Wendell Mayes, who owned KNOW in Austin. "Alton Stewart put it on—he was the engineer for it, and he got in trouble with the government."[93]

Gene Roth, owner of KONO in San Antonio, had a brother who operated an "outlaw" station at the Agriculture and Mechanical College of Texas in College Station. "The FCC walked in on him and shut him down," remembered Roth. "He was broadcasting without a license—just playing music that the Corps liked to hear—eight or ten months until they caught him."[94] George Ing, engineer for KONO, built the station. It did not have an antenna. It was connected to the building's electrical wiring. "It was legal," stated Ing. "It was only a five-watt transmitter. You wired it right into the (wall) receptacles. It fed the radio frequency on top of the 60-cycle current. Anywhere the 60-cycle current goes, the signal goes—he even sold commercials on it." Ing also built the transmitter for an "outlaw" station in Fredericksburg. It was located in a hardware store and operated by the owner. "I did not think at that time that it was illegal," stated Ing. "1930s—five watts because I wanted to make sure that it would not go outside the state. I don't remember the frequency. They just barely got to the city limits."[95]

Jack McGrew was a law student at the University of Texas in 1934:

I worked for an "outlaw" station in Austin. We called it "Capital-X." The transmitter was on rollers or casters, so if they [the FCC] got too nosy about us, we could put the thing on a truck and get it out of sight. We broadcast any kind of programming we could get our hands on, mostly phonograph records. I was pretty desperate. I needed a job. They were located in a hotel which is no longer there. . . . They also owned a couple of outlaw stations in East Texas.

The theory was—such stations were low power . . . could not be heard outside of the state of Texas—so we were not subject to the rules of the FRC. The way they finally got these stations off the air—they sent inspectors into the area and located the tower; and if they could station someone under that tower, or very close to it, they could establish that we were interfering with other stations from out of state, even though our signal was not getting out of state; but an out-of-state licensed signal, on the same frequency, would be wiped out if you were sitting under our tower. That is the way they closed down Chicago; that is the way they closed down the East Texas stations, and the way they closed us down in Austin. They were all made-up gimmick names like "Capital-X." There were a lot of them. The whole operation probably lasted less then six months. . . . The federal marshals closed us up.[96]

The Development of Chain Broadcasting

Operators of radio stations had probably considered forming chains with other stations for as long as they had been broadcasting. American Telephone and Telegraph (AT&T) operated WEAF in New York City, the first station that experimented with "toll" broadcasting. AT&T believed it could increase its profits by "chaining" stations together. It ran its first permanent network line from New York City to WMAF in South Darmouth, Massachusetts, in June of 1923. There had been earlier connections between the two stations on a temporary basis. This first permanent line ran through several cities that soon wanted on the network. By late 1923, six stations had joined the chain. At the end of 1924, the network was composed of twenty-six stations.[97]

About the same time, General Electric and RCA attempted to start another chain through their station, WJZ in New York. Because AT&T refused to lease the new company lines, it was connected by telegraph lines, which were not suitable for broadcast-quality transmissions. Still, by 1925, WJZ fed a network of fourteen stations. Under the leadership of a young administrator, David Sarnoff, RCA, GE, and Westinghouse formed a new company to specialize in network broadcasting. That company's name was Arrow Broadcasting. That was soon changed to the National Broadcasting Company (NBC).

Because of the conflict between the two networks, and after long negotiations, an agreement was reached in which AT&T got out of the broadcasting business, and a group consisting of RCA, GE, and Westinghouse originated all broadcasting activities, including networks, through lines leased from AT&T.[98]

NBC-Red started service on November 15, 1926. It originated from WEAF in New York and was composed of stations that had been on the AT&T network. On January 1, 1927, NBC started a second network. Formed mostly from the WJZ chain stations, it was called NBC-Blue. The terms "Red" and "Blue" came from the colors used by AT&T engineers to designate the lines on company circuit charts leased by each network. By December 23, 1928, NBC-Red was feeding regular coast-to-coast service to fifty-eight stations.[99]

In September of 1926, the Judson Radio Program Corporation was formed by George A. Coats and Arthur Judson to provide programming for radio. Judson had earlier approached Sarnoff with a proposal to provide talent to the networks through his company. When his proposal was ignored, Judson threatened to form another network. Coats and Judson found many stations eager to join a new network.

In January of 1927, Coats and Judson formed the United Independent Broadcasters Network, with twelve affiliates. Because they needed more resources, Judson and Coats persuaded the Columbia Phonograph Company to invest, and together they formed the Columbia Phonograph Broadcasting System. The network broadcast its first program on September 19, 1927. When the phonograph company withdrew its support, Judson found new investors and changed the name to the Columbia Broadcasting System (CBS). The network continued to lose money; and in September of 1928, it was bought by the Congress Cigar Company of Philadelphia, the family business of twenty-seven-year-old William S. Paley. He purchased a station in New York and convinced Paramount Pictures to invest. In one year, the network was making money and becoming a serious rival of NBC.[100]

Chain Broadcasting in Texas

The first Texas station to participate in a chain was WFAA in Dallas. On December 6, 1923, President Calvin Coolidge's message on the opening of Congress was broadcast nationally by a temporary chain of seven stations linked by AT&T.[101]

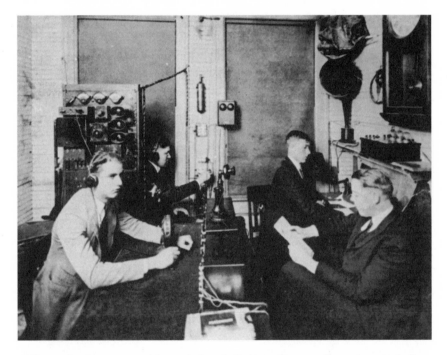

The production crew ten minutes before the linking of seven radio stations, including WFAA, Dallas, into a chain to broadcast the speech of President Calvin Coolidge to Congress on December 6, 1923. Left to right: Charles F. Baker, chief operator of WFAA; C. B. Hobson, long lines chief for Southwestern Bell; an unknown engineer; and Frank Cowan, engineer from Bell Labs. Courtesy
The Old Timer's Bulletin, *Inc. (vol. 24, no. 3, December, 1983),*
official journal for the Antique Wireless Association, Bloomfied, New York

WFAA broadcast the speech on 467 meters. The station's chief operator was Charles F. Baker.

The first radio network in Texas was established through the Magnolene Chain in early 1927. KFDM in Beaumont sent programming to WRR in Dallas for simultaneous broadcast. The Magnolene Chain soon added "links" for WFAA, Dallas; KRLD, Dallas; WJAD, Waco; and KPRC, Houston. On October 3, 1927, the Magnolia Refinery band broadcast a special thirty-minute program honoring the sixth anniversary of WBAP. WJAD was also "chained."[102] In the winter of 1928, the Magnolene Chain broadcast the Katy Band concerts from Parsons, Kansas, using the company's communications system.

A special "tie-up" of stations occurred on December 24, 1927. The Magnolene Chain presented a musical program from Mexico. The studio was located in the Caballo Blanca Inn in Nuevo Laredo, Mexico. The announcer was John Thorwald from WRR in Dallas. On several occasions that winter, KFDM performed multi-network feeds, broadcasting one program over its transmitter while feeding a band concert by wire to the chain.[103]

Throughout its history, Texas broadcasting has produced an unusually large number of networks. A few were one-time special networks, but generally, until 1960, these were meant to be permanent:

Southwest Broadcasting Company, 1933
Ford Dealers Special Network, 1933
Texas Quality Network, 1934
Southwest Broadcasting System, 1935
Humble Sports Network, 1936
West Texas Broadcasting System, 1936
Campaign Network, 1938
Dr Pepper Special Network, 1938
Texas State Network, 1938
Lone Star Chain, 1939
Magnolia High School Network, 1940
Transcontinental Broadcasting System, 1940
West Texas Network, 1946
Texas State-Wide FM Educational Network, 1946
Dixie Network, 1948
Southwest Network, 1948
Texas Baptist FM Network, 1948
Texas Independent Network, 1948
Texas Broadcasting System, 1949
Liberty Broadcasting System, 1950

Progressive Broadcasting System, 1950
Southwestern Collegiate Broadcasting System, 1950
Texas Spanish Language Network, 1951
Cactus State Network, 1952
Texas Plains Stations, Inc., 1952
Negro Radio South, 1954
Sombrero Network, 1954
Serape Network, 1960[104]

Southwest Broadcasting Company

The first attempt at a permanent network was the Southwest Broadcasting Company, established in 1933. It was managed by A. L. Chilton of KRLD in Dallas. Southwest was a regional network based in Fort Worth, with studios in the Texas Hotel. It had two affiliated stations in Dallas and two in Houston, as well as two affiliates outside the state.[105]

Texas Quality (Group) Network (TQN)

The formation of the Texas Quality Group was announced on September 5, 1934, by Martin Campbell, manager of WFAA in Dallas. The network was to begin operations with permanent telephone lines on September 10 connecting WFAA, WBAP in Fort Worth, WOAI in San Antonio, and KPRC in Houston.[106]

The Texas Quality Group was formed to satisfy a need demonstrated by the demand and use of temporary, special "hook-ups." The Boyer Company of Chicago had been broadcasting a thirteen-week, quarter-hour program over WFAA. In January of 1934, Boyer announced that it was extending its radio campaign to KPRC and WOAI through the Texas network. This was one of the first regular programs on Texas Quality.[107] The four stations had earlier been "chained" for special political campaigns or entertainment.

Campbell remembered one of the main factors that prompted a permanent network:

> From time to time we would have special shows—per order basic hook-up. WBAP had *The Light Crust Doughboys* and *Crazy Crystals* back to back. They were on the special hook-up that preceded TQN. . . . They were two of the basic talents at the beginning of the network. They were part of the beginning group when WBAP first put in the lines for the Texas Quality Group. I changed it later to the Texas Quality Network. . . . We underwrote the lines on a full-time basis in the early thirties—probably 1934 or '35. That was the first regular

organized "group" with permanent lines. There were specials—I'm sure—that were special one-time networks other than *The Light Crust Doughboys*. . . . They were for political broadcasting. *The Light Crust Doughboys* were on for a very long time on a special network.[108]

The Light Crust Doughboys

Bob Wills and his Aladdin Laddies had played dances for years. The group had a Saturday radio show from Kemble Brothers Furniture Store in Fort Worth. Wills wanted a more secure program. A friend, Ed Kemble, approached the Burrus Mill and Elevator Company to sponsor a show featuring Wills and his band. The mill did a large amount of advertising of its product, Light Crust Flour. The company agreed to try the band for one month on KFJZ in Fort Worth.

The program was first broadcast in January of 1931. The announcer was Truett Kimzey, station engineer. The program featured Bob Wills, Herman Armspiger, and Milton Brown. On the first program, Kimzey introduced the band, and they played "Twenty-One Years." After "Chicken Reel," Kimzey read a commercial written by Wilbert Lee O'Daniel, president and general manager of Burrus Mill.

The show originated each morning from the KFJZ studios in Meacham's Department Store in downtown Fort Worth. During one of the first programs, Wills casually referred to the band as "The Light Crust Doughboys." Kimzey picked up the name, and it and the famous opening soon evolved. After a couple of notes from a guitar or fiddle, Kimzey would enthusiastically announce, "The Light Crust Doughboys are on the air," and the band would go into their rousing theme song:

> *Oh, we never do brag, we never do boast.*
> *We sing our song from coast to coast.*
> *We're the Light Crust Doughboys from Burrus*
> *Mill.*[109]

> *Like our song, think it's fine?*
> *Sit right down and drop a line*
> *To the Light Crust Doughboys from Burrus*
> *Mill.*[110]

Despite favorable mail, two weeks after the program began, O'Daniel fired the band and canceled the show. He "didn't like their hillbilly music." Because of the response, the program continued without a sponsor. Trying to resurrect the mill's sponsorship, Wills offered to perform any job around the mill. O'Daniel finally

The original Light Crust Doughboys who started broadcasting on KFJZ, Fort Worth, in 1931. Left to right: Bob Wills; a non-member; Truett Kimzey, announcer; Milton Brown; and Herman Arnspiger. Courtesy Marvin Montgomery

agreed to again sponsor the program and pay the band members $7.50 a week, but they had to work forty-hour weeks in the mill after doing their early morning program. After a short time, because of sore and stiff hands, the band gave O'Daniel an ultimatum. They could work in the mill or play for the radio program; they could not do both. O'Daniel agreed to let them stop working in the mill, but they had to stay at the mill eight hours a day and practice for the program.[111]

After a few weeks, the program was moved to 12:30 P.M. on WBAP. Within months, it was on a special network "chained" to WOAI in San Antonio and KPRC in Houston. Because of disagreements with O'Daniel, Wills left *The Light Crust Doughboys* in 1932. He started his own program on WACO sponsored by Jones Fine Bread. During these programs Wills referred to his band as the Texas Playboys. The group consisted of himself, Tommy Duncan, Kermit Whalin, Johnnie Lee Wills, and June Whalin.[112]

Marvin Montgomery heard how *The Light Crust Doughboys* got on a network: "He [O'Daniel] wanted a network of stations. He wanted San Antonio, and he

*The original Light Crust Doughboys and bus in 1931. Left to right: Herman Arnspiger;
Bob Wills; Milton Brown; Truett Kimzey, announcer; Leslie Pritchet; and
W. Lee O'Daniel. Courtesy Marvin Montgomery*

wanted Dallas. They [station administrators] said, 'If you sell an hour's time, we will start a network.' So he sold fifteen minutes to Mrs. Tucker's Shortening, fifteen minutes to Bewley Mills Chuck Wagon Gang—he had fifteen minutes sold to Crazy Water Crystals."[113]

Hoxie Mundine, engineer at WOAI in San Antonio, helped start the network:

Mr. Halff [founder of WOAI in San Antonio] called me in one day. He said, "In the morning, I want you to get your remote equipment—have everything ready to go at the studio in the morning."

He had a cab to take us to the airport, and I said, "Where are we going?"

And he said, "Fort Worth!"

"What are we going to do up there?"

"We're going up to the flour mills—Burrus Mill and W. Lee O'Daniel."

"What are we going to do up there?"

He said, "I'll show you when we get there, and set up the lines to Western Union."

I said, "Western Union!"

He said, "Yah, we want to see if we can use Western Union lines to set up a network."

That was unbelievable to me because they (Western Union) had no lines dedicated for broadcasting. So they had the hillbilly band there—Light Crust Doughboys—so they had lines to all the stations.

He said, "We're going to start this up now."

That was the beginning of the Texas Quality Network. Why they picked on me to go up there when they could have had someone from Dallas or Fort Worth?

They [Halff and other network officials] said, "It'll do."

So they used that a long time. But, boy, when that Western Union guy made a mistake, plugged one of those telegraph lines in, and knocked out those transmitters, they started to think about it. The equalization necessary to overcome the loss was unbelievable, but we managed to get through. Then the telephone company lowered their rates, so they went to that. The phone company rates were too high.[114]

Abe Herman, attorney for WBAP, helped organize the Texas Quality Network. "Halff in San Antonio was the creator of the Texas Quality Network. He sold [Jack] Harris at KPRC [Houston] on joining up. He then went to Dallas and sold Campbell [of WFAA], and then he came over here and sold Harold Hough [WBAP]. . . . Of course, we wanted to be dominant, particularly during political season. You could not run for office unless you bought the Texas Quality Network. You just could not get the distribution. Martin Campbell was the president of that group; Halff was the secretary."[115]

"The network was very informally organized with no headquarters," said Jack McGrew of KPRC. "Any network station could sell programming, and any network station could originate programming, and did. The only instrument exchanged between the stations was a letter."[116]

In October of 1935 TQN broadcast fifteen sponsored programs. Humble Oil and Refinery carried football. Other than sports, there were eleven hours of regularly sponsored programming each week like:

Club Aquila and From the Patio for Gebhardt Chili from WOAI
Chuck Wagon Gang for Bewley Mills from WBAP
Jack Amlung's Orchestra for Crazy Water Mineral Company from
   WBAP
The Light Crust Doughboys for Burrus Mill from WBAP
Ideal Waltztime for William Cameron & Company, Waco, from
   WBAP
Gladiola Gloom Chasers for Fant Milling, Sherman, from WFAA
Texas Artists' Series for Employers Casualty Company from WFAA
Friendly Builders for Lumbermen's Association of Texas from WFAA

Pepper-Uppers for Dr Pepper, Waco, from WFAA

Ice Parade for Southwestern Ice Manufacturer, Dallas, from
 WFAA

Riding with the Texas Rangers for Kellogg, Battle Creek, Michigan,
 from WFAA

Greyhound Traveler for Southwestern Greyhound Bus Lines, Fort
 Worth, from WFAA

Hillbillies for W. Lee O'Daniel's Company, Fort Worth, from
 WBAP

Coca Cola College Night from WFAA

Gulf Presents Ken Millican for Gulf Oil from WOAI[117]

The Pepper-Uppers show started in April of 1935 as a Sunday evening quarter-hour program. Texas Quality stations were the nucleus. The program was soon broadcast on a special network of seventeen stations covering any southern state that had distribution of Dr Pepper. The special Dr Pepper network extended from Amarillo to Greenville, South Carolina.[118]

Marvin Montgomery joined *The Light Crust Doughboys* after TQN was formed. He recalled:

They had taken Pappy's [O'Daniel became famous because of the program; when he ran for governor, people referred to him with "Pass the Biscuits, Pappy."] office and made a little studio to do the transcriptions after they did their broadcast on top of the old Blackstone Hotel. Pappy had been taking the band out to play at theaters, getting fifteen dollars for the appearance, and keeping the money for himself. Pappy also had a deal. For every sack of flour he sold, he made so much. When the Doughboys got going, Pappy was making more money than Jack Burrus.

Pappy was also using workers from the mill to go down to his farm in Aledo to build barns and do different kinds of work on Burrus Mill time. So, unbeknownst to Pappy, Jack Burrus hires Eddie Dune to go over and take his place. Jack goes over to his office and waits for him, and when he comes in: "You're fired, Pappy. Get your stuff and go." And he did.

There were nine members of the Doughboys then. When Eddie went over there, he wanted Dick Rinehart and Bert Dodson to come over and join the Doughboys. They were the two singers of the "Wanderers, a Dallas musical group." Bert Dodson was the manager. He [Eddie Dune] called and asked to hire them, and he [Dodson] said, "If you take Marvin, take all three of them. It'll break the band up. I'm tired of riding around in this old wooden station wagon every night."

That's how I got on with the Doughboys. Three of us went over there, and

Eddie fired six and kept three. So we came down to a six-piece band. He wanted to upgrade the band a little. We were on the Texas Quality Network. We were also on WKY (Oklahoma City), KVOO (Tulsa), and KWKH (Shreveport). We did these by transcriptions. When we were in those towns, we would go up and do a live program on that station. When we went off the air in 1951, we were on 170 stations. . . . We would do our program at the Blackstone Hotel at noon, and then we would go back to the mill and do three or four transcriptions there—same show with different commercials.

Pappy had designed this bus—we went to Hollywood and made this movie with Gene Autry [*Oh, Susanna*]. . . . We drove to Dallas to open the Centennial—1936—where the big stage was across from "Big Tex." They had a building built in a U shape. They had about five stations all glassed-in. Each radio station had their own studio. Everything was live, and sometimes there would be three or four programs going on at the same time. During the centennial, we would broadcast . . . as the Texo Hired Hands.

We were the music on the *Crazy Water Crystals* (show). We went to Mineral Wells every other week and cut enough [shows] for two weeks—at night. They paid us a dollar a program, and we would make fifteen programs in one night. We did it in Mineral Wells in the basement. He [Collins, owner of Crazy Water Crystals] had an orchestra, but he also wanted country music. It was really loose, and we would holler. So, one night, I went to the mike and said, "Mr. Collins, do you know what the old hen said when she laid the square egg?"

He said, "No."

I said, "It said, 'Ouch!'"

After that program, he really jumped down me, "I don't want any jokes like that on this program."

That was really a bad joke in those days. They would not record over because they were using those acetate discs, and one of those discs cost two or three dollars. They could not afford to ruin a disc. They just had to let it go. Dizzy Dean, the baseball player, stayed in Mineral Wells a month or two in the winter, and he was always coming down and listening to us.[119]

Montgomery also told a little-known fact:

This advertising agency, J. Walter Thompson from Chicago, about ruined *The Doughboys*. They turned it into a *soap opera*—1937. This was after Eddie Dune left and before they found Parker Wilson. We had sound effects. We did not play music—just the theme song and maybe one song. Nobody knows about that! It almost took us off the air. We could not act. They brought in some women to do the women parts.

The Doughboys were off the air during the war . . . I was on the radio as the Duncan Coffee Grinders. We were on TQN.[120]

• • •

The Light Crust Doughboys reformed after World War II, but because of the unions the band was forbidden to make transcriptions. That effectively stopped the Doughboys from broadcasting. They continued playing and making personal appearances as the Doughboys and the Texo Hired Hands for Texo Mills. "They would book us as 'The Light Crust Doughboys' to open a supermarket," stated Montgomery, "and at the next town, we would put on a tee shirt that said 'Texo Hired Hands,' and we would do another show." When WBAP-TV in Fort Worth started broadcasting in September of 1948, the group became the Flying-X Ranch Boys. The Light Crust Doughboys with Marvin Montgomery continue to play today.[121] The Texas Quality Network lasted until the 1950s.

Magnolia High School Football Network

In 1935 the Magnolia Petroleum Company broadcast a few Southwest Conference football games. "The next year they got ready to do it, the conference wanted to put the thing up for bids," said Morrell Ratcliffe, advertising agent. "The Humble Oil and Refinery Company bid five thousand per school, and Magnolia did not think that it was worth it."[122]

Magnolia decided to broadcast high school football in 1936, the first year of the AA conference championship games. As the state expanded and more high schools were added, Magnolia broadcast the AAAA and AAA conference championships. In 1938 Magnolia started broadcasting the championship basketball tournament from Austin. They broadcast this series until 1960. Ratcliffe's advertising agency negotiated for Magnolia:

> The thing became so popular that many stations carried the games free just to have the programming. We would pay the line charges if a station carried the game free. Probably 10 percent of the stations carried the game at no charge. . . . These were networks only in the event of a special event. These networks carried no other programming at all. We contracted with the stations and said, "We will pay you $135 for the three games."
>
> I would sit down on Monday morning with my secretary, and we would decide that we would put these seven or eight on this ball game here and we would put these seven or eight stations on this ball game here. We would arrange those, and then we would send Tucker a list and . . . he would order in the appropriate facilities. . . . We would contract with these announcers: Eddie Barker, Wes Wise, Frank Gleiber. . . .
>
> We would sign off broadcasting, "This broadcast is brought to you by your friendly Magnolia dealer at the sign of the Flying Red Horse."[123]

Humble Sports Network

Humble Oil and Refining Company sponsored the play-by-play broadcast of six Southwest Conference football games on the Southwest Broadcasting System (there were a Southwest Broadcasting System and a Southwest Broadcasting Company) in the fall of 1935. Humble began regular broadcasts in 1936.[124] Stan McKenzie, owner of KWED in Seguin, was an announcer for Humble football: "When the network started, they did a Texas-Rice game in Houston, and they tried one of the sports editors from one of the Houston papers. They were not play-by-play people. He was a nice guy, but did a terrible job . . . so the next week they tried the other sports editor, and that was Kern Tips, nicknamed 'Flips.' He was a smash hit."[125]

Ves Box joined the Humble sports broadcasts a few years after it began:

Kern [Tips] began broadcasting when Humble began broadcasting in 1936. Humble had been dabbling with it and used sports writers for announcers with some rather dire results, according to some of the stories I heard. Kern had been a sports writer . . . and was widely followed as a young sports writer. . . . He was selected in 1935 or '36 by Humble to do some trial broadcasting for them and developed into their head announcer. He was head and shoulders above anyone else. He was very particular about the people he worked with—in that they did their job. He had a wonderful vocabulary and could express himself eloquently; could see as much football as anybody, and tell more football, and tell it accurately. Some of us had a tendency to lag behind the play, but he was right up with it—had a great pair of eyes—never used field glasses.[126]

When Box was hired to do football for Humble, he attended a meeting held by Tips, the coach of the announcers and "lead" announcer. The group would meet with one or two of the coaches from the conference and talk about the coming season. At the meeting, the group also reviewed the *dos* and *don'ts* of broadcasting a game for Humble. A Humble announcer was to remain neutral in calling the game. The score was to be given every few minutes. The agency supervisor, who was one of the four persons working the game, had a piece of paper or cardboard with "score" in big letters. Every few minutes he held it in front of the announcer to remind him it was time to give the score. Humble did not want its announcers to mention a player who received a penalty. The *team* was penalized—not the player.

Announcers never gave the name of a player who was injured. In an earlier game a mother listening to a broadcast heard the announcer say that her son was hurt. The woman had a heart attack. Thereafter, Humble announcers never gave the name or number of an injured player. Announcers were not allowed to talk about a fight on the field or anything of that nature. Humble did not allow any comment that would throw an unfavorable light on a team, player, or official. If an announcer violated these rules, "he was gone."[127] McKenzie learned Humble's rules: "You were not a 'homer.' You were nonbiased. They did not like to get criticism that this announcer liked this team or that team. . . . cannot criticize the officials. You did not second guess. You did not say who committed a foul. Who did the clip. You just announced that it [a team] got a fifteen-yard penalty for clipping. You did not criticize a player. You did not announce an injury."[128]

Box usually announced the "second-most-important" game:

If there was just one game, Kern did it. . . . Everyone recognized Kern as the number-one announcer. He was the best radio football announcer ever. I was the number-two man, and I always worked the second-most-important game in the conference. If SMU and TCU were playing for the conference championship, that was Kern's game.

We had from thirty-five down to ten stations on every network. Humble boasted that if you were in the state of Texas on a given Saturday afternoon, you could hear any game played by any Southwestern Conference team. That was not necessarily true for the University of Arkansas because Humble did not have distribution in Arkansas.[129]

"It was a public relations thing for Humble rather than a money-making thing," said McKenzie. "I think that we had twelve commercials during the entire game. In the early days, if you had a commercial scheduled for the first quarter and there were no time-outs, you did not make up for that—'Scratch It!'"[130]

After the first couple of years, Humble used the Texas Quality Network and the Texas State Network. The most important game with Kern Tips was on TQN; the second most important game with Ves Box was on TSN.

Lone Star Chain

The Lone Star Chain (LSC) started operations on September 26, 1939. "The network was composed of twenty to twenty-five regional stations," stated Clyde Melville, managing director. "TQN was used to carrying political programming. LSC was made up of lower-wattage stations but had equal coverage. The LSC carried a little more commercial activity than did TQN."[131]

The operating committee for the Lone Star Chain was Harold Hough of KGKO in Fort Worth, Tilford Jones of KXYZ in Houston, and O. L. (Ted) Taylor of KTSA, San Antonio; KGNC, Amarillo; and KRGV, Weslaco.[132] LSC was the third major radio network in the state. In Dallas–Fort Worth, TQN programming was always on whichever station, WFAA or WBAP, was on 800 (820) kilocycles. LSC was always affiliated with whichever station was on 570 kilocycles. The Texas State Network originated at KFJZ in Fort Worth and was affiliated with WRR in Dallas.

Texas State Network

The history of this network can be traced through a long progression of stations in Fort Worth. KFJZ, started by W. E. Branch in 1922, continued into the 1930s and eventually became the flagship station of the Texas State Network. WPA, the first station in Fort Worth, founded by the *Fort Worth Record,* became WFQB, then KSAT, then KTAT. For a very short time KTAT was the flagship station of TSN.

The formation of the network is most closely identified with the name Roosevelt. Elliott Roosevelt, son of President Franklin Delano Roosevelt, founded the Texas State Network. "When Elliott Roosevelt came down at the suggestion of Amon Carter," said Abe Herman, "he fell in love with Ruth Coogins, a local girl here. He divorced his wife and married her—moved down here."[133]

Ruth Roosevelt purchased KFJZ for $57,000 from R. S. Bishop in June of 1937. The sale was approved by the FCC on April 14, 1938. Elliott was president of the station and Ruth vice-president. Prior to the purchase, Elliott had been vice-president in charge of sales for Southwest Broadcasting Company. He was vice-president of Hearst Radio, Inc., and in charge of stations in Oklahoma City, San Antonio, Waco, and Austin.[134] According to Pete Teddlie of WRR in Dallas:

> Roosevelt—he was at a handicap because he knew nothing—absolutely nothing about radio. It fascinated him. . . . Gene Cagle of KFJZ sent him over and said to take care of him, show him around, and tell him what everything was— the copy department—everything.
>
> He was having opposition from his dad. He thought I could convince his mother enough that she would override Franklin and give him the money. I went to Washington. I went to the White House—and I talked to his mother. Eleanor was for it. . . . His dad was against it . . . [I] told her it was a lucrative thing—Dallas was growing bigger than Fort Worth . . . she asked a lot of questions about the financial end of it.[135]

Elliott Roosevelt wanted to operate a national radio network. On August 2, 1938, he, Harry A. Hutchison, and Pat Murphy chartered the Texas State Network, Inc. Its first broadcast, on September 15, 1938, was at the open-air Casa Mañana and was attended by 5,000 people. The program featured Bob Hope,

Texas Governor James V. Allred, Lou Preston and his band, and a 300-voice choir. One hour of the two-hour program was broadcast nationally on the Mutual Broadcasting System.[136]

In July of 1939, the FCC approved Ruth Roosevelt's purchase of Tarrant Broadcasting Company, operator of KTAT. The price was $101,570. That station transmitted with 1,000 watts on 1240 kilocycles, while KFJZ was 250 watts in daytime and 100 watts at night on 1370 kilocycles. Because the FCC did not allow one person to own two stations in the same market, Ruth Roosevelt surrendered the license for KFJZ.

When it was learned that a Dallas group was applying for the frequency of KFJZ, she quickly received permission from the FCC to change the call letters of her new station, KTAT, to KFJZ. On August 16, 1939, KTAT had become the flagship station of the Texas State Network, and eleven hours later the call letters KTAT were dropped, and KFJZ, on a new frequency, again became the flagship station. The network head was Elliott Roosevelt. KFJZ was managed by Gene Cagle. Its commercial manager was Charles Meade, the program director was Roy Duffy, and the publicity director was Forrest W. Clough.[137]

Roosevelt tried to build a statewide broadcasting empire. He tried to lease WRR from the city of Dallas. He did lease the station in Paris, Texas. "He would come over there and talk to us, and he had a security guy with him," remembered Weldon Jeffus, station engineer. "He (security man) would make us go in the studio and sit down, and then he would bring Mr. Roosevelt in. Roosevelt would make his speech and he would leave, and then you could leave. . . . He would give a pep talk about . . . better sales or putting out a better signal."[138]

In July of 1938 the largest radio network in Texas history was formed when President Franklin D. Roosevelt, father of the network's owner, gave a talk over thirty-one Texas stations. FDR spoke in the garden of his son's home near Benbrook outside Fort Worth.[139] Network employees were in attendance. "We were all invited out for a barbecue," remembered Buddy Cruse, KFJZ and TSN engineer, "and we all got to meet the president."[140]

In 1939 Roosevelt tried to form the Transcontinental Broadcasting System. The network was to begin on January 1, 1940. A full day's schedule was planned, including a broadcast of the Cotton Bowl football game from Dallas. Helen Wombolt, TSN staff, remembered the network: "Transcontinental Network came into being when I was with TSN—and it never hit the air. They had it all set to go on January 1, 1940. December 31, 1939, I was at home, and Mr. Roosevelt called and told me to go to the station right away and program for tomorrow. He said there would be no network feed for tomorrow. . . . We had a whole block that was going to be fed by this network. They hired a program director from New York, and it was to be the fourth national network."[141]

Stan Wilson, station staff, never understood Roosevelt's approach to broad-casting: "His philosophy of operating a network was a little ridiculous at the time. Too many people worked there. They had a staff orchestra feeding sustaining programming down TSN. They had a whole house full of vice-presidents."[142]

Dave Naugle worked for KFJZ and TSN in the 1940s:

TSN did a lot of plays in 1941 and '42 written by Horas Busby, who turned out to be LBJ's speech writer. Somebody got an idea for a drama and someone would write it. They were kind of like soap operas. They did have soap operas at one time, but not when I was there. They had continuing soap operas when Elliott Roosevelt was in full swing. They had a staff of about 150 people at the network.

He would go off and see a good-looking hatcheck girl, and he would say, "How would you like to come to work for us as vice-president?"

They were forever showing up and coming to the receptionist and saying, "I'm so and so, and Mr. Roosevelt hired me to be a vice-president."

She would say, "You can sit over here on the couch until we can find you an office."[143]

According to Wilson, about the time World War II started, Roosevelt "saw an opportunity to get out" and sold KFJZ and TSN. "Gene Cagle went to the own-ers of the station and network and said, 'I can operate the Texas State Network at a profit.' We had a building down there which housed the vice-presidents. We had a whole bunch of vice-presidents. Everybody who had a function was a vice-president. From that day forward, he [Cagle] had only one vice-president. That was one way he got it on an even keel. He fired the orchestra. You can imagine the cost of something like that."[144]

Cagle made out a list of who was to be fired and then checked into a hospital for a week. He stayed where people could not find him. Everyone was fired who did not have a contract preventing it. According to Naugle, Cagle's actions saved the network, which continues today.[145]

Jim Lowe worked at KFJZ and TSN during the 1940s:

We had two boards—the KFJZ and TSN board. The TSN board was where you had Porter Randall come on at 7:30 A.M., and then repeat a little later for different legs of the network. We would play Gladiola commercials to one leg of the network and instrumental music to the other leg. . . . We had the south leg of the network; and we had the east leg, and then the west leg of the net-work. There was no north leg. The north leg of the network was WRR.

Anybody who walked in with money could buy a block of time. We had an old country singer called Tex Lee, and he would just show up at 2:30 in the afternoon with his guitar and the money. He was sponsored by "Sparkellite," which was some sort of thing like Crazy Water Crystals or Hadacol. . . . He would come and bring whatever was thirty minutes in those days—maybe thirty dollars.

Cagle had a thing he called "Businessman's Bounce." At night you could play something slow or opera, but in the daytime hours he wanted it to have a beat. Boyd Kelly had a thing for Hildegard. I would type the list, and he would approve it; and he always wanted you to play a Hildegard record—and more Hildegard records got broken over there because nobody liked Hildegard. He would call up sometimes and say, "How come you don't play that Hildegard record?"

"Boyd, that thing got broken. That's four times this month that Hildegard record got broken."

One program was called *The Shopping Reporter.* That was a brokered thing by a man called Roy Duffy. . . . He would be on for forty-five minutes in the afternoon—what would be traffic time now. . . . We would play a Bob Wills record—he would have two spots between each record; and sometimes if there was a bridge in the record, he would fade it out, run spots in there, and then fade it back up—so in thirty minutes, you could get in thirty spots.[146]

KFJZ ran a large number of commercials, according to Dave Naugle:

One of the differences between WFAA and KFJZ was that I would read four or five commercials in an eight-hour shift at WFAA. Over at KFJZ, I would read that many in fifteen minutes—maybe more. I would ring a bell between commercials to separate them . . . just one spot after another—ring a bell and read another one. Gene Cagle came in and picked up the log after listening at home; and he just scratched out one commercial after another. "I told them not to put that many commercials in here."

I remember many times having twelve or thirteen commercials in a fifteen-minute period. When we were disc jockeys, I'd get so frustrated trying to get the stuff in. You had so many minutes and so many commercials, and you're supposed to play music. I'd drop the needle down on the very end of the song, the very end and play ·he last eight seconds of it; and say, "Oh, I put the needle on the wrong end." I'd say on the air "I'll fix that up" and play another commercial on tape. Just anything to get another commercial in. Some were on ETs, some were live, and some on tape. Next time we would give the weather: "The weather is going to be fair and mild—high of 90—tonight's low will be about 70—We'll be right back after this word from 'so and so.'" It was really terrible, but we were number one. That was the amazing thing.[147]

• • •

Stan Wilson sold advertising on KFJZ. He would sell a politician a quarter or half hour. If there were any questions about the content of the speeches, the station would have it checked by an attorney. When the speech was given, the salesman would sit in the control room "with his finger on the button." If the politician got off the prepared speech, he would be cut off. Salesmen had to literally "ride herd" on the speech of a candidate to which he sold time. This was how Wilson first met Lyndon B. Johnson. At the meeting Johnson told Wilson, "Stan, you're meeting the future president of the United States."

Wilson sold time to a candidate for the office of sheriff in Fort Worth. Homer Casey was running against a man named Alexander. Casey was "quite a cut-up." He told Wilson, "Listen, Wilson, I'm going to tell you Izzy Fred is behind Alexander; and I'm going to let the people know it."

Wilson said, "Like hell you are. I've got a nervous finger."

Casey went on his broadcast and said, "There's a very well-known, famous businessman behind my opponent. I ask—Is he afraid?—Is he Fred?—Is he Fred?"

For one speech Casey discovered that Alexander had booked time one day from 7:30 to 7:45 P.M. Casey booked 7:15 to 7:30. At the end of the program Casey said, "Now my opponent is going to follow me—immediately following this broadcast. So I'm going to ask him these specific questions; and if he wants to be honest with you, he's going to answer them."[148]

Many stations had the inevitable "station clown." At KFJZ it was Wally Blanton. He played a practical joke on Porter Randall, one of the most popular newscasters in Texas. Randall was all business—very professional. One day Blanton "set up" the times on all the clocks in the station. When Randall arrived to prepare his newscast, he looked at the clocks, believed he was a little late, and hurriedly got his copy together.

The station had a monitoring circuit that fed sound into Randall's office as well as most rooms in the station. The circuit did not go out over the air, but it usually fed whatever was being broadcast. This day, at the proper time according to the advanced clocks, the engineers fed over the monitoring circuit into Randall's office the end of the program that usually preceded his newscast, reinforcing the idea that it was about to start. Randall took his news and went into the studio. Over the monitoring circuit in the studio the introduction to Randall's newscast was given; he put his hand up to his ear as he always did, and he started reading the news.

As Randall read, Blanton entered the studio and started taking Randall's pants off. Then he set fire to the news script. Another person entered the studio and pasted together what sheets remained. Randall, hand on ear, read on. As he got to the point where there was little left to read, his only comment was, "Ladies and gentlemen, I can see this is going to be a very difficult broadcast." He never laughed. He just kept reading what copy was left. Soon, Randall was informed of what was happening.[149]

Another KFJZ announcer got caught by his own joke. He was reading a spot for a lawn mower. Instead of saying the price was "150 dollars," the announcer jokingly said, "150 potatoes." A man walked into the department store with 150 potatoes, and the store had to sell him the mower.[150]

Stories of similar happenings permeate broadcasting. One radio news announcer, while on the air, had colleagues enter the studio and start to remove his clothes. As the newscast progressed, so did the disrobing. At the end of the newscast, there was the newsman, standing all alone in the middle of the studio in his underwear, but "still reading the news."

Another newscaster started reading a newscast in a glass-enclosed studio. As he progressed, the lights in the surrounding halls went out, then the lights in the control room disappeared, and then the ceiling lights in the studio went off. At the end of the newscast, the announcer had his cigarette lighter out, lit, holding it as close to his copy as he dared, but "still reading the news."

According to Chem Terry of WBAP, there were always people who wanted to "break up" an announcer:

Ken McClure was a famous newsman. He was known all over this end of the country—and loved. He was sponsored by the Magnolia Oil Company every day at noon. . . . When I started, they said, "Now, we're getting close to the news. Here's your copy. *Say,* 'Here's Ken McClure with the news. It's Magnolia news time.' *Don't say,* 'It's Magnolia nose time. Here's Ken Manure with the clues.'" Now a guy with all that pressure on him, what's he going to say? They did every new announcer that way. They did it on purpose. I read that *so slowly.* . . . Ken knew what was going on, and he came on with a chuckle.[151]

At one time, Terry was the "color man" for football games on KBST in Big Springs. The sponsor sat in the booth and over Terry's shoulder read *each word* of the commercial as Terry read it. The slogan of the sponsor was "To better serve your baking needs, a better bread you need is Meads. Often buttered, but never bettered." "You try saying that in a cold air booth ten or twelve times during a game," said Terry.[152]

Radio Talent and Performers

Talent from Texas, which provided most of the live programming for the state's broadcasting industry, started in the 1920s, greatly expanded during the 1930s, and lasted into the 1950s. *The Light Crust Doughboys,* starting in 1931, exemplified the connection between program development and networks. *The Doughboys* necessitated the formation of the Texas Quality Network, and the establishment of networks demanded the creation and development of more talent and programming so chains could justify their existence. The 1930s was one of the most important periods in the development of Texas broadcasting talent.

The Doughboys may have been the most popular radio program ever originated in Texas. Bob Wills started his career there. At times Tex Ritter played with the Doughboys. In the 1950s, Tennessee Ernie Ford, Slim Whitman, and Hank Thompson played with the band. Even Walter Cronkite announced a program in 1934.

Cecil Gill, "the Yodeling Country Boy," was a popular country and western singer and radio personality starting during the Great Depression. Gill's first broadcast was over KFYO in Abilene on an amateur program from the Palace Theater. He came to Fort Worth and originated shows on KTAT, WBAP, and KFJZ. Karl Wyler started his career in El Paso over KFXH in 1922 when he was sixteen. He was known as "the Happiness Boy," who rattled off humorous anecdotes between songs. Wyler joined the administration and production staff of KTSM when it began broadcasting in 1929. He continued to performed as "Karl the Kowhand."[153]

In 1928 a country singer named William Boyd started performing on WRR in Dallas with a group called the Cowboy Ramblers. Boyd and his group performed for more than a decade. Later, Boyd moved to Hollywood and made "B" westerns as Hopalong Cassidy. After World War II, Boyd was again a disc jockey on WRR. Earnest Tubb started with a show on KONO in San Antonio in the late 1920s. Trumpeter Harry James played in house bands on WRR in Dallas and KFDM in Beaumont before going to Hollywood.[154]

WFAA in Dallas originated a very popular and long-running program called *The Early Birds.* "I came from the East," said Earl Cullum of WFAA, "and they began telling me about this show which was broadcast from 7:00 to 8:00 A.M. I told people, 'Oh, yeah. Back East, like in Kentucky at WHAS, they did not bother with daytime programs . . . it was the bottom of the Depression.'" *The Early Birds,* with Jimmy Jefferies as master of ceremonies, started during the Great Depression, and "its popularity was unbelievable," stated Cullum. "People would ask, 'Did you hear Jimmy Jefferies this morning?'" The show's theme was *Happy Days Are Here Again,* played by Eddie Dune and the orchestra. During the 1930s and 1940s WFAA did not use records; all programming was live.[155] Other acts on the show were "Hack and Willy," Elmer Bockman, Ben McClusty, and an act called "King of the Ditty Singers." Dale Evans was a singer on the show before she started performing in motion pictures. *The Early Birds* entertained Texas audiences into the 1950s.[156]

The Stamps Quartet was a popular program originating in Dallas on KRLD. It was the product of the quartet's organization, headed by Frank Stamps. He and the organization printed and sang songs especially written for the group. At one time, the organization consisted of three performing quartets. During the 1950s, Jim Reeves started performing at KGRI in Henderson. Whenever he was in the vicinity, he would drop by Carthage, and Bev Brown, owner of KGAS, would talk him into doing an impromptu show.[157]

KFJZ in Fort Worth had *The Songs of Carol Laden* and *Poetry by Margie Boswell*. While working at WBAP in Fort Worth, Chem Terry did a late-night show called *Terrible Terry's Stomping Grounds*. Frances "Flo" Helm, director of women's programs on WBAP, helped create soap operas for that station; one was called *Helen's Home*. Ellen "Bells" West Becker and Howard Carrollway worked with that show. After four years, Helm and the show moved to the national networks in New York City. Helm later returned to Fort Worth and wrote *Fruit Express* and *School of the Air*. Around 1938, WBAP had a late-night program called *Black Night*, written by Virginia Wilkins. The program was so gruesome and intense that Wilkins would come to rehearsals and "break out in a cold sweat." WFAA in Dallas programmed a soap opera called *Clare Lou and M.*

Until the Second World War, WBAP had a twenty-one-piece orchestra directed by Gene Gaugh that played on many programs, like *Variety in Rhythm*. The station originated an *Amos 'n' Andy* type show called *Slow and Easy* with two performers who sang, played the piano, and performed skits in three or four character voices. KTAT in Fort Worth also had an *Amos 'n' Andy* type program called *Honeyboy and Sassafras*. Ginger Rogers was a singer on WBAP before she went to Hollywood. Ted Gouldy, WBAP staff, did as many as thirteen broadcasts a week on programs like *Saturday Morning Roundup,* and *What's the News.*

WRR in Dallas had a religious program called *Albert Ott* and another called *Vanda* who read poetry. The station broadcast *Kiddies Club,* in which young acts came in and auditioned on Friday and performed on a show broadcast from the Melba Theater on Saturday. Linda Darnell performed on the show before she went to Hollywood. WRR aired *Pet Time,* where owners of lost pets would come by the station and describe their animals. *The WRR Players* did a program in which they dramatized wrecks for the automobile association.[158]

Around 1949 a young Elvis Presley played on *Houston Hoe-down.* He did the show every other week for a year.[159] When Stan Wilson was manager of WACO, he had a performer named Hank Thompson. As a child living in Waco, Thompson started performing on a live talent program broadcast by WACO on Saturday mornings from the stage of the Waco Theater. It was sponsored by Jones "Fine" Bread and produced by Mary Holliday. Thompson also became the talent on other programs, Wilson remembered:

We paid Hank fifty cents a program. He was a talent on *The Fairway Grocer and Market* (show). "Hank the Hired Hand" we called him. I called Hank in and said, "Hank, you're a good-looking kid, and once you get those braces off your teeth, I really think that you could make something out of yourself; but I don't think that you're going to make it as a singer and guitar player."

Many years later—1953—he [Thompson] drove up to the television station I was running, and the secretary said, "There's a man named Mr. Thompson out here to see you."

I walked out to the lobby, and it was Hank—boots and six foot five.

He looked down at me and said, "You know, I never did take your advice. . . . Come outside." He had this big bus—*Hank Thompson and the Brazos Valley Boys.*

I said, "You're really traveling first class."

He said, "I'm in that gold Cadillac behind it."

Hank married a girl who worked in the corner drug store in downtown Waco where Dr Pepper was first made.[160]

The program *Doctor I.Q.* originated for years from the Majestic Theater in Dallas. The show was originated by Lee Segall, a Houston advertising agent. It moved to the national networks but occasionally would return to Texas on tour. "We would all go down to the Majestic Theater," remembered Dave Naugle of WFAA, "about six or seven of us in different places in the audience." Naugle was one of the voices who would say, "Doctor, I have a lady in the balcony."

"Who is she and where is she from?" asked Doctor I.Q. The reward for being on the show was "Give that woman ten dollars, and a box of Mars Bars." Lew Valentine was the original *Doctor I.Q.* When Valentine quit the show, Jimmy McClain took his place.[161]

On November 19, 1939, the University of Texas at Austin began a program called *Radio House.* The university had no transmitter, so programs were distributed over transmission lines or ETs. *Radio House* programming was heard over the Texas Quality Network, the Texas State Network, KTBC in Austin, and other stations.[162]

A very popular local show that started in 1947 in San Antonio on KONO was called *So You Wanna Be A Cop.* The creation of Jack L. Pink, it ran ten years on Sunday evenings at 9 P.M. The production crew was composed of Bill Allert, interviewer; police officer Myles Hirsch; and Rocky Rhodes, radio technician. On Friday and Saturday evenings they drove a bright red station wagon, "Big Red," around on police calls. The station wagon had a Brush "Sound Mirror" recorder mounted inside with a microphone on a 250-foot cable. The microphone went with the police officers answering the call and made a sound record of the event. The natural sound of police answering calls was the program. The first years the program was recorded on a wire recorder that did not permit editing. Then the show started using the Brush with "paper-backed" magnetic tape. By the middle

1950s, it was estimated that the program had used 4,000,000 feet of recording tape. Some weeks *So You Wanna Be A Cop* had an 87 percent share of San Antonio's radio audience.[163]

KFJZ had a program called *The Insomnia Club*. It ran from midnight until one in the morning. Dave Naugle hosted another rather macabre program:

> *The Texas Pharmaceutical Hour* . . . was written by Forrest Clough, who was in a wheel chair from polio—he used to do a program where they rang "The Bell of Death" and announced deaths all over the state of Texas on the TSN network. They had a gong with a button on it—and press the button and "Bong!" "The Bell of Death rings for . . ."—and you would read the name, where he lived, when he was born, and everything. I did that program a lot. It was an on-air obituary. It may have been part of another program, but I remember pressing that bell eight or ten times on a single show, and reading those things—anybody they had names for.[164]

J. Frank Norris

In 1924 Rev. J. Frank Norris was pastor of the First Baptist Church in Fort Worth. He obtained the license for KFQB, a descendant of WPA. During the next twelve or thirteen years, as the station's ownership kept changing, Norris continued to have an interest in each. When KTAT was sold to Elliot Roosevelt, Norris included in the contract a clause which gave him specified broadcast times on Sundays. He had this free time until he died. Jim Lowe, who worked with Norris, remembered:

> He got 11:00 to noon on Sundays. It was his forever. He also wanted . . . 10:00 to midnight on Sunday nights. Sometimes . . . he would do it from the church. . . . Most nights it would be kind of quiet, and he would come down there—and we would play religious music—and when he decided he wanted to talk, he would sit in there by himself—and sometimes with his wife. He would sit there sometimes and carry-on for thirty minutes.
>
> He would look up and wave at you—and on the air, he would say, "Sonny (he did not know my name), go get me a Dr Pepper, would you? I'll pay you when you bring it." I would go get it, and then on the air, he said, "Thank you very much. Those Cokes are terrible. Don't ever drink Cokes; they're bad for you. Stick to Dr Pepper." He would burp on the air and take a swig—a character—most of the time I did not know what he was saying because I did not listen.[165]

In later years, Norris purchased time on station KWBC in Fort Worth to simulcast his program from KFJZ. According to Lowe, "It might have been the world's first simulcast."[166] Johnny Smith, engineer for KFJZ, remembered Norris:

Norris was owner of KFQB at one time. Nobody would buck him, not even Amon Carter—and he would not buck Amon Carter. He had an hour at noon on Sunday, and then he had two hours on Sunday night from ten to midnight. When he sold it [the station], that was in the contract. We didn't get rid of him until he died, and that was after we put on television.

Somebody was always giving him a new car because he would do commercials for the car. . . . One specific night he said, "I've got myself a new Chrysler, and, boy, it is a dandy. Let me read you something about it. It removes stains on the seat if you run something on it." He read the whole owner's manual to the car.

Sometimes he might not talk for two hours, and we would have a transcription set up in the studio. It might be 11:05 P.M. or something, and he'd be talking along and say, "I'm tired; change the radio." That was the cue that he was through and to start playing his transcriptions. We would pick up from anywhere; it did not matter.

He was famous because he shot a guy . . . killed him in his office. He got out of that, and he burned his church down one time—that was the story.[167]

Norris was just one of many early radio ministers. One station employee was shocked when he saw a preacher who, moments before, had been crying and sobbing—then, off-the-air, joking and laughing with his friends. Richard (Cactus) Pryor of Austin helped with a program for Brother Billingsly, who had a daily religious show on the station in Alice. "He was one of these 'criers.' 'Lord, help me; pray for me; God, pray for me,'—and he would look at me and wink. He ran away with the church choir soprano."[168]

Other Early State Networks

On March 5, 1938, Elliott Roosevelt helped organize a seven-station chain designed to handle political broadcasts. No name was given for the network. A three-station hook-up for Ford Dealers in the Southwest started on September 6, 1933. *The Feel of the Ford Revue* originated at WFAA in Dallas. It was fed throughout the state as well as to two stations in Oklahoma. The Dixie Network, formed in 1949, was headquartered at KATL in Houston. The Southwest Broadcasting Network formed and issued a rate card on February 1, 1935. The network listed thirteen stations, eleven in Texas, which could be bought for $1,734 an hour.[169]

In 1946 Arnold Wittman, director of the school plant division of the Texas State Department of Education, planned to establish a 43–FM station educational network in Texas. In 1950 the students and faculty of eleven southwestern colleges and universities attended a meeting establishing a Southwestern Collegiate

Broadcasting System. One of the speakers at the conference was Mary Holliday of WACO. In 1948 six Texas Baptist organizations organized an FM network. The headquarters were at Mary Hardin Baylor College in Belton. Associated with the network were Howard Payne College, Brownwood; Buckner Orphans Home, Dallas; Wayland Baptist College, Plainview; Southwestern Baptist Theological Seminary, Fort Worth; and San Antonio Baptist Association, San Antonio.[170]

James G. Ulmer

During the 1930s, Texas broadcasting experienced some very interesting and unusual events, some legal and some not. Near the end of the decade, another personality tried to influence illegally the state's broadcasting industry.

Dr. James G. Ulmer started in the radio business at a station in Tyler in the 1930s. He steadily acquired control of numerous stations. While driving from Austin to Houston on February 8, 1940, Ulmer was "astounded and appalled" to hear that the FCC had just revoked the license of every station he controlled. Some were KOCA, Kilgore; KSAM, Huntsville; KAND, Corsicana; KRBA, Lufkin; KNRT, Palestine; and KTBC, Austin. The commission alleged that Ulmer and Roy G. Terry, chief owner and manager of KOCA, held undisclosed interest and ownership that were never revealed to the commission. On February 13, 1940, the FCC ordered revocation of the license of KGKB, Tyler, for "hidden ownership, operation, and control."

Ulmer gained control of stations by prevailing upon a small group of local businessmen with excellent reputations to organize a partnership. Ulmer would control the important details and have his lawyer, James H. Hanley, former radio commissioner, file the papers with the FCC. After a construction permit was issued, the partners entered into a contract authorizing Ulmer, or one of his co-workers, to finance, construct, and operate the station. In this manner the partnership assigned their license rights to Ulmer without the knowledge or consent of the commission. The partnership made no capital investment and received no income. All profits went to Ulmer.[171]

Jack McGrew was working for KFDM in Beaumont in the 1930s when the station's management changed:

> Gillium leased the station from Magnolia with the FRC's knowledge and permission, but then he subleased the station to Roy Terry and Dr. Ulmer from Tyler. When Magnolia got around to selling the station, the FCC learned of his subleasing arrangement, which had never been filed with them, and they gave Magnolia considerable trouble about it although Magnolia was innocent. Gillium had subleased it to Ulmer without saying anything to anybody.

When Terry and Ulmer came in, they "revolutionized" the station. "Hit 'em"—"Go get 'em"—both way type of operations. Announcers were supposed to stand three or four feet from the microphone and shout at the top of their voices—and it was practically wall to wall commercials. It was really bad. They thought that that was the way to get people's attention—to yell at them. They still do that . . . listen to the average car commercial on television. They are yelling at you.[172]

In January of 1943, at the beginning of Ulmer's problems, he sold KTBC in Austin to Claudia Alta Johnson. That was the beginning of the media empire of Claudia and her husband, Lyndon Baines Johnson.[173]

Bev E. Brown, past owner of KGAS in Carthage, remembered how one station rid itself of Ulmer:

He [Ulmer] was one of the original founders of the Texas Association of Broadcasters. Ulmer . . . had a guy named Roy Terry in Kilgore running the station. He [Ulmer] wasn't on the license in any of these other places because they had overlapping signals.

Somebody turned it in to the FCC, and Dr. Ulmer went up to Washington and testified: No, he didn't own any part of KOCA in Kilgore.

So the next time he came over to Kilgore to pick up his thousand-dollar check, which he got each month, Roy Terry said, "You don't have any thousand coming."

Ulmer said, "Sure, I do!"

"No, it's right here in the record. You don't own any part of this thing."

This is how Roy Terry came to own KOCA in Kilgore.[174]

The problems associated with Ulmer, the border stations, and the outlaw stations exemplify an independent mentality believed by some to exist in Texas and Texans. It helps explain why individuals in the industry, early in radio and later in television, showed a great spirit of innovation.

As the 1930s ended, Texas broadcasting was a thriving industry. It had added many new stations; strengthened its programming, particularly with the help of national networks and the formation of local state networks; made tremendous technical progress; and eliminated many problems or had them eliminated by regulatory and enforcement practices of the FCC.

Radio broadcasting seemed ready to face the 1940s. Then, the industry was confronted with trying to continue its high level of service to the public with government restrictions, loss of personnel, and other problems created by the Second World War. After the war, radio faced its most severe challenge to its dominance and prestige: television.

CHAPTER 3

The War and Television

1941 to 1950

The most important event in Texas broadcasting in the 1940s happened on September 29, 1948, but it started in 1934:

> All eyes focused on a small panel of ground glass. There was a flicker of light— orange and black—and then a face appeared. "This is television station W5AGO," announced an unknown voice. W5AGO, *the Southwest's first television station,* was on the air. The experiment was featured in the 1934 Southwestern Exposition and Fat Stock Show in Fort Worth. Although many hundreds of people saw this demonstration, television was not ready.[1]

Television in the Lone Star State actually started fourteen years later when Frank Mills stood before a microphone and announced, "This is WBAP-TV, Fort Worth."[2]

With this utterance in 1948, the first television station in the Southwest began regular broadcasts. Preceding this event, radio broadcasting endured the Second World War. During that conflict, radio grew slowly; in many ways it stopped growing. The causes were government restrictions, lack of equipment, loss of personnel, changed priorities, etc. At the end of the decade when growth could have continued at the same rate as in the 1920s and 1930s, it did not. Radio grew, but slower. One reason was its first real competition: television.

"There was no reason for radio to almost die except for stupidity," stated Jim Byron, WBAP news director. "When television came, we didn't do much about our radio. We did not promote it. We were like so many other stations that had television, we thought that when television came in, radio was going to get hurt. But it needn't have been that way. We integrated radio into television, and radio became a step-child."[3]

After the war, until the first telecast of WBAP-TV, television in Texas spent three years struggling to get started. When materials and equipment finally became available, television was ready. Near the end of the decade, the public became aware that television was coming. Stories of it appeared in newspapers; television stations were being built; receivers could be seen in stores; and soon, usually in large cities, residents in the neighborhood had a "TV" in their home and an antenna on their roof.

War Radio

Dave Naugle of KFJZ in Fort Worth was on duty December 7, 1941. "I was actually in the teletype room when the bells started ringing—about eight or ten of them. 'Flash!—Japs Attack Oahu.'" The station began receiving telegrams from the U.S. government telling the staff not to give the identity of the town in which it was located and not to give the weather. Stations were told how to act when

Truett Kimzey's demonstration of mechanical television over W5AGO, Fort Worth, in 1934, broadcasting to the North Side Coliseum during the Fat Stock Show. Courtesy KXAS-TV, Fort Worth, Texas

people wished to enter "after hours." When a person came to the door and wanted in, station personnel were to go to the door and exhibit a gun so that person could see it. If the person still wanted in, then he or she was allowed to enter. Stations were required to keep a gun at the transmitter.[4]

Frank Mills ran out of announcers at WBAP in Fort Worth. He worked twelve- and fourteen-hour days to cover for missing staff. The station replaced men by hiring women broadcasters. Kathryn Reynolds joined the engineering staff in 1942. Marion Ringler Allen was assistant to the continuity director and "Gay Cooke's" on many programs. Muriel Sproules, Ellen Gallagher, and Eileen Flake continued jobs in administration while helping produce shows. At WRR in Dallas, the production staff was all women. Earl McDonald, a college student at Southern Methodist University, was the first man on the station's staff after the war ended. McDonald was "broken in" by Freddie Mercer.[5]

Because of war restrictions, stations could not purchase new equipment. "We had to patch things up," stated Ves Box of KRLD in Dallas. "Gas was rationed. We did a lot of promotions for clean rest rooms instead of products. It was bad policy to create a demand for a product that was in short supply."[6]

Some stations reduced the power output of the transmitter to 90 percent of full power to extend tube life. "During World War II there was a[n alert] system based on a thousand-cycle tone," remembered Bill Bradford of KSST in Sulfur Springs, "and everybody built their own detectors that detected the tone. If you heard the tone from your key station, which in the Dallas area was WFAA, you monitored that station."[7]

After the war the government installed a Conelrad System, in which the emergency signal was to have the key station's transmitter go off for five seconds, on for five seconds, off for five seconds, followed by a tone. "Remember the radios with the little triangles?" asked Bradford. "Everybody [stations] who had a National Defense Emergency Authorization would discontinue operations and switch, and come back on the air without identifying their call letter or city— come back on the air on 640 or 1240 kilocycles. This was to deprive the enemy nuclear bomber from riding in under radar and navigating by radio stations."[8]

Frequency Modulation

The war stymied the development of Frequency Modulation (FM) radio. Edwin Howard Armstrong started developing a static-free radio after the First World War. Armstrong was inspired in 1923 when he was told by David Sarnoff, "I wish someone would come up with a little black box to eliminated static." For the next ten years Armstrong experimented to that end. In March, 1934, at the invitation of Sarnoff, he installed his transmitting equipment in RCA's experimental labs in the Empire State Building. A year later he was asked to remove it. RCA had decided to shift its experimentation to television. In 1936 Armstrong was granted a license for an experimental FM station. W2XMN, a 50,000-watt FM station, was situated in Alpine, New Jersey. In the fall of 1939, the FCC removed Channel 1 from the television band and gave it to experimental FM broadcasting. In May of 1940, the FCC authorized commercial FM operations.

Then FM encountered two crucial and almost fatal setbacks. Just as commercial expansion was imminent, the Second World War started. Like television, FM was "put on hold." After the war, when growth could have resumed, the FCC devastated FM by moving it from television's Channel 1 frequencies of 43 to 50 megacycles up the spectrum to 88 to 108 megacycles. Now, all prewar equipment and transmitters used by 47 stations and 500,000 home receivers were useless. FM essentially started over; it almost disappeared. In the late 1940s and the 1950s, either FM became a high-quality simulcast of the station's AM programming, it became "radio of the classics" playing classical music, or licenses were returned to the FCC. FM had become media's unwanted stepchild. The stigma lasted for decades.[9]

On October 15, 1945, WFAA in Dallas launched W5XIC, the first Frequency Modulation "development" station in Texas. Soon, KERA became the first FM station in the Dallas–Fort Worth area.[10]

Times Publishing Company of Wichita Falls entered the FM market on December 23, 1946. KTRN, the first FM station in that area, transmitted with 250 watts. Higher power was expected in the summer. Programming for the first few days included story recitations by famous actors, news, special features and comments, and a remote broadcast of Handel's "Messiah" from a local church.[11]

In El Paso, KVOF, operated by Texas Western College, was one of the first FM stations. That station started as WTCM (West Texas College of Mines) on October 5, 1946, by thirteen women enrolled in a broadcasting class. It broadcast to the campus by "carrier current" for many years. When the FM station began operation in 1950, it became KVOF-FM, "The Voice of Freedom."[12]

Just prior to the war, WFAA in Dallas announced plans to broadcast the newspaper by radio. The paper scanner was to be located at the radio studios, with recorders, which received the broadcast and printed the newspaper on an 8.5" x 11" page, located across town. The news would be transmitted over W5XD, WFAA's ultra-high-frequency short-wave station.[13]

One postwar AM station was KVET in Austin, which began on October 1, 1946. The founders, all World War II veterans, were Sherman Birdwell, future Texas education commissioner; R. L. Phinney, future IRS director; J. J. (Jake) Pickle, future representative to the U.S. Congress; Ed Clark, future ambassador to Australia; Willard Deason, future U.S. interstate commerce commissioner;

J. C. Kellam, future president of the Texas Broadcasting Company; W. E. Syers, future freelance author; and John Connally, future governor of Texas.[14]

Liberty Broadcasting System (LBS)

Although Texas had had a long history of radio chains, it was just after the war when people were ready to relax and listen to something not quite so serious that the largest and most popular state-based network was formed. The Liberty Broadcasting System furnished the nation "American's pastime" on a regular basis.

"My grandmother used to tell me that she would hear me walking up and down in the alley in the back of our house in Shreveport broadcasting play-by-play," remembered Wes Wise, sports broadcaster and onetime mayor of Dallas. "I would keep a score card of the previous night's Shreveport game, and I was re-creating it. I never dreamed that I would re-create games on the Liberty Broadcasting System." Wise joined LBS shortly after Gordon McLendon began the most sophisticated and popular "re-creations" of sporting events in broadcast history.[15] McLendon, however, was not the first.

Jack Bell of KDET in Center re-created sporting events when he attended the Radio School of Broadcasting in Dallas:

> About 1938, WRR was on at that time and *Bill Boyd and the Cowboy Ramblers* were on the air . . . out at the fair grounds. . . . Saturday was your big day. I would kind of make out like I was an announcer. . . . I used to mimic the announcers. You would walk in . . . and you could see them in the studio.
>
> 1941—in my trade school, we went to *The Early Birds Show* . . . and they [WFAA] would pick certain commercials or announcements that they would let us do live, on the air on that morning show. . . . They had a lot of fun. They introduced you as being a student at this Radio School of Broadcasting and someday you will be hearing him on the radio.
>
> Eddie Hill was one of the instructors in sports. We got to re-create games. We didn't have a teletype or anything—we just made it up. I would make up an SMU vs. Texas game. I would have the lineups. We had some sound-effect records and an old wire recorder, the first one I had ever seen.[16]

Bell later became program director at KDET in the 1950s. One of his jobs was to announce sporting events along with selling advertising. Sometimes Bell had only sold a few commercials for a game by the time of the broadcast—maybe enough sponsors for the first quarter or half. Bell would go to the game and start the broadcast. "During a time out . . . I would get up, and if there was anybody in the stands who were sponsors [on the station] that I knew, I would hit them up . . . to sponsor the second half." According to Bev Brown of KGAS in Carthage, Bell would yell out in the stands and over the air, "Hey, Joe, you'll take this next quarter, won't you?" Then he would look around and see another supporter and yell, "Joe's got this quarter. Why don't you take the third quarter?" This was right in front of "Joe's" friends and family. "A person sitting around with his friends," said Brown, "you know he's not going to say no."[17]

Sporting events had been broadcast for almost as long as there was radio in Texas. The rebroadcast of game information, in some form, started in the 1920s. On Thanksgiving Day, 1921, the station at the Agriculture and Mechanical College at College Station transmitted a coded account of a football game for other stations to receive and transform into an account of the game. Harold Hough started broadcasting baseball on WBAP in Fort Worth in 1922. Some games were broadcast by having a person at the ballpark relay a description of the action by phone to a person at the station. The announcer then conveyed that to the radio audience. Although these were not referred to as "re-creations," they had similar characteristics. Jack McGrew did "re-creations" in the 1930s at KFDM in Beaumont: "We got our baseball coverage from out of town from a 'sounder.' We were doing it long before Gordon McLendon. . . . We did not have all the color. He really made a show out of it. The telegrapher would sit there at a typewriter, and as the stuff came out of the sounder he would type it out. I would lean over his shoulder. All it consisted of was 'balls' and 'strikes' and 'a hit to right field.' As he wrote it, I read it."[18]

"I helped Glen Brown re-create Austin Pioneer baseball games," said Stan McKenzie of KWED (Keep Working Every Day) in Seguin. The station had one person at the ballpark taking notes on a score card, and the information would be sent back by Western Union. The announcers were about an inning and a half behind the actual play. "They would telegraph who was at bat, where the ball was hit, if it was a two-base hit or three-base hit, and who fielded the ball . . . using '6 to 3,' or '5 flies out to number 9 in the outfield.'" The station added background sound. McKenzie believed the audience really thought the announcers were at the ballpark.[19]

Sometimes teams played where there were no telegraph or telephone lines. The station sent a person to the stadium and had him record an inning or two, go to his car, drive to the nearest telephone, and call the station. "I remember one time I got caught up and they had not called," remembered McKenzie. "I had a guy on first base and I didn't know what was going to happen. So I finally devised a plan where the guy at first tried to steal second, he knocked the bag loose at second base, and they had to call time to repair the bag." One ballpark had a railroad running beside it, and a few times per game the sound effects engineer would "run" a train by the stadium.[20]

Grady Maples, who broadcast baseball games for KFJZ in Fort Worth, was refused permission one year to broadcast from LaGrave Field. Maples went out to the ballpark parking lot, climbed a telephone pole with a microphone, hung on the pole by a belt, and broadcast the game. Zack Hurt and Tommy Mendeno used two pencils to imitate the sound of the bat for the games they re-created on KFJZ in the 1940s. Later, in the 1950s, Hurt moved to KXOL in Fort Worth and, according to Chem Terry, who was part of the announcing staff, continued to re-create baseball games:

"Popcorn!" "Peanuts!" Just like you would hear people at a stadium—just noise. Over here I had an applause record. . . . I had another turntable that I would run my commercials on if I had one on a disc (ET). Augy (Nararoo) was in one of the studios . . . and he had a little wooden dowel that hung down by a string. He would hit it with a little rod and it sounded just exactly like the "crack" of a bat. Every once in a while he would hit his desk or something and go "thump" and "Ahhh, we nearly caught one up here in the booth, Chem." Every once in a while I would say "Cold Beer!" "Peanuts!" "Get your peanuts!" "Souvenirs!" "Programs!"

Augy would go out to where the ticker was. Remember those old bell-shaped tickers? That's where the game came in. It was . . . coded, like a "3" would be the third inning; "T" would be top half.

Now if the ticker tape breaks down, you get a fellow out there trying to "show out" to the crowd, or you get a dog on the field, or "have you seen that flag? Man that flag is going to blow off of there. That thing's flapping. . . . Everybody is watching that flag. Nobody is watching the game. The game's stopped. . . ."[21]

Bob Hicks of Odessa remembers one re-created game in which Bob Byron "filled" for fifty minutes because it was raining at the ballpark.[22] Zack Hurt of KFJZ re-created a game while broadcasting from the grand opening of a Worth Supermarket in Fort Worth in a roped-off area surrounded by "Wheaties" containers sitting on top of a flat-bed trailer truck. The audience loved it.[23]

The best and most sophisticated "re-creations" were those of Gordon McLendon on the Liberty Broadcasting System. "He made that such an art when he started it," said Chem Terry. "Nobody doubted him—[the listeners] thought that his 're-created' games sounded better than when he was at the game itself." McLendon first broadcast a sporting event as a student at an Atlanta "Rabbits" High School football game. He borrowed a public-address system from his father's movie theater and described the action. As a teenager, driving in his family automobile, McLendon would practice announcing by pretending he was at a football or baseball game.[24]

McLendon began his professional career in 1947 when his father, Barton R. McLendon, became half-owner of KNET in Palestine, Texas. "He started doing 're-creations' in Palestine," remembered Wes Wise. In November of 1947, McLendon and his father bought a station in the Oak Cliff section of Dallas. They changed the call letters to KLIF. The station was licensed for "daytime-only" operations with 1,000 watts on 1190 kilocycles.[25]

McLendon decided that broadcasting major-league baseball on a daily basis was his "hidden weapon" against the well-established 50,000-watt stations. He began on November 9, 1947, by re-creating a professional football game. McLendon wanted to "create fixed times for sports listening so the audience would become habitual." He also determined that re-creating a game in his studios was cheaper than going to the ballpark.[26]

On March 21, 1948, McLendon re-created his first baseball game. It was an exhibition game between the New York Yankees and the St. Louis Cardinals. He hired a man in New York City to listen to the radio broadcast and teletype him "Ball!" "Strike!" "Fly-out to right field!" McLendon then dramatized it. At first KLIF only broadcast New York City teams because there were three: the Yankees, the Dodgers, and the Giants. One team usually played every afternoon.[27]

Wes Wise was hired to help broadcast games after the network started. Wise was working at KNOR in Monroe, Louisiana, which carried the games from LBS. One day Wise received a phone call from Louisiana Governor James Noe:

"I've just been talking to my son-in-law Gordon McLendon. You know, you met him a couple of weeks ago when he was here."

I said, "Yes, Sir."

He said, "He's very interested in you."

I said, "Oh! I didn't know that he ever listened to me."

He said, "He listened to you quite a bit the last time he was in town. He was impressed."

I said, "I'm sure glad to hear that, Mr. Noe. . . . I think that Gordon is one of the best announcers I've ever heard."

He said, "I'm glad to hear you say that because he wants you to come to Dallas and be his assistant."

There was, I'm sure, stunned silence. I said, "He's never even heard me do sports, Mr. Noe."

He said, "He thinks that you have the talent. He thinks he can teach you to do those ball games."

I said, "Well, I'm going with a young lady in Monroe that I think a lot of."

He said, "Now look, son! You forget that young lady and you go up to Dallas."

Within a week, I got in my '39 Ford and came to Dallas.

He [McLendon] liked radio, and he loved to be on the air. KLIF was in the basement of the Cliff Towers—in Oak Cliff. It was right after the war and people were hungry for entertainment, especially baseball. As soon as he started the games they caught on and people were coming to him, wanting on the network. He would say, "Yes, you can for a certain fee." It was very paltry by today's standards.[28]

The network spread by word of mouth. During the first year the operator of the station in Denison approached McLendon. Its afternoon audience had disappeared. People were listening to the games on KLIF. The owners asked if they could "hook on," pay a little fee, and carry the games. Then came Tyler, Mineral Wells, Mt. Pleasant, Waco—until by the end of the first year McLendon had a network of approximately fifty stations. On the day it stopped broadcasting in 1952, the Liberty Broadcasting System had 458 affiliates: *the second largest radio network in the country.* LBS also broadcast professional football on Sunday afternoon, Louisiana State University games on Saturday nights, and Miami University games on Friday nights after KLIF was licensed to broadcast past local sunset.[29]

On days when there were no games being played for LBS to re-create, McLendon might do a historical "re-creation," such as the Jack Johnson/Jim Jefferies boxing match or a football game from the 1920s. McLendon's favorite "re-created" historical event was a July 24, 1886, baseball game between the Brooklyn (Trolley) Dodgers and the St. Louis Browns. Special features were a batting count of five balls and two strikes, rumors that first basemen were considering using gloves, foul balls that caused vendors to spill full trays of beer steins, recognition of the attendance of well-known baseball fans like Mark Twain and Harriet Beecher Stowe, a foul ball that left the ballpark causing the umpire to call a five-minute time-out to retrieve the ball, and a post-game interview with St. Louis third baseman Arlie Neff. McLendon talked to the "real" Neff, age 91, by telephone.[30]

"At the start I just went to the Dallas baseball park" explained McLendon. "I took the extreme crowd noise, I took the gentle crowd noise, and I blended them. Later on I got very sophisticated. We had the crowd noise from the park itself. . . . We played the national anthem from Ebbitt's Field; it was with Gladys Gooding." During the broadcast four turntables were used. Two played general crowd noises and two played excited crowd noises. The sound engineer would fade between them to "fit" what was happening. The announcers had headsets and could hear the background sounds, and they would react to the rise and fall of excitement in the crowd noises.[31]

Wes Wise remembered his first day at LBS:

• • •

I walked into the Cliff Towers Hotel and said, "Where are the KLIF studios?"

They said, "Right over there."

There was a new sign that said, "KLIF." You walked down about ten steps and you opened a sort of opaque glass door type thing. The first thing I saw was a hand-painted sign that said, "Liberty Broadcasting System's *Game of The Day* with Gordon McLendon and Wes Wise." I've wondered to this day if Gordon did that for my benefit; to make me feel good because he was that type of person.[32]

Wise received instruction from McLendon on things he had to learn to re-create games the LBS way:

"You've got to use your imagination. You've seen plenty of baseball games. You know how long it takes the [pitched] ball to hit the bat, the bat strike the ball and it go to the second baseman, and how long it takes the second baseman to throw to first. You've got to imagine all that timing. You know how long it takes a home run to get out there."

That score sheet was very vital. . . . You had to look at that diamond and use your imagination pretty well. You could not get into a different world. You would lose your concentration on what was coming in on the teletype. . . . That was part of the fun and the fascination. . . .

The sheet said, "S1C," "Strike one called"; "B1OS," "Ball one outside." This came out on a paper roll. She [Nancy Golf] is keeping track of the base running. You had to keep the balls and strikes in your head, and seldom did you lose the count, but if you did, you could scan the sheet. . . . A good operator in the stadium would send "DiMaggio goes back to field it and shakes his head as the ball goes over the fence." Very few would do the shaking of the head thing. . . . That was the kind of thing that we added that we did not get off the wire. Things like "He backs out of the batter's box and knocks off his cleats." We started to learn certain idiosyncrasies of certain players.

Tom Malarkie did our commercials. We would have Tom take a wastebasket, and like a public announcer say, "Next batter—Tommy Hendrik." He would be in the announcers booth but he would have a special LBS microphone. We didn't have it through the whole broadcast, but we would have it now and then to make it more realistic. I remember Gordon saying one time "Tom, you're going to have to put your face deeper in the wastebasket."

When a single was coming up we would put up one finger for the sound-effects man, Creig Latask, so he would anticipate that this was to be a single. The baseball bat—for a single we would hit it just slightly. If you wanted a double, you hit it a little harder. If you wanted a home run—"Bam!"

He [McLendon] was big on "color" and things about the players. . . . The telegrapher at the stadium had a lot to do with how good the "re-creation" was—and our broadcast was. A good telegrapher knew baseball, and he would say "He got him on a change-of-pace pitch on that third strike," instead of "strike three called." We paid Western Union, and we had our own wire. We didn't have a say of who was on the other end, but he was at the stadium where the Western Union operators were.

At the beginning of the game we would always say, "This is a major-league broadcast-by-wire re-creation." A lot of people did not know what this meant. They did not know that these were re-creations. I have been asked many times "Did people, when they found out that they were re-creations—that we were not actually at the ball games—did they resent that?" The exact opposite happened. They would tune in even more to see if they could catch us in a mistake—to bet someone next to them that we weren't really at the baseball park.

Sometimes in the last year—1951—some were done live and some in the studio. Probably two-thirds were done in the studio and one-third at the ballpark. Nobody could tell the difference. People would make bets on which ones were live and which ones were re-creations.

If the wire goes out, or if the information becomes garbled, which did happen, then you had to get the "dog on the field and the umpires chasing the dog." Gordon's favorite was the "fight in the stands." . . . We had all kinds of stalls. He would come up with some just for fun.[33]

Once, McLendon had Lou Galling, nicknamed "old aches and pain," foul-off 109 straight pitches while he was waiting for the teletype to come back. One of the lighter moments on LBS was when Dizzy Dean, new football "color," asked to do some play-by-play. Dean re-created a 65-yard run into "He's going around the end, he's at the 30, the 40, the 50, the 55, the 60, the 65!" McLendon kicked Dean under the table. Dean corrected himself "Naw fans, he's coming back now to the 40, the 30."[34]

The Liberty Broadcasting System furnished more then baseball games. On October 2, 1950, LBS scheduled ten-and-a-half hours of programming to affiliates in all forty-eight states. One program was a musical minstrel show. LBS broadcast *Disc-Jockey Round Table,* which featured a new disc jockey from a different city each day. Later, McLendon added news programming and commentators like Raymond Gram Swing, Joseph C. Harsch, and John Vandercook. At one time, Liberty broadcast a soap opera.[35]

The Liberty Broadcasting System ceased operations on May 15, 1952, after McLendon lost a $12 million civil suit against organized baseball. In early 1952, the club owners announced that they would severely limit the number of afternoon games that could be carried, they refused to allow any nighttime broadcasts, some teams refused to allow their games to be carried, owners demanded new restrictions covering the selection of announcers and sponsors, and they forbid LBS to broadcast in the Midwest and Northeast.[36]

"The baseball clubs came to the conclusion that this was killing the attendance at their minor-league baseball parks," stated McLendon, "because they said my versions of the games were so much more colorful than their broadcasts. That made the minor-league baseball clubs look kind of pale by comparison."[37] These actions by baseball owners "killed" the Liberty network but did not stop McLendon. He started the smaller Kickerbocker Broadcasting Network, which re-created games, but only in Texas.

A new direction was initiated by KLIF in May of 1953. McLendon, who credited his friend Todd Storz with its invention, began a "Top-40" format on KLIF. Station manager Bill Stewart began the new format with a "gimmick," a trademark of McLendon's stations in their "Top-40" years. On opening day KLIF played Ray Anthony's "Dragnet" theme for twenty-four straight hours. KLIF's new format helped establish the fast-talking, exuberant, zany, motor-mouth "deejays" who played the top-selling popular records and entertained listeners with shear craziness and humor. On-air personalities included "The Weird Beard," "Jimmy Rabbitt," "Charlie and Harrigan," "The Big R," and "Mark E. Baby." Within six weeks, KLIF's share of the Dallas audience rose from 2 percent to more than 30 percent.

With KLIF's spectacular success, McLendon added the format to other stations: WRIT, Milwaukee; KTSA, San Antonio; KILT, Houston; KEFI, Shreveport; WAKY, Louisville; WNOE, New Orleans; and KNOE, Monroe, Louisiana.[38] In the late 1950s, by certain audience measurements KLIF was "the most popular radio station in the country." McLendon's innovation did not stop. In 1961 he took control of sales for an "All-News" station in Tijuana, Mexico. XTRA beamed its twenty-four-hour news format into the Los Angeles metropolitan area. McLendon originated KADS, an "all Want Ads" formatted station. He started Radio Nord, the first "pirate" radio ship broadcasting from the North Sea into the European Continent that did not have popular commercial radio broadcasting.[39]

According to Wes Wise, broadcasting sports was McLendon's favorite activity: "McLendon once said to Nancy Golf, 'Of all the things that I have ever done in my life, by far the greatest . . . years of my life were those years of doing the baseball games on the Liberty Broadcasting System. The days of the Liberty Broadcasting System were like a huge fish leaping out of the ocean to catch the rays of the sunshine for one fleeting moment and then sinking back into the sea, never to be heard from again.'"[40]

The Coming of Television

The word "television" was used around 1907. The idea of "pictures by air" or "distance seeing" had been known and written about since the nineteenth century. An artist in *Punch* in 1879 showed two people sitting in front of a fireplace watching a sporting event on a screen above the mantel. Cartoonist Albert Robida of France predicted "living pictures" bringing images of sports, culture, and even war into the sanctity of the home. Around the turn of the century, television was the subject of a Tom Swift novel.[41] A fantasized concept of television was used in the 1930s chaptered movie *Radio Ranch* with Gene Autry.

During the early part of this century, experiments were carried out in two different systems of television: mechanical and electronic. John Logie Baird in Great Britain and Charles Francis Jenkins and Ernst Alexanderson in the United States were advocates of a mechanical system. This system used the "Nipkow Disc," invented in Germany by Paul Nipkow. It used a rotating wheel in both the camera and receiver to dissect and then reassemble the image.

Vladimir Zworykin, a Russian emigrant, and Philo T. Farnsworth were the leaders in the development of electronic television.[42] In 1923 Zworykin demonstrated a crude all-electronic television system using a camera tube called the "Iconoscope." Farnsworth filed a patent application in 1927 for his system, which used an all-electronic "Image-Dissector" camera.

Some experimenters formed businesses. On July 2, 1928, Jenkins began a regular schedule of broadcasting "Radiomovies" (motion pictures) and "Radiovision" (live images), from Anacostia, Maryland. During this period, other stations installed their own "Radiomovies" equipment built by Westinghouse. Jenkins built a movie studio to produce "silhouette" movies. At first, "Radiomovies" could only reproduce shadow images. Jenkins formed a company to market kits for receivers and transmitters. One of his television sets cost $60. Later, half-tone movies were transmitted using a sixty-line image on a wavelength of 46 meters to an estimated audience of 20,000.[43]

In the late 1920s, the Federal Radio Commission reserved four 100-kilocycle channels for experimental television stations in the United States. Its report referred to people who watched television as "Lookers-in." Other names for viewers were "Teleseers," "Audobservers," "Telegazers," "Visioneers," "Ingazers," "Beholders," "Opticizers," and "Inviders." In Great Britain, France, Germany, Japan, the Soviet Union, and the United States, experimentation continued.[44]

On May 10, 1931, Don Lee's station W6XAO transmitted an image from one side of a room to the other by all-electronic equipment. On December 23, 1931, that station started regular telecasting: one hour a day, six days a week. W6XAO was the forerunner of KTSL-TV in Los Angeles, California.[45]

In 1936 the Radio Corporation of America "signed on" experimental station W2XBS, which became WNBT-TV. In February of 1937, Guy Woodward, supervisor of the mail department at WBAP, received a publicity packet about NBC's experiments in all-electronic television with artists wearing orange, brown, and red paint on their faces; spotlight pouring brilliant light in eyes; microphones hanging from pulleys skimming silently overhead; and great black boxes with glass eyes memorizing every move of performers.[46]

The Establishment of Television in Texas

All eyes were focused on a small panel of ground glass. There was a flicker of light—orange and black—and then a face appeared. "This is television station W5AGO," announced an unknown voice. W5AGO, *the Southwest's first television station,* was on the air. Its builder and owner, Truett Kimzey, engineer for KFJZ, had spent two months building the transmitting station. His experiment was featured in the 1934 Southwestern Exposition and Fat Stock Show in Fort Worth.[47]

Kimzey was on a trip to New York when he made an investment in the future. "I thought television was just around the corner," said Kimzey, "and sunk all my savings—$1,500—in the equipment." The equipment was very crude because the television camera as it is known today had not yet been invented. Performers stood in a darkened room before a battery of ten photoelectric cells while dozens of tiny shafts of light were thrown over their features through a revolving scanner disc. The performer's image was reflected into the bank of cells. The receiver had a similar disc revolving at the same rate of speed, and the picture was projected on a ground-glass panel. "The performer sang or talked into a microphone of another radio station," explained Kimzey, "but since electricity has no loss of motion, the sound and picture reach the receiver at the same time and there is perfect synchronization."

Some of the first television performers were Cecil Gill, the yodeling country boy; Nancy Jo Nolte; and Helen and Ellen Prestidge.[48] Gill was a well-known radio performer in Texas. The Prestidge sisters were friends of Kimzey. They were known as "The Harmony Twins" and had sung on KTAT, KRLD, WRR, and KFJZ in the Fort Worth–Dallas area. "Mr. Kimzey was instrumental in having us perform on the first remote broadcast on television from the studio downtown to the Exposition and Fat Stock Show," stated Ellen Prestidge. "That was quite a day."[49]

Kimzey installed his television transmitter atop the Commercial Standard

Building at Seventh and Main Streets in downtown Fort Worth, the studios of KFJZ. Earlier television experiments had operated over telephone lines, but never over the air. "The pictures weren't perfect by any means. They were clear enough to recognize people on the screen," said Kimzey. The "Televisor" would successfully transmit the head and shoulders of a subject or two or more persons standing close together. Kimzey was working on developments that he hoped would televise a larger area.[50] Johnny Smith, an engineer at KFJZ, remembered seeing one of Kimzey's demonstrations: "I saw the transmissions from the Trinity Life Building downtown out to the North Side Stock Show. I can just vaguely remember being there and a sign saying, "Come In and See Television." I thought it was a picture on film. It was actually on the air. . . . I saw a screen with a flying spot scanner of some sort. It was just somebody talking; it might have been Truett."[51]

J. R. (Buddy) Cruse, an engineer at KFJZ, remembered a different television demonstration: "It was an exhibition at the Fat Stock Show, and it created a lot of interest. Everybody wanted to see it and see themselves on television. . . . It was the closest thing to television at that time. It was a rotating disc. You could see details pretty well. It was black and white, and the focus and sharpness was not there, but you could see this lady . . . up on the screen. It was in a darkened room almost like a movie theater. When someone would get on there, everybody would laugh."[52]

Winston O. Sparks of Fort Worth observed one of Kimzey's demonstrations:

[It was] in the exhibit building during the Fort Worth Stock Show. I was just a bare faced kid running around eating all the free samples of fresh biscuits. . . . On one particular display—something was moving like a fan; a slow-moving fan. . . . Then about twenty-five feet away there was another screen showing what was being transmitted over here. It [the television camera] was a wheel. . . . The sign explained, "What you're seeing here is being transferred through a wire over to this other screen." It talked about what would be available in the future. Someday you would be able to see people from whatever contraption this was, from somewhere else, and look at it on the screen. Lot of people would not believe it. They would say "It's not coming from across town. That's just an old movie they got running up there."[53]

Kimzey was wrong; television was not just around the corner; it was fourteen years away.[54] Lawrence Birdsong of Longview saw a demonstration in Dallas "where the telephone exhibit was . . . of the State Fair of Texas, probably the centennial. We paid two bits and went in. This screen had lights around all four sides just like a dressing room mirror. . . . Right around the side, we could look over and see them projected on the screen. That was my first television."[55]

George Ing, of KONO in San Antonio, attended a demonstration in the late 1930s. "Someone came to San Antonio and demonstrated a flying spot scanner right across the street from KONO at the Central Catholic School. I read about it in the newspaper," stated Ing. "It was just a whirling disc in a darkened room. He was not transmitting a picture over wire or over the air. He was picking up cartoons. It did not impress me that much."[56]

As a teenager in 1929, Jack McGrew, future general manager of KPRC in Houston, wanted to build a television. He and a friend, "Ribs" Good, both tinkered in radio. Together they built "the best radios that either one of us every owned," said McGrew. "We used what was called 'peanut tubes'—a small vacuum tube—very small, but quite efficient for their day." The two friends started reading articles in *Popular Mechanics* and *Popular Science* about transmitting pictures through the air. "We were aware of scanning discs, and we even considered building such a device, but we could not figure out what we would watch if we built it. Where are you going to see a program?"[57]

Television in the 1930s was very primitive. Different manufacturers had different systems. Some used a line-scan of 300 or 400 rather than the 525 lines adopted by the National Television System Committee (NTSC) on April 30, 1941. The Radio Corporation of America (RCA), General Electric (GE), DuMont, and others were manufacturing equipment, mostly on different standards. The equipment was not compatible or interchangeable. An RCA television set would not receive the signal of a station using DuMont equipment. "They were trying," explained Rupert Bogan, WBAP engineer, "to come up with some means of developing the transmission of this thing from the camera to the transmitter and on to the air. Of course, the television receiver was very primitive, too."[58]

Real interest to get television for Texas started at the end of World War II. Harold Hough, manager of WBAP, and Abe Herman, attorney for Carter Publications, went to Princeton University in 1946 for a meeting of the National Broadcasting Company's affiliates. At the meeting David Sarnoff, chairman of the Radio Corporation of America, gave a lecture promoting television and facsimile. Herman thought television was a little like movies; but after Sarnoff's presentation, Herman recommended that Carter Publications develop television, not facsimile.

The electronic rave at that time was facsimile. The NBC people told the affiliate representatives that if they did not apply for a frequency modulation (FM) license and develop facsimile, they might lose their amplitude modulation (AM) affiliation. The representatives of WFAA in Dallas believed what they had heard and decided that facsimile, not television, was the real future. WFAA's decision to continue developing facsimile, which it was developing just before the war, almost resulted in its elimination from the field of television.[59]

Jack McGrew attended a meeting of NBC affiliates in Atlantic City, New Jersey. David Sarnoff told the group that he believed television was destined to become a stronger medium than either radio or newspapers. It might become stronger than both combined. He warned that any radio station or newspaper should seriously consider moving into television. McGrew took the comments seriously. He returned to Houston and reported to former governor Bill Hobby and his wife, owners of the *Houston Post* and KPRC. "We tried to estimate," McGrew wrote, "the length of time required to develop a circulation of sufficient size to attract advertisers, how long the proposed station could be expected to lose money, and just how much money might be lost before such an operation became a viable enterprise."[60]

Herman and Hough returned to Texas from a National Association of Broadcasters meeting in Atlantic City in 1946. They began talking television to Amon Carter. "I rushed home, went in to see my boss, and tried to deliver word for word the ideas the General [Sarnoff] had given us," said Hough.[61]

"I can remember when we had silent movies," Herman told Carter, "and I remember when they applied talk to them; and the difference was between night and day." "If you go in there and build a television station, and have 'um talk out there where you can see and listen to it, I think it'll make money," he said. "We think that it is the coming thing, and if you will just advance us the money, we'll sure build it."[62]

Carter replied, "Well, the General seems to be quite bullish on television."

Hough countered, "Bull nothing, he's elephant."[63]

Shortly thereafter, Herman, Hough, and R. C. (Super) Stenson, director of engineering for WBAP, went to New York. General Electric, one company building early television equipment, had television station W2XB operating at Schenectady. The broadcasters took a special train to observe one of the few functioning stations in the country. When the group left the train, personnel from the station took their photograph. The film was rushed back to the station and developed; and when the group reached the General Electric facilities, the group's image was broadcast over the air.[64]

Bob Gould, one of three persons working at W2XB, remembered the WBAP group coming through on tour. "But I was not aware of who they were. Super Stenson, Harold Hough, and the whole gang were up there observing: everybody came to Schenectady to observe this new thing—television." Gould showed them the mercury-vapor, water-cooled lights. "We would show them the cameras we had," said Gould, "the console equipment, the projectors; everything that General Electric was trying to sell to people starting television."[65]

Carter Publications decided to go into television and instructed Herman to prepare an application for a construction permit. Obtaining a permit was simple in those days, not the three-year ordeal it became in the 1950s. It took a three-cent stamp. Carter Publications could have had their construction permit a year sooner if not for the expense and shortage of television equipment.[66]

When Carter Publications filed an application, the company believed it was the first in Texas. It was not. On October 23, 1944, Interstate Circuit, Inc., of Dallas had filed for the first construction permit in the state. Interstate and its president, Karl Hoblitzelle, had been giants in the motion picture theater business for decades. Hoblitzelle was to own 36.5 percent of the stock in the station. Other stockholders were R. J. O'Donnell of Dallas with 10 percent, John R. Maroney of Dallas with 3.5 percent, and Paramount Pictures Inc. of New York City with 50 percent. J. C. Skinner was the applicant's engineer.

Interstate proposed a 410-foot antenna transmitting with 25 kilowatts visual and 12.5 kilowatts aural. Two DuMont cameras would be located in two studios in the Republic National Bank Building at 1313 Main Street in Dallas. The station was projected to cost $234,500. The mailing address was the Majestic Theater on Elm Street. The station would broadcast seven days a week, with the following schedule on Sundays:

11:00 A.M.–12:00 P.M.	Church services from the studio
3:00–3:30 P.M.	3 reels short subject
6:00–6:15	Newscast from the studio
6:15–6:30	Travelogue
6:30–7:00	Film entertainment
7:00–7:30	Music and vocal from the studio
7:00–8:00	Film entertainment
8:00–9:00	Church from the studio
9:00–9:30	Orchestral from the studio[67]

In 1946 the opening of Interstate's Wilshire movie theater in Dallas was telecast throughout the lobby on closed-circuit equipment specifically purchased from DuMont. The performance included speeches and entertainers such as "Little Willie," a singer and dancer. The cameraman was Bob Chambers. Interstate was not granted a construction permit for Channel 8. Instead, it was granted to Tom Potter, who built KBTV. The equipment was sold to KRLD in Dallas.[68]

Carter Publications's application was one of three in Texas when it was filed. In 1946 Carter Publications in Fort Worth and Chronicle Publishing Company in San Antonio joined Interstate. Since World War II, doubts about television had prompted fifty-seven applicants in the country to withdraw. No application was filed for Houston. The WBAP application was uncontested. "WFAA officials laughed," said Abe Herman. "They decided to go with FM and facsimile." Martin Campbell, general manager of WFAA, "made a mistake."[69]

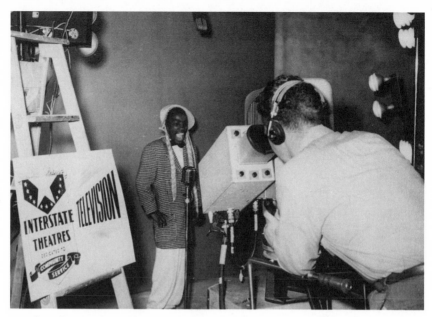

Little Willie, singer and dancer, and Bob Chambers, cameraman, at the closed-circuit demonstration of television by Interstate Theaters during the opening of the Wilshire Theater in Dallas in 1946. Courtesy Paul E. Adair

When Clarence Bruyere started working at WFAA, one of the first things he heard was, "Martin Campbell said that we were not going to go for television . . . that FM was going to be the thing of the future, and he had us submit a license, and it was called KERA." Bruyere did not hear that directly from Campbell but from employees. "I heard that this cost him his job," stated Bruyere.[70]

Jack McGrew remembered a story he heard from Campbell:

Purely to aggravate Hough—they were still mortal enemies, more or less; they ragged each other all the time—Martin Campbell thought he would try to trick Hough into applying for a television permit. So he let the word out that he and his attorney were going to Washington to file for a television construction permit. And indeed they were going to Washington, but for some other reason. Hough got the word and immediately recruited Herman, and they flew to Washington. Martin was on the train. They [WBAP] filed for a construction permit. Martin had no intention of filing for a permit at that point.

Martin [Campbell] regaled Jack Harris and me with this story some time later. Harris and I were sitting in his dining room in Dallas and he is telling us this story on the night that WBAP-TV is to go on the air. We're sitting there watching the television set—they had trouble, and Martin was just rolling on the floor. All he did incidentally was to deliver to the *Fort Worth Star-Telegram* an exclusive license because shortly after that the FCC froze television applications and nobody got on the air.[71]

Television for Texas

On Friday, June 21, 1946, Carter Publications was granted a construction permit for Channel 5, which at that time was a center channel and generally considered most desirable for television reception. Channel 5 would be broadcasting with a power of 30.4 kilowatts with an antenna height of five hundred feet. The station was expected to be operational within the year, in time for next season's baseball and football games.[72]

"We got our permit early, but what were we to do with it?" said Harold Hough. "Folks were saying be careful—it's too risky—why hurry, and the expert advice to play possum came from some of the strangest places." Carter Publications had its construction permit for nearly two years before building the station. They kept renewing it. They were not sure they really wanted to go into television because they knew it was going to cost a great deal of money.[73]

Choosing the site for the studio and transmitter was the job of the engineering staff. Leonard Saye, chief maintenance engineer for WBAP, considered three locations in the Fort Worth area. The first location was a downtown block already owned by the *Star-Telegram*. The second was near the railroad yards, so refrigeration could be available for cooling purposes. The third was a seventy-four-acre field near the White Lake Dairy.[74]

The land near the dairy was selected, but there was a problem: the price was too high. Abe Herman informed Amon Carter, "We found the land we want for the station, but the owner wants $450.00 an acre."

Carter fired back, "That's outrageous! Who owns that land?"

Herman returned, "You do, Mr. Carter." Carter had owned the land for years, and the dairy ran its herd on it. The newspaper owned a piece of property at Fifth and Taylor Streets in downtown. The two parties agreed upon a trade. Carter Publications and Channel 5 received seventy-four acres, on which the station was built, and Carter received the downtown land, which he later sold for a million dollars.[75]

Carter, Hough, and Herman inspected the site where the building and tower were to be erected. Hough was surprised. "The landowner did not seem to be exactly pleased with my tower location." The three climbed through the fence and walked out into the field. It was 110 degrees in the shade, "but you could leave the shade," stated Hough. The field contained a herd of cows. A large Jersey bull left the herd and was moving in their direction. Hough told Carter to "Scat!"

Carter told Hough, "Forget that bull. He won't bother us."

The bull, pawing the ground, came closer.

Hough turned to leave, saying, "I'm gettin' out of here. I've got a wooden leg and that bull doesn't know who you are." "That bull doesn't care that you are Amon Carter." They safely rolled under the fence by a ten-yard margin.[76]

Once the site had been selected, the engineers had to determine for the FCC how far the station's signal would reach. Johnny Smith, engineer, described Channel 5's attempt to determine coverage:

The chief engineer, "Super" Stenson, was very much business. It had to be in the early part of '47. We were working at the maintenance shop down on Barnett where we made all the transcriptions, delayed soap opera programs, and did maintenance on the equipment used in the control room and remotes.

On this particular day, Mr. Stenson came over and said, "We need to go out on the east side of town and we will be gone all afternoon."

He told the other fellows in the shop we'd be back late. I couldn't figure out where we were going. We get this roll of butcher paper and a sack of nails, and we came out here in this field where this tower is now; climb the fence. He told me that the paper had to be put down just right; it had to be running exactly north and south, and there had to be a cross, east and west, right here at this point where the stake was in the ground. We used nails pushed through the paper into the ground to hold the paper down. The pilot from the Richey Flying Service would fly over and take these pictures, one going north, one going east; and he was taking a picture of that elevation which was five hundred feet showing the horizon in the four directions. It showed what the coverage would be if you had an antenna sticking up in the air five-hundred feet above the ground. We spent the afternoon getting the paper down, keeping the wind from blowing it away, and getting the pictures made. We got through and rolled the paper up. . . . We started back to town and I just didn't know whether I had the right to question the old man about what we were doing. You know, he's the boss. But I could not figure out what is all this for.

I said, "What is it they're going to do out there in that field?"

He said, "That's going to be the site of our television tower. And that location is being done for the FCC."

I said, "A television tower. What are you talking about? What is television?"

He said, "Well, we're going to go into the television business, and television is something that you broadcast through the air just like radio; as a matter of fact, people will be able to sit at home, and we'll broadcast movies right through the air."

I thought, "Ah, phooey, the old man's off his rocker."

I really didn't believe it. But I was told to keep it hush-hush because we'd been given a permit to build the station, and KSD in St. Louis had been given a permit at the same time; so we had a race . . . as a matter of fact, we won.[77]

Smith helped get the stations' equipment ready:

When they started building this building out there, there was the biggest hole in the ground you ever saw. I couldn't figure out why such a big building, and it turned out to be about 80 to 90 percent radio studios.

We started getting equipment in great big wooden crates. You'd open one up and it would say, "Camera Control Unit," and you'd say, "What's that?" Our job was to take the equipment, see if we could figure what plugs into what, and then turn it on to see if we could make it work. Every time you opened a piece of equipment there would be an instruction book and there would be a photograph of the way the thing was supposed to look after it was hooked up. You could see that there was a cable running from the power supply to the control unit, and there was another cable from the control unit to the camera; and you start looking around, looking for what kind of cable fits this plug. That's about all we knew about it.[78]

On June 20, 1948, a preview of television was arranged by WBAP-TV. The show was a closed-circuit feed from Channel 5's mobile unit to television sets in the Keystone Room of the Hotel Texas. Seeing their first telecast were WBAP and *Star-Telegram* officials, representatives of RCA Victor, and television dealers from around the area. Harold Hough, now vice-president in charge of broadcasting for Carter Publications, presented the broadcast. The program was picked up by Channel 5's cameras in the Centennial Room of the hotel, with the mobile unit sitting out on the street. Hough introduced the program as giving the audience a glimpse of the type of telecast that might be expected. The talent for the show was a band called the Flying X Ranch Boys, known on radio as the Light Crust Doughboys.[79] Frank Mills was master of ceremonies:

Mr. Carter had all the big shots in town. They were in a dinner in the Crystal Ballroom. I was to M.C. this twenty- or thirty-minute program from one of the hotel rooms. I don't know if they had any air conditioning; it didn't make any difference because by the time you turned on all these incandescents, it was just like an oven.

They kept telling me, "Now, Mills, you don't go on the air until you get the cue, and you won't get the cue until you see the red light on the camera."

I said, "That's all I need to know; don't get excited about it. Just give us the cue; that's all; then we'll go."

We stand around and we stand around and we stand around, and finally I go to the floor man and I said, "What's going on?"

He replied, "I haven't heard from the truck."

I said, "Guys, let's do something here to relieve the tedium; let's just do something for Mr. Carter personally. How's that? Fine."

So, I'm grimacing and just a bunch of junk coming out here, and I'm really teasing Carter. "Okay, Amon, you got all those tin-horns down there"—this kind of thing—"Hey, boys, let's hit it."

And they'd go through some number or chorus; and somebody would get up there and crack it up, and we'd fall out laughing. We had one clown who was always coming out with something; he'd walk up there in front of the camera with the microphone standing there; and he'd get off some corny joke and "haw, haw, haw."

All of a sudden Johnny Smith burst through the door, and his face was red. He had run up the stairs; we were on about the second or third floor, and he hadn't stopped. "You're on the air! You're on the air!"

I said, "Come on, Johnny!"

"The two [Tally] lights are out; the phone's out!" he exclaimed.

Back in front of the microphone I said, "I'm sorry, Mr. Carter. We're just up here rehearsing and having fun, and we'll take it from the top now. You ready, boys?"

I thought, this is the beginning and the end of me in television.[80]

Mills never heard about the incident. He was astonished because he knew the picture and sound were going to the remote truck and to the television sets in the ballroom.

One staff member hired that summer was Robert Gould, as chief of production. Gould was one of the two staff members with previous experience in television. W2XB in Schenectady, New York, had hired Gould in 1939 as camera operator and later producer/director.[81] In 1948, on the advice of Duff Brown, director at WRGB-TV (W2XB), Gould wrote Hough explaining who he was, what he was doing at the time, and what he could do for Channel 5 and asked Hough about employment. Gould received a letter from Hough stating that he and Abe Herman would be in New York City in two weeks and requested Gould to meet them at the Lexington Hotel. Gould's job interview was unique:

Hough was a man who never took his hat off. He wore a hat forever. He had a wooden leg . . . he lost [his own leg] as a boy peddling papers in Oklahoma City; a train ran over his leg. I didn't know Harold Hough. He had a yellowish white shirt on. He wasn't disheveled looking, but wasn't neat looking; he just looked like an old country guy that put a suit on and everything didn't fit just right.

He was surrounded by top-notch executives from ABC and NBC because he represented both networks at that time on radio. I didn't know any of them. I was a country boy in tall cotton at that point. Abe Herman was there. He's got a booming voice; he scared me the way he talked—shouted all the time. We sat around and had drinks, and they were carrying on conversations, half of which I couldn't understand because I hadn't been exposed to that kind of business.

Finally Mr. Hough said, "I'm getting hungry. I'm going to order up some Southern fired chicken." Pretty soon a mountain of Southern fried chicken comes up; we're all sitting around eating chicken, nothing formal, and Hough says, "Getting stuffy in here." He throws up the window on Lexington Avenue; he's chewing a chicken bone and looking out the window—and he's throwing the bones out the window.

I said to myself, "There's my kind of man; he's my man."

They finish the chicken and he says, "All you guys, get out of the room. I want to talk to this boy." And so he got them all out. The only question he asked me was, "Can you direct *The Flying X Ranch Boys?* They're a local group, Western artists, that we have on staff at the station; we'll do a show with them." He says, "Can you direct?"

I said, "Sure, I can direct them, Mr. Hough."

Then he said, "Then we've got a deal if we can get together on the salary." We didn't argue too much about the salary. It sounded pretty good to me. He said, "If you'll come with me, you'll never regret it."

And as long as he was alive, I never regretted it. It was just a handshake. . . .[82]

Other personnel added to the television staff that summer were George Cranston, Jim Byron, Seymour C. Andrews, Rupert Bogan, Phil Wygant, Roberta Connolly (Bobbie Wygant), Tom Bedford, Johnny Smith, Frank Mills, Bud Sherman, Guy Woodward, Russ Thornton, Lillard Hill, Jim Turner, Pat Barnett, Clint Bourland, Johnny Hay, Bob Grammer, and others.

In August 1948, WBAP-TV signed the first dual network affiliation in the United States. Channel 5 would be affiliated with NBC and ABC. Programming from the two networks used a comparatively new process called "Kinescope." This technique used motion picture film shot off a master television screen while the program was in progress. The developed film was then flown to affiliates and televised a few days or weeks after the show originated. Live network programming was not expected in Texas for more than a year. Coaxial cable, which would eventually bring live network to Channel 5, had been laid, but its use was restricted by a shortage of specialized equipment.[83]

The decision was made that sports and movies would be the main programming. Movies were a natural. A movie takes up a lot of time; it has a story line.

The station's personnel tried to persuade the Southwest Conference to televise more football games than planned. The personnel approached the Dallas and Fort Worth high schools about telecasting their games. Some administrators agreed when they realized that if they could not get people to the games, those people might watch the games on television. The station needed the programming, and plans were made to broadcast three high school football games a week on Thursday, Friday, and Saturday nights. All home games of Texas Christian University would be televised on Saturdays.[84]

As of August 16, 1948, the following applications had been filed or granted in the state.

Amarillo
    Amarillo Television Company: application for Channel 2
Austin
    Austin Television Company: application for Channel 8
Beaumont
    Lufkin Amusement Company: application for Channel 10
Corpus Christi
    Corpus Christi Television Company: application for Channel 6
Dallas
    A. H. Belo Corporation: application for Channel 12
    Texas Television: application for Channel 10
    City of Dallas: application for Channel 10
    KRLD Radio: construction permit for KRLD-TV, Channel 4
    Lacy-Potter Television: construction permit for KBTV-TV, Channel 8
    Variety Broadcasting Company: application for Channel 2
Fort Worth
    Carter Publications: construction permit for Channel 5
    Television Enterprises: application for Channel 10
Houston
    Harris County Broadcasting Company: application for Channel 13
    Texas Television Company: application for Channel 4
    Houston Post Company: application for Channel 4
    W. Albert Lee: construction permit for KLEE-TV, Channel 2
    Shamrock Broadcasting Company: application for Channel 13
San Antonio
    Express Publishing Company: application for Channel 12
    San Antonio Television: construction permit for KEYL-TV, Channel 5
    Southland Industries: construction permit for WOAI-TV, Channel 4
    Walmac Company: application for Channel 12

Mission Broadcasting Company: application for Channel 12
Waco
Waco Television Company: application for Channel 11
Wichita Falls
Wichita Falls Television Company: application for Channel 3[85]

On September 30, 1948, the Federal Communications Commission froze all applications for Very High Frequency (VHF) television channels. For the next four years, until April 14, 1952, the FCC studied the growing shortage of allottable channels, color television, and educational use of media. The only stations allowed to be constructed and operated were those that had been granted construction permits or were already on the air. In Texas, one television station was on the air: WBAP-TV, Fort Worth. It had been broadcasting one day. Five other Texas stations had construction permits.

Telecasting Begins

Carl Simpson, manager of E. E. Dabney Hardware in De Leon, was delighted. For the first time since he had become a television dealer, his television set produced something other than electronic snow: it had a picture. At 11:21 A.M. on September 15, 1948, WBAP-TV engineers energized the transmitter and broadcast a test pattern. People watched the still picture with music. Telephone calls came from Dallas, Waxahachie, McKinney, Denton, and De Leon. Reception was reported good up to a thirty-five- to forty-mile radius. De Leon, at eighty-seven miles, was the farthest known city with reception. Test patterns were scheduled daily from 11 A.M. to noon and from 4:00 to 5:00 P.M. Except for experiments, this was the first television signal in Texas and the South.[86]

Serious problems still existed. The building was not completed, and the station would go on the air unfinished. "We started putting the equipment in the television control room before the room was finished," remembered Johnny Smith. "Those glass panels across the front of the control room were not there; it was a raw concrete floor."[87] There were holes in the floor where engineers were going to set equipment. They used a two-by-six-foot metal bench that RCA sold the station to hold equipment because they had to temporarily wire the control room to get on the air. The engineers checked everything. RCA sent engineers to help, but they left early.[88]

Jack McGrew of KPRC in Houston visited WBAP-TV:

Before they ever got on the air, I went to Fort Worth on the bus. I knew Hough and George Cranston quite well. We were good friends. They invited me to

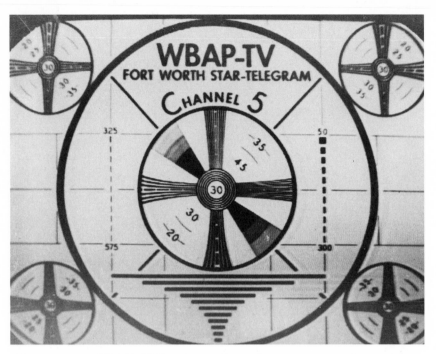

The test pattern of WBAP-TV broadcast on September 15, 1948, except for experiments, the first television signal in the South. Courtesy KXAS-TV, Fort Worth, Texas

come out to the station. Harold took me out there himself to show me around. The thing that startled me was that there was construction dust everywhere. They had all this equipment sitting on the loading dock, and the air was heavy with construction dust. I said to myself, "If that dust gets in that equipment, there's going to be hell to pay."

They had not moved their projectors inside yet; they were still sitting on the dock. They showed me their projection room. In those days they were using film. That was all that was available. The projection room was fire proof, and I asked, "Why fire proof?"

Hough said, "Because the film material is nitrate and it can burn."

I said, "We haven't used nitrate for some time."

I was impressed with the huge overhead doors in the studio. . . . I learned sometime later that one of the reasons for them was so Amon could ride in there on his horse without getting off.[89]

During September the first Zoomar lens in the Southwest was installed on a camera assigned to the remote unit. The fourteenth such lens was the product of Dr. F. G. Back, and it took four years to develop mathematically. The glass had aged eight years to prevent warping. Only twenty-four $7,500.00 Zoomars were manufactured per year. They had been used for approximately one year.[90]

Chem Terry, WBAP-TV announcer, remembered one of Amon Carter's visits to the new facilities:

> They were some of the finest facilities you could find. Mr. Carter came out to inspect them, and he walked into the big studio—all kinds of equipment in there—millions of dollars in there.
>
> He looked around and said, "Harold, come here."
>
> Mr. Hough came over and said, "Yes, Mr. Carter."
>
> Carter said, "Clock! Clock! Clock! Three clocks in this studio. What do you need three clocks in here for?"
>
> Harold said, "Mr. Carter, we have to keep the exact time of when we get on and when we get off."
>
> Carter said, "People on the air can't see them."
>
> Harold said, "Yes they can. They can see them."
>
> Carter said, "Well, that seems pretty extravagant to me."
>
> After all the money he had spent out there, he could not see the need for three clocks in this huge studio.[91]

Harold Hough gave simple orders. He would say, "Do it!" He did not say how or why—"just get it done." Hough wanted a newsreel on opening night, and orders went to Jim Byron, news director of WBAP radio. Byron's reaction was one of dismay, but he soon reconciled himself because he had a production staff. Byron knew nothing about television or film but had seen newsreels in motion picture theaters. The newsreel he chose was like *The Pathe News;* thus, *The Texas News* was born.

Byron assembled his staff. "I happened to be sitting directly across the WBAP news room in the old Medical Arts Building," stated Doyle Vinson, news staff, "so when he looked up and saw me, I became the first member of the [television] staff." Other members selected knew as little about newsreels as Vinson did. In September the staff received camera equipment, film, and other accessories. Jimmie Mundell, James Kerr, and Phil Hopkins were hired as cameramen. It was later discovered that *The Texas News* was created out of a misunderstanding. Byron thought Hough had ordered a newsreel. Hough only wanted some type of news program for opening night. In September, Lillard Hill was chosen the voice of *The Texas News.*[92]

The Truman Broadcast

At 2:18 P.M. two muffled rings on the telephone inside the WBAP remote truck signaled that the studio was calling. Larry Dupont, production staff, answered and, after a brief moment of silence, announced, "We're on the air." The date was September 27, 1948. The occasion was a brief visit of President Harry S Truman to Fort Worth during his campaign for re-election. Television owners saw a crowd shot and a speaker's platform at the Texas and Pacific Railway Terminal Building in downtown Fort Worth. The weather was warm and sunny, and fifteen acres of people welcomed the president.[93]

Amon Carter and Harold Hough decided to televise the president's speech even though it was scheduled two days before the station's official opening. Abe Herman advised, "If Mr. Truman wins the election, you'll have no problems. If he loses, you could be in trouble."[94]

Staff Engineer Rupert Bogan decided the telecast was part of the station's test period. "You had a construction period—you built the station. Whenever you get it built, you wire the FCC for permission to make test." The FCC sent WBAP-TV a wire authorizing signal test. "You're in a test period. That's what we were in when we picked up Truman." Channel 5 was running tests. [95]

Officially, the station could not program, and Herman thought it illegal. The administration made no such claims; they just did it anyway.[96] Johnny Smith was a cameraman:

> To tell you, we didn't know all the refinements. We did things that are absolutely hilarious by today's standards. We're standing down there about an hour and a half before time to go on, and we're trying to decide who's going to run the audio and who's going to be a cameraman and so on.
>
> During the course of the morning, Gene Reynolds and Frank Mills showed up; they were supposed to be the announcers of the show. Larry Dupont was the director that was supposed to be making all the decisions.
>
> They asked Larry, "Where are the announcers supposed to be?"
>
> He didn't know. Well, they had to be someplace where they could see, have a microphone, and describe events until the speaker started talking. They didn't have a place, so one of the fellows goes over in the TP building and comes up with a great big toilet tissue box. This box is about three by four by four feet. We ended up setting that box up on top of the truck and cut a hole in the side of it. The announcer was going to stand on the ladder that goes from the truck up to the roof of the truck . . . be inside the box, peep out, watch the proceedings, and describe it on television. That was the first announcer's booth on a television remote. The next couple of days we kept hearing about phone calls that people had made to our manager, George Cranston, wanting to know what that bunch of television people were doing. WBAP had a truck down there with a great big paper box setting [on] top of it, and viewers simply didn't know what that was for.

*On September 27, 1948, two days before the official opening of Channel 5,
WBAP-TV's remote unit televised the speech of President Harry S Truman
from downtown Fort Worth. This was the first television program in the South.
Courtesy KXAS-TV, Fort Worth, Texas*

I happened to be assigned to running the camera up on the roof. . . . I was
going to get . . . a twenty-five-inch lens. The idea was that I was supposed to
get the first shot of the train coming into the yards. Now here comes the train,
and they kept hollering at me on the headphones, "Which car is he in?" How
do I know? So I decided to focus on the first one—the one that had the little
platform across the back. And I just followed that train . . . and the paper the
next morning said, "Cameraman spots Truman on the horizon and followed
him all the way into the TP (Texas and Pacific) station."[97]

Frank Mills was chief announcer for radio and now television:

This was our first exposure to real live television. Every dealer had sets all over
the place, in the windows, and you could walk around downtown and see
people ten deep standing around display windows watching the program.

"I'll do radio and put Bud Sherman on television." I told Bud, "You're going to do television."

He said, "What are you going to do?"

I said, "I'm going to do radio."

"Oh, hell! I don't know anything about television," replied Bud.

I said, "I don't know anything about television either; the people out there watching don't know anything about television; so we're all even. You do it; see you later."

We got all set up and tested the mikes. We're only this far from going on the air—you can hear the train coming, and the engineer at my elbow says, "Hey, Sherman wants you."

"What's the matter?" I asked.

"Well, I don't know. Something is out over there," he said.

So I run over to see what the problem was, and Sherman isn't there. When I turned around, there was Sherman waving at the radio mike. I was so mad, but I didn't have time to get him and send him back.

So I try to do this thing, and I had been told time and again, "You can't do it like radio; you've got to do what's on the monitor." Problem was it was a real bright day; and where they had the dang monitor, the sun was washing out the picture. The picture looked like this white table cloth. I told an engineer, "Forget me! If I can't describe what's going on up there and you guys keep up with me, we might as well close it up." He disappeared in a flash and came back with a carton about so high. He cut the bottom out of the darn thing, put it over the monitor. I had to get underneath that darn thing where it was dark, read the screen, and tell them what was happening.[98]

Roger Dickey was ready for the Truman telecast:

A friend of mine who I bought my parts from wanted me to go to an electronic trade show in Chicago in 1947. I came across a kit: a ten-inch television set. It was put out by RCA, or had an RCA circuit. You could not buy a television at that time. You might buy one in other areas, but not here. Nobody had a television set in Grand Prairie. I told Howard Clint that I wanted to buy that kit through him. Thirty tubes in that set; all the parts and a little wooden cabinet. When I got back home it wasn't too long that my kit arrived. I preceded to build that set. I'm not bragging, but the day I turned it on, it worked fine. I never had to do a thing to it. I saw that broadcast of Harry Truman. I had the only television in town. I had it working long enough to pick up test patterns. When I found out that they were going to broadcast Truman, I set it up in the window of my shop. There was a bunch of people standing out there watching that television. We were downtown on east Main and had quite a bit of traffic there. Shortly after that they started to come in. The first set we sold was a little Motorola seven-inch set; that was all we could get. I started repairing televisions. You build a thirty-tube television set and you learn how to repair them.[99]

The telecast was received by four hundred television receivers throughout the Dallas–Fort Worth area. The president, accompanied by his wife and their daughter, was met by Amon Carter, Congressman Lyndon Johnson, and other dignitaries.[100] Built for the speech was a temporary wooden platform with banners and steps. Bud Sherman was standing at the bottom of the steps when the president and Carter started up the stairs. When Truman was halfway up, the Marine band started playing the National Anthem. The president stopped, held his hat over his heart, and stood there in a staunch military attitude until the music finished. Turning to Carter and speaking softly, he said, "You know, I've heard that a thousand times, and every time I do, it sends chills up my spine."

Then the president turned, put on his hat, and continued up the stairs. During the next thirty minutes, Truman spoke, and the Dallas–Fort Worth area watched the first television program in the Southwest.[101]

Opening Night: WBAP-TV

The building was 80 percent completed. Hallways were muddy pathways where workmen put planks so people could walk. There was a large opening at the top of the studio. Studio doors had not arrived. No linoleum or tile was on the floor. Concrete dust from unfinished floors rose and fell whenever someone walked. Dust settled on equipment and stung eyes and throats. Windows in the control room had no glass, and a large section of silver-painted cardboard served as a door. Weeks before, during a rainstorm, the staff had rushed to the station and thrown tarps over equipment standing under the unfinished roof. People walked through mud because parking lots were not finished.[102]

Newspeople worked diligently off packing boxes and wooden planks in the prop room. Engineers had difficulty keeping equipment working. It overheated because the air conditioning was not working properly. The transmitter was over on the west side of the hall, and all cables running from the control room went through the basement, which was crowded with stacks of tin, tin covers, and vending machines. Only the remote cameras had arrived, so they were used in the studio. The RCA studio camera had not been built. One camera from the remote truck set on a sawhorse in the west side of the studio because men were plastering on the east side. The staff built flats for sets in the garage or strung lights in the

Amon G. Carter speaking during the introductory program of WBAP-TV on September 29, 1948. Seated behind him are "Super" Stenson, George Cranston, Bob Gould, and Harold Hough at the desk. Courtesy KXAS-TV, Fort Worth, Texas

finished part of the studio, even though only enough lighting equipment had arrived for one side and the end of the studio.[103]

Nevertheless, it was September 29, 1948, and WBAP-TV, *the first television station in the Southwest,* was going on the air. At one minute before 7:00 P.M., Harold Hough seated himself at a desk. Amon Carter took off his Shady Oaks hat. R. C. ("Super") Stenson, George Cranston, Seymour Andrews, and Bob Gould took seats, and Frank Mills took his place before the microphone. "This is WBAP-TV, Fort Worth," Mills announced.[104]

A group of reporters from the Associated Press, United Press, International News Service, and the local newspapers, as well as correspondents from *Variety, Broadcasting,* and *Time* magazines watched from the Presidential Suite in the Worth Hotel. Local restaurants took reservations for television parties, and home set owners invited friends and neighbors over for the evening. Department stores stayed open, serving refreshments to customers who came to watch.[105]

After Mills's introduction, all persons on the set spoke briefly. Carter's script for opening the station was:

• • •

Ladies and Gentlemen—Tonight, we of the STAR-TELEGRAM wish to present a PREVIEW OPENING of Television Station WBAP-TV. In doing so, we feel we should call your attention to the fact that the new STAR-TELE-GRAM Radio and Television Plant in the Meadowbrook area is not complete, and for this reason we will have our FORMAL OPENING later—then, we can invite you to visit the New Building, but it is NOT READY TO RE-CEIVE YOU NOW.

IN THE MONTH OF MARCH, 1922—Mr. Hough—(here you will have to ad-lib what you wish to say in your own easy way).

Include:
$200.00 FOR A STATION THAT WAS TO BE WBAP. From a ten watter, it grew to a fifty thousand watt Clear Channel Station.

IN 1938 KGKO WAS ADDED TO THE STAR-TELEGRAM ACTIVI-TIES.

NOW — TELEVISION — Which after all, merely means THE WORLD IN PICTURES IN YOUR HOME. IT IS SIGHT TO YOUR RADIO. We have tried to equip the NEW STATION with all the LATEST ELECTRONIC EQUIPMENT. $500,000.00 worth—I hope it was worth the money.

We hope the new Television Station will be of service to the good folks of Fort Worth and Dallas, and a large part of Texas. IT IS NEW TO US AND TO YOU, and we trust you will be patient with the staff in its initial effort. Our PROGRAMMING will grow and we trust it will grow sufficiently to justify your attention to it, which of course we will GREATLY APPRECIATE, and will be our reward.

Thank you Ladies and Gentlemen.[106]

Carter ad-libbed the middle part of his speech. "We had set aside $300.00 to launch a radio station. When it opened, I didn't know if anybody listened or not. One day, a card came from as far away as Mineral Wells. After more cards followed, we knew radio had arrived. Tonight we're adding sight to sound. I believe television's here to stay." The speeches made by Carter and staff lasted nine minutes. At 7:10 P.M. Channel 5 started an NBC introductory program lasting twenty-three minutes.[107]

Telephone calls told of good reception. One call was from Highland Park, in Dallas. The engineering staff was astonished. When the station tested the transmitter, the staff did not believe the station would cover Fort Worth. Carter had a television set at his home, and reception was reported to be good. Johnny Smith stated his disbelief: "That was clear on the other side of town!" Television was straight-line transmission. A person standing five hundred feet above ground would see just the tops of hills. The engineers thought that television signals were like seeing, and anyone not living on the top of a hill was out of the reception.[108]

As the NBC dedication film ran, Mrs. Jack Hester of Everman phoned to talk about her picture. "It's coming in fine," she said. Her husband, on another phone, interrupted, "Wait a minute, Nancy. It just went off."[109]

At 7:26 P.M. WBAP-TV plunged into darkness. In the confusion, floor men tripped over cables, dignitaries groped around the control room, and telephone calls swamped the switchboard. "It was truly a dark moment for television," stated Bob Gould, production director. "We called the power company immediately and learned that shortly after 5:00 P.M., a truck had smashed into a power pole near the station. It wasn't until 7:26 P.M. that they could safely turn off the power in the area to repair the damage."[110]

"What a time to die!" said Martha Grammer, sales staff. "It was only off seventeen minutes—but it seemed like an eternity. We had quite a job explaining to the viewers that the blackout wasn't due to the failure of our transmitter equipment." In Dallas, Jack McGrew and Jack Harris of KPRC in Houston were having dinner with Martin Campbell, manager of WFAA. When Channel 5 went off the air, Martin found it very funny. He enjoyed all the problems his competitors were having getting their station started.[111]

Jack Rogers, publicity staff, had just told forty newsmen in the Worth Hotel that television was a great new medium and what a great picture they were receiving, when the picture faded. Power was restored at 7:43 P.M., and the opening night's programming continued. Mills had to announce the WPIX-TV filmed newsreel from New York. He did not know how he could talk for fifteen minutes with the dust in the air. The workmen had been sanding all afternoon because the floor had dried improperly. No tile was laid because the floor had buckled. The dust circulated around the studio with the air conditioning system. Mills stood a foot from the monitor. He would rub one eye, watch the picture, and try to read the script. Then he would rub the other eye and try to read.[112]

Everyone was excited. Lillard Hill, the voice of *The Texas News,* had run out and bought a blue shirt because that color telecast better. Light blue telecast as white. White objects looked dirty. Talent could not wear checks because the picture shimmered. Hill read the first local newscast. He was seated at a regular table. The floor director pointed at him and he read five minutes of news with no film.[113]

The control room was full of people. "It sounded like a laryngitis epidemic," remembered Rupert Bogan, staff engineer, who ran the camera controls. "We had to whisper so the sound would not be picked up in the studio."[114] The large glass windows between the rooms were not installed.

The evening's movie was *The Scarlet Pimpernel,* sponsored by Stripling's Department Store. Representatives of the store and advertising agency were present. The introduction before the movie was a short film concerning the store. When the film came on, it was upside down, and the end of the reel was being shown first. Amon Carter went berserk and, without looking, ran across the new studio. He almost fell to his death in a twelve-foot opening into the basement. Johnny Hay and Bob Gould grabbed him as he was about to step off. The standby organist, one carryover of radio, "filled in" while the projectionist rewound the film. The organist did not fare better than the film. A hastily set-up organ and camera produced a view of the back of his head.[115]

The last program of the evening was *The Texas News,* with highlights of President Truman's visit two days earlier. The show, sponsored by Burlington Lines Railroad, introduced the original voice of the *News,* Lillard Hill.[116]

That viewers did not really understand television quickly became obvious. One viewer was having trouble seeing the programs. She phoned complaining that she could not see a thing. Receptionist Judy Meade asked what kind of set she was watching. The woman answered, "Why, my regular radio set, of course."[117]

Mills was at the open house a few weeks later when the building was finished:

Lights up, food, drinks, what have you for these people circulating around. Mr. Carter had invited anybody who was anybody out there, and so I'm standing around in the main studio. It suited me fine—no speeches. We're all trying to answer their questions.

This one woman came up to me and said, "Where's the film?"

I said, "It's in the film room across the hall."

"No, I mean in the camera," she questioned.

I said, "What camera?"

"That camera," she replied.

I said, "It's a television camera. There's no film in there."

She continued, "You can't tell me there isn't any film."

I said, "It's electronic." I'm trying to tell her something I don't know anything about. Finally, I said, "Look, lady, if there's film in that damn thing, how is running this film through here exposed on me standing over here going to come out to be me on your screen?" I continued, "It doesn't develop in there."

"Oh, yes, it does," she said.

I don't know if she was stoned or what, but I had about fifteen minutes with her. I was just about to lose my mind when some other guest came over, called her by name, took her by the arm, and took her out. She was looking all over the floor for the film that had come out.[118]

• • •

When the building was planned, Hough had said, "Make it big enough to run a herd of cattle through." It was *the first facility in the United States built especially for television.* There were three studios. The main studio was eighty-two feet long, forty-five feet wide, and twenty-eight feet high. The second studio was thirty feet by twenty feet by twenty feet. The third studio, which was the film projection studio, was fourteen feet wide and eighteen feet long. "Video lane" consisted of two fifteen-by-twelve-foot doors on opposite sides of studio #1. When opened, they allowed anything up to twelve feet square to move through the studio.[119]

The station finally received studio cameras. They were called studio cameras even though they had the same electronics as the field cameras. They were dressed up with a little three-inch red stripe around them. The field cameras had their power supply in a suitcase-type container. The studio power supplies were mounted in a rack. Studio #1 had two TK-10A and one TK-30A RCA cameras. One TK-30A was located in Studio #2. Camera cables were hidden in Q-ducts in the floor running from the control room down the entire length of the studio. "We had this old field stuff, and two of these old cameras, I think, were actually manufactured in 1946," said Rupert Bogan. "They put out a very poor picture, and I never did get those things to working properly. I worked on those things every week for ten years and never did get them where they would come up to the quality picture that the other cameras were putting out."[120]

WBAP-TV eventually had seven cameras, priced at $26,800 each. The first pickup tubes were 2P23's. They had a high infrared sensitivity that would take the clothes off talent. If people wore certain types of clothes, the clothes might not show up on the screen. There were occasions when women looked like they were not wearing blouses. When a person wore a blue coat, the monitor showed the coat as plaid. Not knowing if their eyes were fooling, the engineers rechecked their equipment but found that the phenomenon persisted. After the show ended, questioning disclosed that the coat originally had been plaid but had been dyed blue. The infrared-sensitive tube penetrated the dye and revealed the original look of the fabric.[121]

The camera's sensitivity caused problems with makeup as well. Red and orange televised as white. Lipstick had to be brown. Unless the lower lip was darker than the upper, the lights made the lower appear washed out. Television makeup used a special pancake resistant to heat from the lights. Blonde women required a dark pancake, or their eyes faded out. Clean-shaved men were given five o'clock shadows.[122] Camera tubes lasted three hundred hours and cost twelve hundred dollars. On remotes, the infrared sensitivity showed no transition between black and white and gave no shades of gray. Grass looked white. Skin washed out. The next generation of tubes had no infrared problem, but their sensitivity was lower. This caused higher light levels in the studio.

One of the worst pieces of equipment was the Telop. The art department could not make 35mm slides, so everything was on Telop cards: four by five inches and handmade. Each was artwork requiring lettering, a sketch, a drawing, or even a cartoon. For some ads or promos, someone would tear something from a newspaper, paste it on a card, and stick it in the Telop. The picture was so poor from some cards that it took imagination to see anything on the screen. Cameras used with the Telop had an Iconoscope pickup tube like DuMont cameras. These tubes scanned from an angle rather than directly in front of the target, causing a trapezoid effect in the image. One camera control adjustment was for trapezoid correction. To augment the Telop, a camera in the studio was pointed at title cards. This arrangement was used often because the Telop could not handle the workload.[123]

The staff soon discovered that even some of the station's administrators did not seem to really understand how things worked. The station was off the air many times in the early years because of technical problems. "They would just go black," stated Chem Terry, staff announcer. "About two seconds after it went off, Mr. Cranston [station manager] would call Tommy Thompson, the night director, and say, 'Tommy, What's the matter?'"

"We're having some technical problems, Mr. Cranston. We'll be on the air as soon as possible."

Cranston would say, "Well . . . get someone and make an announcement."[124]

Sales

The first commercial on WBAP-TV was for Day and Night water heaters; it was to run at 7:38 P.M. on opening night.[125] Channel 5 usually had time to sell. "I can't tell you when the station got in the black," said Roy Bacus, sales manager. "At first, no one at the station ever really knew if television would ever make money."[126]

WBAP-TV had guidelines for advertising. Beer commercials could not run adjacent to the news program. Liquor commercials were not allowed on Sunday or near children's programming. No personal or medical products ran. Channel 5 did accept direct advertising, requiring the audience to call the station to place orders. Martha Grammer, secretary in sales, at times had three people in her office answering phones and taking orders. Sometimes staff members in the studio answered phones.[127]

Network programming was received by delay on kinescope. One local jewelry advertiser refused to pay a bill in February because the station ran the program with his Christmas sales special in January. The station had no control over these programs, and dealers did not understand the problem. Until live networking reached Fort Worth in 1952, the station ran two or more one-minute spots between programs. The sales department would schedule all the commercials they could sell. If needed, there was always room for another spot in a time slot. Before live networking, the station's programs might start minutes late. The newspaper schedule would list the program at 9:00 P.M., but the program might actually start at 9:05 or 9:06 P.M.[128]

Advertising rates were low, but so were salaries. Russ Thornton started in the news department in 1952 at $50.00 a week. "Salaries were so low that many employees could not afford a television," stated Luther Atkins, director of special events. "We couldn't afford it. I remember driving to a friend's home to sit and watch *Laurel and Hardy*." When the conversation centered on television at another party, Atkins and his wife both could not join the conversation about their own profession. Clint Bourland, news staff, did not have a set until 1952 because it cost four to five hundred dollars. No Dallas news staff member owned a set. They would do their stories, put the film on the bus for Fort Worth, later go to the Brass Rail Bar, buy a beer, and at 6:45 P.M. or so, watch *The Texas News*.[129]

Programming

Bob Gould was director of programming. "It was easier to create something you could not do because your mind would just go bananas, but you had to get back to the local situation. You had only two cameras and people limited in numbers and experience, so you had to whittle an idea down to size to handle it. No plays which required rehearsing were produced. Most shows were unrehearsed. Directors had programming ideas that could not be done—just too big for Channel 5's situation. Creativity was lost. I'd say, "Hey, guys, that's a good idea, but we can't do it."[130]

Channel 5 used movies because they were the cheapest way to program the greatest amount of time. Film and live were the only choices. To go from one live program to another all day long could not be done. There had to be film breaks. Local productions were simple. There were only two projectors, the Telop, and two or three cameras. Scripts were rough at best. The director controlled the entire program as producer/director. Shows like *Bobby Peters*, a children's program, were mostly ad-libbed. Peters did not know exactly what he was going to do beforehand; he had a rough idea. The director knew what commercials were in the show and when they should run. Peters would perform, the director would go to a commercial, and while the commercial was running, Peters would decide what he wanted to do next.[131]

Early network programming caused problems. Networks were not precise about program timing. There was no assurance when a show would end. Programs from DuMont or NBC sometimes ran forty to forty-five minutes when they were scheduled for twenty-eight. For that reason, Channel 5 had local talent to "fill" after network programming. If programming ran short, the staff would roll out the organ for William Barclay or Ted Graves. When an emergency occurred, some production member grabbed the phone and yelled, "Barclay, get the hell down here!" The station could also fill with *Snaders*. These were three- to five-minute films of performers or musical numbers. When faced with extra time, the director would call the projectionist and have him load a *Snader*. Another popular time filler was the *Industry on Parade* series of films.[132]

The station purchased and used devices that ran film in an endless roll. They mounted in the projector film gate and could run for any length of time. One film was of an elephant going into a lake and then blowing water out his trunk. Others had scenes of giraffes and monkeys. These films had no point except to fill time and keep some picture on the screen. The audio technician would play music with the pictures. The station used these films before regular programming started for the day or to fill a programming void; they might run for fifteen or thirty minutes. Another device was a kaleidoscope placed in front of the camera lens. "Can you imagine sitting and watching a television set with a picture of a kaleidoscope going on it?" said Bogan. "We put it on the air. People would look at test patterns back then."[133]

If a filmed program were running long, there was a different solution. The director could tell the projectionist to leave the film running during commercial breaks. When Jim Turner complained to Bob Gould that commercials during *Six-Gun Theater* were causing the show to potentially run long, Gould said, "Well, the program has been coming off on time each day." "The only thing the audience missed was part of the horse chase," said Turner. Stan Wilson, manager of KFJZ-TV in Fort Worth, invented a device that would speed up a movie projector. "You speed up the movie a little, and you get more time for commercials," explained Dave Naugle, staff announcer. "We called it the 'Wilson Movie Gooser.'"[134]

By December, 1949, WBAP-TV was producing eighteen regular studio programs:

> *Dream Kitchen Time*—Alice Walter dramatized modern kitchen operations and planning
> *Fashion Reflections*—Nora Lou Greene described women's wear
> *Flying X Ranch Boys*—Western music and comedy
> *Gardening Can Be Fun*—Discussion of latest gardening and farm techniques
> *Here's to Your Health*—Specialists explained diseases, symptoms, prevention, and cures

Hoffman Hayloft—Western talent with square dancing

Melody Shop—Musical comedy

Playtime—Mary Parker told stories and played games with children

Rhythm and Romance—Music by selected guests

See-Saw Zoo—Children's puppet show

Skillern's Sports Preview—Interviews with sports personalities

Stump Us—Audience phoned in names of songs for Barclay to play

TCU in Revue—Faculty and students described and dramatized campus activities

Vesper Hour—Music from choirs of Fort Worth churches

What Is It?—Teams of guests tried to guess objects

What's New, Ladies?—Wilma Rutherford kept career girls and homemakers up to date

William Barclay Presents—Barclay, staff organist, introduced musical guests

Your Song and Mine—Musical requests by telephone[135]

Remotes

A prime source of early programming was remotes. Friday night, September 30, 1948, the second night of telecasting, WBAP-TV attempted to telecast its first football game, the game between Fort Worth's Paschal High School and Amarillo High at Farrington Field in Fort Worth. Bud Sherman, sports announcer, did the play-by-play. As the show began, the station lost the picture. "All of a sudden," remembered Sherman, "I had a little old voice in my headset coming from the truck down below saying, 'We're not on the air.' 'We've lost our picture.' I didn't know when we were going to get the picture back, and I needed the practice, so, I went ahead and finished that game with audio." There were no interviews after those games because Channel 5 was not equipped for that. All audio programming came from the announcer's booth. Commercials, all for the same sponsor, were read by Sherman. Later, the program might be switched to the studio for live or film commercials.[136]

Sherman recalled another problem he encountered while trying to announce a baseball game early the next spring:

We didn't have a broadcasting booth, and it was a cold night. We were sitting there in the open air. There was a north wind coming in on my back. It got cold; it got colder; and it got the coldest. Finally, in the middle of the seventh inning, I got up and walked down to the clubhouse to warm up. I knew they had a heater in the clubhouse. As I started out again, I started having a chill, and I said, "That's stupid." I didn't go back. I just got in my car and went home. . . . The crowd mike carried the game for the last innings. I didn't get any static from the station.[137]

Sherman was a popular sports announcer and enjoyed meeting his viewers. One sponsor, Lovera Cigars, had Sherman light up a cigar on the show and say, "If you meet me on the street, ask me for a Lovera." Sherman quit going to town; he could not carry enough cigars.[138]

Humble Oil Company negotiated college football rights. Humble approached Channel 5 in early 1948, before the station was on the air, ready to telecast football. Humble's staff was amazed to see the cameras working and cards with "Humble" written on them superimposed over a shot of the field. The Humble staff had everything planned. They knew precisely when they wanted a commercial run and made arrangements to hold up play. They knew what they wanted, and Channel 5 telecast it for them. Commercials were from the press box or the studios. WBAP-TV learned football from Humble; Humble learned television from Channel 5. Humble was innovative, using an end-zone camera, pre- and post-production meetings, and staff evaluations for the next game.[139]

Johnny Smith, remote engineer for WBAP, met many unusual people while working on the station's remote crew:

Television was so new to people. The first couple of nights we were out at the wrestling matches, I couldn't believe this man who came up to the truck. He was obviously excited about something. It turned out that his name was Theo. He was a Hungarian who had a cafe across Exchange Avenue [Theo's Cafe]. He had one of the first television sets, and he had it up on a shelf in his restaurant and bar. People would come in to watch television and see the wrestling matches. Well, not knowing this and who he was with his horrible accent that I couldn't understand, I finally understood that he was trying to say that his television receiver was not working; and he wanted us to come over and fix it right then. We kept trying to tell him that we didn't have anything to do with repairs, that we broadcast a signal; and that's all we have to do with it. He said, "No!" He thought that television was like a utility and that the television station would come out and fix it just like the telephone company fixes your phone. He ended up going into a rage because we would not stop what we were doing, take our earphones off, and go over there to work on that television receiver. How would he know any better at the time? He bought the set, and he thought he had a guarantee that it would work. We later became good friends with Theo. A couple of guys on the crew would go by when they came

James Byron, news director of WBAP radio and television, was founder of The Texas News. *Courtesy KXAS-TV, Fort Worth, Texas*

to work the matches to see if his set was working all right, and he'd give them a beer. They helped him along with his set, and we turned out to be good friends.[140]

On remote telecasts the staff quickly adjusted to people's misconceptions about television. Many would inquire, "Where do you have the film?" Cameraman Bill Larinson of WBAP-TV answered the problem by obtaining a spool of bad 16mm film. According to Johnny Smith, Larinson took his camera side down and threaded the film through the tubes. He left it and closed the camera. Then, when anyone asked where the film was, he opened the side of his camera and showed them. The people left happy, because now they knew the secret of television; it was really film.[141]

The Texas News

A very popular program on WBAP-TV from the first day was *The Texas News*.[142] During its first months, the newsreel ran early, around 6:30 P.M. to 7:45 P.M. Then it moved to a permanent time: 10:00 P.M. There was no minimum or maximum time, but the staff did not like a show under ten minutes, although some were only seven and eight. The station devised a format that adjusted with the newsreel length. After October, 1949, the newsreel was followed by *Weather Telefacts.* If the news ran short, the weather could expand. *News Final,* following the weather, was an announcer reading national and international news. This segment could also adjust, as could the next: *Sports with Sherman.*

The news department did not employ people who were just reporters. The person filming the story was the reporter. The staff was not chosen because they had "golden tones" but because they were real journalists.[143] Clint Bourland was a member of the news staff:

In those days the elite corps of people were the film editors because they were also the story writers for the newsreel, and that's what I was. That was the happiest time in my life because you had no reporters to fool with. It told the story in the newsreel format. The reporter was subordinate; you never saw him. The voice itself was an anonymous voice; so in your writing, you could get away with a lot more things: anonymously. What I liked about the newsreel format, first of all, was that you edited the picture story and had no written material. You just edited what looked good, and then you sat down and wrote it. That was discipline. It didn't take any more talent to write that stuff than it would to write anything today, but it took iron discipline. If you had a picture of the Dallas County Sheriff come up fifteen seconds deep in your story, by God, your script had to say "Dallas County Sheriff Bill Decker" at fifteen seconds. And many times you would rewrite that thing five and six times to get it down to the timing.[144]

Russ Thornton, a news staff member, recalled:

It was well-written. The pictures told a story. We didn't do it like the network or most people do it now, where you sit down and write the script, and then you try to figure out how to visually match that script. We edited a picture story that told in a logical sequence what the hell was going on. Made you feel like you were there and seeing it happen—used the cut-away as a bridge so you didn't think you'd missed anything. Then we wrote to those pictures, so that when you saw somebody, the narrator was letting you know who you were seeing or what you were seeing. It was not like it is now, where they use visuals to illustrate something somebody has written—this to me is confusing many times. They'll be talking about a person; and I'm seeing two people on the screen, and I don't know which one he is.[145]

• • •

When the newsreel was ready, Lillard Hill and staff sat down and rehearsed. Hill would have cues such as pictures or changes of scenes, and he would have a script that more or less followed the film. The staff rehearsed the show in the news room with a regular 16mm projector. Other times, there was no time for rehearsal because the staff worked until the very last minute. Despite the department's organization, there was frequently someone racing down the hall at the last minute, film in hand, as the clock hit 10:00 P.M. Many times, Channel 5 "rode" station identification for thirty or forty seconds, waiting for the projectionist to thread the newsreel. Then the staff worried about film breaks. The humidity or other conditions affected the film cement, and splices would separate in the projector. If the film broke after the film gate, the show kept running, and the film spilled on the floor. If the film broke before the gate, Hill would say, "One moment, please," and music would be played. The theme of *The Texas News* was the *Broad March Theme*. It was the most identifiable news theme in Texas. Each story had its own theme music. *Dark Intruder* was always played for burglary stories.[146]

Jim Byron, news director, recalled why the early *Texas News* programs no longer exist: "Our first news was a newsreel—*The Texas News*. Well, the first night we went on the air, we decided that the best way was to break the newsreel down and put the clips in separate files so they could be referred to. So we have nothing to show what our first newsreel looked like. We do not know what the order was, but these things were not important at that time. We did not know that we were making history. We felt fortunate that we could get through the day."[147]

"We had fewer sacred cows in this news room than I had ever seen in any organization that I've worked for," stated Clint Bourland. "When I was with the [Dallas] *Herald,* they had a list of a hundred people that you didn't offend. At Channel 5, you didn't poke fun at the old man, old man Carter, and you didn't poke fun at his projects."[148]

The everyday working of the newsroom was under the direction of Doyle Vinson. He had the ideas and creativity.[149] If Vinson kept the department running, Byron was the brains. "I don't know anyone who worked for that man who didn't consider him a giant," said Bourland. Station managers tried to bring Byron to heel because they thought they were in charge of the station. Managers soon found no one controlled Byron. He ran the news department the way he wanted because the administration at Carter Publications had faith in him. No station manager could undercut him. At a *Star-Telegram* meeting Amon Carter asked, "Jimmy, who do you answer to? Who's your boss out there?"

Byron answered, "Mr. Carter, I don't answer to anybody. I figure that I have all the authority I need to do my job; and if I exceed that authority, I imagine I'll hear from you."

Carter answered, "Well, you're doing good, Jim. Keep it up."[150]

Byron was a stickler for details. He read every radio and television news script. Anything incorrect would be called to the attention of the person responsible. "If you said that the First National Bank was *located* at Fifth and Main," said Bourland, "he would jump you about that." Technically, a building was located one time, when built; thereafter, it was *situated* at that location. Bud Sherman made a grammatical mistake one night. "I had misused the words 'imply' and 'infer.' I had used one when I should have used the other," admitted Sherman. "Byron would step out of his office and say, 'Bud, you got a minute?' Of course, you had a minute when the boss says, 'You got a minute?' You'd go in there, and he'd have your script."[151]

Alex Burton, news staff, received one memorable critique from Byron:

He would come by your desk and say, "You got a minute?" Which means, now! I want to see you! When I got to be the anchor guy, I never got any directions on how to do it; I just did it. He came by my desk one day and said, "You got a minute?"

I said, "Yes sir." I followed him into his office and there was nothing on his desk but the previous night ten o'clock newscast. It was spread out like a fan and there were great big blue marks, question marks, and exclamation marks over every piece of copy.

He said, "Sit down."

I sat down. He sat down at his desk and took out a cigarette. He was smoking at that time. He smoked Chesterfield. He took out his cigarette holder, got a cigarette, put it in there, lit it, took a puff, looked out the window, and said, "Tell me, Alex. Would you rather be doing something else?"[152]

WBAP-TV's newsreel was extremely popular and won many awards. "For general excellence in television newsreel coverage and handling," *The Texas News* won the Outstanding Television News Service Award of the National Association of Radio News Directors in November of 1949 in New York City. Byron accepted the award three of four years between 1949 and 1952.[153]

Weather Telefacts

Harold Taft, Walter Porter, and Bob Denny were American Airlines meteorologists. Channel 5 was one year old when Taft noticed the station did not have a weather show. He talked with the others, and they decided they could use weather briefing techniques used by Armed Services pilots. They believed television was a natural for weather. The three approached Program Director Bob Gould and proposed a weather show. No station had a program like the one proposed; it did not exist in the country, not even at NBC. Gould told Hough, and the reaction

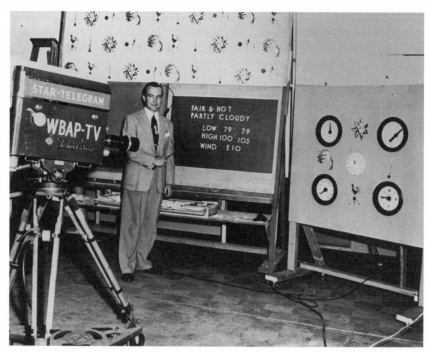

Walter Porter on the set of WBAP-TV's Weather Telefacts, *the first television weather program in the nation. Courtesy KXAS-TV, Fort Worth, Texas*

was "Hey, that's a good idea." The program premiered on Halloween night, October 31, 1949.[154] *Weather Telefacts* was *the first television weather program in the nation.* Scheduled after *The Texas News, Weather Telefacts* ran approximately five minutes. Taft, Porter, and Denny needed no training in weather presentation. Which camera was on and the general routine were all the staff had to tell them. There were no contracts; just a handshake. Gould never had written contracts with any talent.[155]

Channel 5 installed the first television weather station in 1953. This consisted of an outdoor transmitter that indicated temperature, barometric pressure, wind direction and velocity, and relative humidity to active dials located in the studio. Besides an evening weather show, WBAP-TV gave viewers a twenty-second look at the dials so they could keep informed about current conditions.[156]

The title *Weather Telefacts* was short for facts about the weather. All ideas came from Taft and his peers. There were no other shows to copy. While Taft helped develop the program, he had never seen a television weather presentation. Taft rarely saw Channel 5's programming or the weather show because for many years he did not own a television set. "In my field, I didn't need anything to go by," stated Taft. "You know, give me a map, a stick, and some chalk; and I'll tell you about the weather. I'll tell you things you didn't know." Taft never aimed at an audience. He presented the weather. He hit the middle of the road by showing a broad scope, and an interested person could pick up what he or she wanted from Taft's presentation. "The message could tell Mother to put a jacket on the kid, but not a heavy one, because he will drag it through the mud on the way home, or inform construction supervisors that tomorrow would not be a good day to pour concrete."

The program was always live and flexible. The three meteorologists took as much time as needed. One program ran seventeen minutes. If there was a problem, they could stretch. The station hired professional meteorologists. In later years, other stations hired nonmeteorological personnel. "These nonprofessionals all fall into the same trap," said Taft. "After these people have done the weather for three or four years or so, they begin to think that they know more about it than the professionals do. I hear some of the damnedest explanations you have ever heard in your life coming off the tube, even today; just makes you cringe."

Taft began weather watchers, people who reported weather conditions at their locations, because rainfall reports came from the airport. Complaints centered around why Taft did not give the rainfall at their house or why their town was not on the radar scope. The only complaint Taft received from station administration was from Amon Carter. He phoned one night, "This is Amon Carter."

"Yes, sir, Mr. Carter," answered Taft.

"I watch the weather; like it real good," Carter stated, "but you mention Dallas too damn much."[157]

Television in Houston

Jack McGrew of KPRC in Houston returned from a 1947 Atlantic City meeting where he heard David Sarnoff advise media companies to seriously consider going into television. He reported to Bill Hobby, owner of the radio station, and they discussed applying for a television license. Hobby decided to participate. An application for Channel 4 in Houston was prepared and filed on January 21, 1948. That was the channel recommended for a prospective NBC affiliate. The application was late. W. Albert Lee, owner of hotels and a laundry in Houston, had submitted an application several months earlier. The FCC had allocated four channels to Houston. Any applicant who was unopposed, a citizen of this country, and not a convicted felon, was virtually assured a television license. On January 30, 1948, nine days after Hobby and the *Houston Post* Company filed for Channel 4, Lee was issued a construction permit for Channel 2. The station would be KLEE-TV. Lee started KLEE-AM in February of 1948. He also received one of the first frequency modulation (FM) construction permits in Houston; it was never used. Within a month there were three more applications filed for the remaining television channels assigned to Houston. They were from KTRH (The Rice Hotel), the service of the *Houston Chronicle,* owned by Houston financier Jesse Jones; KXYZ, owned by Houston oilman Glenn McCarthy; and KTHT, owned by former Harris County Judge Roy Hofheinz.[158]

Paul Huhndorff, the engineer who built KLEE radio, took a trip to the East Coast to observe television: "In March of 1948, I went to Syracuse, New York, to General Electric. . . . I went to all the factory places. They still had the Iconoscope cameras when I went to Schenectady, New York, to see KRGB-TV. They had seminars on television, and they were educating us into what television was all about. We went from there to New York City and went through the DuMont plant, then through NBC studios, and then to Camden, New Jersey, the RCA plant."[159]

Huhndorff purchased General Electric and DuMont equipment. RCA was much more expensive than other manufacturers, and he did not like some of their selling tactics:

I had a RCA salesman tell me that if I didn't buy RCA equipment, I would never have another job in television. I got into the back door of television. Lee decided that since I did not have any experience in television, he was going to hire a consultant out of New York. He had worked for DuMont. . . . We were having trouble getting the transmitter to operate like we wanted. Albert Lee came to me one day and said, "You're not going to get on the air by the first of the year."

I said, "What makes you say that?"

He said, "'So and so' said you're not going to get it on the air."

I said, "I'll tell you what. You turn your television set on next Saturday and we'll have a test pattern on." That's when he [Lee] let that guy go.[160]

The studios of KLEE-TV would have been in the top of the Sterling Building in downtown Houston, but the top five stories of the building would have had to have been remodeled. Lee and an associate, Julian A. Weslow, ordered a Quonset hut constructed at Post Oak Road near the Pin Oak Stables. The building was started in September of 1948.

Huhndorff supervised the construction of the facilities. He explained: "I'll tell you how they wound up in a Quonset hut. He [Lee] had seen a bank that was in a Quonset hut. He said, 'Why can't we build the television station like this?'"

I said, "You can do it any way you want."[161]

Television was first demonstrated in Houston in 1948 at the Construction Industries Exposition at the Sam Houston Coliseum. Visitors had a chance to see themselves on television. They also saw live models with faces smeared with vari-colored concoctions of television makeup. KLEE-TV's remote truck, which had been rushed to Houston, had one camera at the main Coliseum entrance to show the people entering and one camera roving around the Coliseum picking up booths and exhibits. Television dealer J. G. Bradburn offered customers a four-page information booklet titled "The Truth About Television." The booklet gave answers to consumer questions such as "Can I buy a tube or screen to attach to my radio to get television?"[162]

KLEE-TV first broadcast a test pattern with full power on December 20, 1948. The station operated with 16 kilowatts visual and 8.4 kilowatts audio. The 537-foot tower was located behind the Quonset hut studio. Originally, Channel 2 was affiliated with CBS only. It soon added affiliation with NBC, ABC, DuMont, and Paramount networks. Opening day was to be January 1, 1949, at 6 P.M. The first few minutes were to be devoted to "flashing test patterns so owners of television sets may get them in focus to receive the images clearly when the first real program goes on." At 6:05 P.M., owner W. Albert Lee was to make a brief appear-

The studios of KLEE-TV, Houston, in 1949. The original Quonset hut studio was the rounded-top building on the far left next to Channel 2's tower. The smaller rounded-top building was the second studio, added a year after the first. Courtesy Paul Huhndorff

ance to officially open the station. At 6:15, *The Alan Dale Show* from the DuMont Network was to be presented. The station actually got on the air three hours and fifteen minutes late because of trouble with the transmitter.[163] Huhndorff was responsible for getting KLEE-TV operational:

> We were supposed to go on the air about 6:00, but we had a water leak about 4:00. We had this plastic tubing, and it had a tendency to get brittle. . . . You were supposed to be able to handle the stuff just like copper tubing but without the danger of accidental electrocution. One of the Saran cooling lines burst. Water started spraying all over the inside of the transmitter. We put some people to work bailing out the water-logged transmitter and some others to try to patch the line. . . . We had to "re-engineer" the insulation system. If the copper tubing had come into contact with any part of the power gird, someone could have been killed or badly injured. . . . We kept working at it and working at it; and the time got past us.
>
> They decided that since I was the one who knew about it . . . I was the one to go on the air and tell about it. We had an announcer, but he did not know what was going on. We turned the transmitter on and found out that we could raise the power and not lose it. The test pattern was on, or maybe the call letters. We had about four or five hours of programming material.[164]

At approximately 9:30 P.M., a voice came from the speakers of television sets across Houston. "There's been trouble, plenty of trouble!" The voice was that of Huhndorff. With this, KLEE-TV, Channel 2 in Houston, began telecasting.[165] Approximately two thousand television sets watched the belated opening. A crowd waited in front of Fred Wyse Clothing Store at 912 Main, eager for the programming to start. The crowd finally saw *Make Mine Music* with the Tony Mottola Trio from the Columbia Broadcasting Company; an audience participation show, *Winner Take All*, with Bud Collier; *Knobb's Korner*, featuring Stan Fritts, Hope Emerson, and Jo Hurt; a children's program with Hope and Mory Bunis called *Lucky Pup*; *Places, Please*, a comedy show; a cooking demonstration, *To a Queen's Taste*; a fashion parade; and a sports program with Dick Altman, sports director.

Staff members were Marion (Bud) Johnson, chief of operations; Ken Bagwell, program director; and Bernard Brink, television consultant.[166] The programming schedule for KLEE-TV on Friday, March 31, 1950, was:

12:00 noon–4:00 P.M.	Test Pattern
4:00	*Woman's Page*
5:00	*Corn's A-Poppin'*
6:00	*Kukla, Fran and Ollie*—NBC

6:30	*Mohawk Showroom*—NBC
7:00	*Hoffman Huddle*
7:30	*We the People*—NBC
8:00	*Impromptu Theater*
8:35	*Wrestling*
10:00	*Scandinavian Salute:* "Youth and Summer in Sweden"
10:30	*News Bulletins*
10:35	Coming Attractions
10:40	Sign-off.[167]

At first the station was on the air five days a week from 6:00 to 9:00 P.M. The engineers spent three hours every morning just to "count down" the sync generator—make it work. For the first few months, the only live broadcasts were remote sporting events.[168] Huhndorff worked with the remote unit:

Lee had a lot of stuff going on. Albert Lee and Morris Siegel were good friends. Siegel was the wrestling promoter. Lee wanted beer advertising, and so he talked Siegel into threatening the beer people that if they did not buy advertising on the television station, they were not going to sell beer in the city auditorium—that kind of thing.

We had an old truck for a remote unit and spare axles everywhere. The truck was not used to the weight of all the equipment, and it kept breaking axles. A couple of times we were parked outside the city auditorium, and we would have to jack the truck up and put on a new axle right there. We had one remote one day; then we had one that night. We had to get a wrecker to haul us across town, backwards, because of a broken axle. We finally had to get a new truck.

To transmit the signal from remote sites to the station for telecast we bolted a microwave dish to the side of the tower. One of my jobs was to climb the tower and adjust the receiving dish each time we did a new remote. That got old in a hurry during the cold, wet winter of 1949. So we designed and build our own dish control system operated remotely from inside the studio. To make the system work, we rigged two war-surplus aircraft prop pitch motors to the dish and ran the control wires into the building.[169]

We did not do much from the studio because there was not a lot to be done. We had some film. The networks were not around. We did a lot of remotes. We did fifty-two wrestling matches a year, seventy-seven baseball games, and twenty high school football games.

We built the first part [the Quonset hut], and later added another studio to

The remote unit of KLEE-TV, Houston, in 1949. Left to right: *Ivan Smith, camera; Mort Dank, director; Harold DeGood, engineer; Carroll Wilson, engineer; Don Leeding, engineer; Charles Hunt, engineer; and Rosenberg, engineer. Courtesy Paul Huhndorff*

the back. It looked great, and it was reasonably priced. We had two studios and a big door between them, and you could pull it down and have two different studios, but there was not much sound proofing between them. We had one studio camera, but we had a remote truck and we used cameras out of it. . . . The one original camera in the studio had an optical viewfinder just like a film camera. The studio camera was the first camera General Electric ever built. They did a modification later and put an electronic viewer on it. We only had one lens on the studio camera, so all you could do was "dolly in" or "out," or "pan." The DuMonts had four lenses. We started with two DuMonts in the remote truck. I think we added one more later. Then we bought one of the old black zooms.

We did not go on the air until about 6:00 in the evening. We ran test patterns most of the day. We spent most of the day making the sync generator work. They used to be a whole rack of equipment, and now they are a chip. Tubes didn't have the stability that you get out of IC [integrated circuit]. Later, we would leave the equipment on all the time because when you turned it on, as it heated up it would change. The more you left a piece of equipment on, the more stable it became. We left the cameras on as much as we could, but you did not want to burn up the IOs [image orthicons] because they were too costly. Seems like they were around a thousand dollars.

Early television cameras couldn't deal with shadows. In order to eliminate them, we poured on the light. The banks of incandescent lights put the temperature at substantially above tolerable. However, costs had to be held in check according to Albert Lee, so there was no air conditioning.

We had a Teloptigon; some called it a Beloptigon. We had trouble with the film chains like crazy. GE designed the film chain with a small Iconoscope. The Bell and Howell projectors worked all right, but the Iconoscopes were the 1850A, the small version. An engineer came down with equipment in the trunk of his car and spent two months in Houston. He rebuilt them putting in the large Iconoscope.[170]

During the first year there were only about 15,000 receivers sold in the Houston area. In order to sell advertising, KLEE-TV had to keep its rates low. Rates were lower than those charged by several Houston radio stations. Lee was losing $30,000

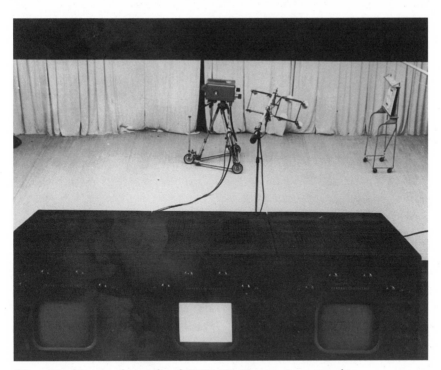

The original Quonset hut studio of KLEE-TV, Houston, in 1949 and its one camera, as seen from master control. Note General Electric's first studio camera with its optical viewfinder and one lens. Courtesy Paul Huhndorff

a month, and he had no major interest to absorb such losses for very long. Within a year, Bill Hobby, owner of KPRC, learned that KLEE-TV might be for sale.[171]

KLEE-TV Becomes KPRC-TV

Jack McGrew, manager of KPRC, felt that the only way the *Houston Post* and KPRC could get into television without extended hearings with the *Houston Chronicle* and others was to try to buy out Albert Lee. In the late 1940s the FCC was operating under a policy favoring any applicant not identified with a newspaper on the theory that it was encouraging diversity in the market. KPRC and KTRH were both affiliated with newspapers. The other two applicants for the remaining channels were not. This policy might have led to a direct contest between the *Houston Post* and the *Houston Chronicle*. Both newspapers could have been "passed over." Because of the "freeze," buying an existing station was the only way KPRC could get on the air.[172]

McGrew traveled to Chicago in 1947. He had been invited to a demonstration of Channel 7, the ABC station there. The station's programming that night consisted of a youngster, thirteen years old, sitting on a stool, playing a guitar, and singing cowboy songs. His mother accompanied him on the piano. That was the entire programming on Channel 7 in Chicago that day. "I figured we could do better than that," reasoned McGrew:

> You must remember that nobody knew anything about this. Nobody knew how to operate a [television] station. Their [KLEE-TV's] schedule ran from 5:00 till 11:00 at night. We figured that that was the way it was going to be forever; that that was all television would ever consist of because radio would still dominate the daytime. Why did we think that? We had no background. Nobody had any background. That is what everybody was doing, and we figured that was the way it was going to be. We also figured that we would lose this rigid format of fifteen [-minute], thirty [-minute], or one-hour programs— that we would start one television program, it would run until it stopped, and then we would start another television program regardless of the clock. We did not realize that the networks were going to continue to operate as they always had with radio.[173]

According to McGrew, another event helped convince Bill Hobby to buy KLEE-TV:

> About this time young Bill Hobby, a student at Rice University, became ill and was bedridden. The governor called Jack [Harris] one day and said, "Don't ya'll own a couple of television sets?"

Jack admitted that we did. So he said, "Could I borrow one and put it in Bill's bedroom so he would have something to watch during these long hours in bed?"

Jack said, "Well, of course." What else could he say? So, guess whose set wound up in Bill's bedroom. When Lee went on the air, we were able to make one concession. We bought two little Zenith round-screen portable television sets. Harris took one set home with him, and he had assigned the other to a station's engineer. They were going to sit there, watch, and decide what KLEE-TV was doing wrong. I later got the engineer's set.

So, the governor would come home in the afternoon and go up to see Bill, and he would be watching the television set. And the governor would spend more and more time watching that television set and less and less time talking to Bill. He finally called Jack and said, "Do you suppose we could buy that thing?"

Jack said, "Well, at least we can try."[174]

In the Spring of 1950, the *Houston Post* filed for assignment of license with the FCC. This created open dismay among the other applicants for television channels in Houston. They were in shock. Now, KPRC-TV would be the only television station in Houston. The *Houston Post* Company assumed ownership on June 1, 1950. On July 3, the call letters were changed to KPRC-TV. The purchase price was $743,000.[175]

KPRC-TV scheduled a television fair for the Fourth of July holiday. Fifty-thousand people came to see Red Ingles and his Natural Seven, Carol Bruce, June Christy, the Mel Arvin Trio, Gypsy Edwards, and Curly Fox and Texas Ruby. Eleven-year-old Tommy Sands made his television debut. The crowd saw television on the newest model receivers: priced from $99 to $2,495. Screens on table models averaged six inches. Console screens were usually eight by ten inches. The biggest attraction was the audience's chance to see themselves on television.

On that day in 1950, there were 26,000 television receivers in Houston. Six months later there were 53,000. One year after the fair there were 100,000 sets. Two years after the fair, in 1952, there were 200,000, and KPRC-TV was the only station on the air. Within three months of purchasing KLEE-TV, KPRC-TV was making money. Within one year, it was making more money than the radio station.[176]

One of the first things that changed conditions at KPRC-TV was the installation of air conditioning in the Quonset hut studios. Channel 2 continued to "pick and choose" from the best network programs, as it was affiliated with all four major networks. Channel 2's lineup of network stars included Sid Caesar, Imogene Coca, Jack Benny, Milton Berle, Bob Hope, Groucho Marx, Danny Thomas, Red

Skelton, Arthur Godfrey, Jackie Gleason, Gary Moore, Dean Martin, Jerry Lewis, Phil Silvers, Perry Como, and Ed Sullivan. Local programming included *Darts For Dough; Most Wanted Men,* a video lineup of criminals wanted by the FBI and the Houston Police, produced by Bob Gray; and the most popular live prime-time show in Houston, *Curly Fox and Texas Ruby.* Recruited from radio along with comic sidekick "Pancho," *Curly Fox* was a *Hee-Haw*–type program televised before a live audience. *Talent Shop* featured pianist Johnny Roya and Paul Schmitt and the TuneSchmitts. One program presented a new talent represented by Tom Parker: a young Elvis Presley mixed country music with rhythm and blues. Schmitt was not impressed. He told "Colonel" Parker, "Elvis is not what television is looking for."[177]

Ten days after the *Houston Post* assumed ownership of Channel 2, an unusual event happened. The Texas League Houston Buffaloes baseball team was playing a home game at Buff Stadium. Press-box facilities did not include room for Channel 2's play-by-play announcers and equipment. The announcer sat in a roped-off row of seats behind home plate. One "cover" camera was also in the area. Dick Gottlieb, KPRC-TV sports announcer, was describing the game when a man stepped over the rope and sat down beside him:

> The man sat down in an empty chair next to me. He sounded drunk when he said, "Dick Gottlieb, I gotta' talk to you, right now!"
>
> I put my hand over the microphone, motioned him away, and said, "Not now, sir."
>
> I turned back to look at the game and he pulled my elbow again. He almost pulled me out of my chair, and said, "Dick Gottlieb, I gotta' talk to you, right now!"
>
> I guess I got mad; mad at the ushers for letting him get up into the roped-off area, and mad that he was interrupting the broadcast. I put my hand over the microphone again and said, louder than before, "Not now, sir!"
>
> I started describing the play on the field when, all of a sudden, there was a gigantic explosion. Blood was all over the place. My audio engineer Lee Bennet was covered with blood. I had blood on me. There was blood on my score pad and on the counter in front of me. When I looked around, the man was slumped over the counter, sliding to the floor. The ball players all stopped and turned; staring up toward us.
>
> The cameraman operating the camera at the end of the row to my left, maybe ten feet away, said to the director on his talk circuit, "A man just shot himself here!"
>
> The director, Gene Osborne, in the truck downstairs said, "Let's see it," and

the camera turned in my direction. For maybe five or ten seconds, the picture of the man was on screen.

Stadium employees quickly carried him to an emergency vehicle and we managed to get the game under way again. I did finish the telecast, but didn't feel very good. They gave me some smelling salts. I didn't think I needed them, but maybe it helped. They tell me that for a minute or two, right after the gunshot, I kept saying to my wife over the air, "I'm all right, I'm all right!" I also understand that a justice of the peace watching the game on television called his office downtown and ruled the incident a suicide, without ever leaving home.[178]

San Antonio Television

"T-Day" arrived in San Antonio at 6 P.M. on Sunday, December 11, 1949. A formal application had been made on March 6, and a construction permit was granted on May 28, 1948.[179]

On June 21, 1949, 1500 dealers and their salespeople assembled at the Gunter Hotel, where they discussed plans to bring television to San Antonio. Speakers at the meeting were Hugh A. L. Halff, president and general manager of WOAI-TV; Charles L. Jeffers, director of engineering; J. R. Duncan, program director; Jack Kessler, assistant general manager and sales director; and Dallas Want, promotion manager. A film, *Magic in the Air,* which explained television studio operations, was shown.

On September 12, 1949, the officers and personnel of Randolph Field witnessed the first local demonstration of television. The program used WOAI-TV's "Telemobile" with new-generation image orthicon pickup tubes. Four days later, two hundred boxes of television equipment were unloaded at the station. On September 28, at 1:35 P.M., Jerry Lee announced the station's identification over a test pattern: "This is WOAI-TV . . . testing."[180]

WOAI-TV's first-day broadcast schedule for December 11, 1949, was:

1:30	Test Pattern
4:45	*WOAI-TV Is Born*
5:00	Dedication Ceremonies
5:20	*SMU–Notre Dame Flashback*
6:00	*Johnny's Tree House*
6:15	*Telenews: Austin Williams*
6:30	*This Is Show Business*
7:00	*Curtain Time*

| 8:00 | *Three in a Family* |
| 9:00 | Sign-off[181] |

Preceding the dedication was a documentary film on the construction of WOAI-TV. The dedication featured Mayor Jack White and members of the San Antonio religious and military communities. *Johnny's Tree House* was a fifteen-minute live studio program for children featuring Johnny ("Chip Off the Old Tree") Dugan. *Curtain Time* presented talent from the San Antonio area.[182]

WOAI-TV was another accomplishment of Southland Industries and its founder, owner, and chairman of the board, G. A. C. Halff. He was instrumental in the formation of the radio station in 1922.[183]

Television for Dallas

In December of 1947, the FCC assigned five television channels to the Dallas–Fort Worth area: channels 4, 5, 8, 10, and 12. Channel 5 was licensed to WBAP-TV. Channel 4 had been assigned to the *Dallas Times-Herald* and would become KRLD-TV. Channel 8 had been licensed to the Lacy-Potter Television Broadcasting Company. Tom Potter and Rogers E. Lacy were granted the license over Interstate Theaters. Lacy died before Channel 8 became operational. Channel 10 had been sought by T. L. Carrisan, a real estate promoter. In December of 1947, Channel 12 was filed for by WFAA and the *Dallas Morning News*.[184]

KBTV-TV, Channel 8, started broadcasting on September 17, 1949, as the first television station in Dallas. Tom Potter, who owned four radio stations in East Texas and Louisiana, as well as seventy-five oil wells, was *the only individual in the United States to own a television station*. Potter had become interested in television years before when it was only an idea with a few engineers. He foresaw many possibilities for education and entertainment. "I am proud to join the ranks of those pioneers who have brought television into the American home," stated Potter. "We will do our utmost to live up to the heritage that, in only a few short years, these men have created."[185]

KBTV (the "-TV" was omitted when the station's call letters were written in Potter publications) was located at 3000 Harry Hines Boulevard. This was several blocks from an earlier proposed site on a hill overlooking the Trinity River just north of downtown Dallas. Earlier, Potter had been refused permission by the Dallas City Planning Commission for a five-hundred-foot tower located atop a building in the Lakewood Shopping Center northeast of downtown. Potter and Lacy had earlier proposed to locate the station on top of a new ultra-modern hotel. Each room in the forty-seven-story hotel was to have a television set installed to receive the programs of the station. The "equipment studio" was to be located

G. A. C. Halff, founder of WOAI, San Antonio. Courtesy Hoxie Mundine

above the forty-seventh floor. The hotel was to be located on the block bounded by Commerce, Ervay, Jackson, and Lane Streets.[186]

Opening night ceremonies at KBTV included speeches by Potter and Alben Barkley, vice-president of the United States. A crowd of 5,000 people heard the speeches and then watched a 2½-hour variety revue. The climax was a gigantic fireworks display.[187] Present was Tom Potter's son, Ted Potter. Ted remembers that later, when he would be at the station, he was always being drafted into being "one of the kids" sitting in the bleachers during the station's children's programs.[188]

KBTV was a complete DuMont technical facility. Channel 8's tower on Harry

Hines was 340 feet tall, and the transmitter operated with 27,100 watts of power. The transmitter was a 112-tube DuMont, the first of its kind. KBTV was originally affiliated with DuMont, using its "celluloid network," which used kinescopes. The station also signed contracts with Paramount Pictures and United Artists. Channel 8 operated with a large amount of local live programming and a large staff. It broadcast four hours of programming daily.[189] KBTV's schedule for Thursday, January 26, 1950, was:

2:00	Test Pattern
6:00	Local news
6:05	*KBTV Newsreel*
6:15	*Time for Beany*
6:30	Serial: *Fighting Marines*
6:50	*Bob Stanford's Preview*
7:00	*Vincent Lopez*
7:15	*Top Views in Sports*
7:30	*Backstage with Norris*
7:45	*Famous Jury Trials*
8:15	*What's on Your Mind?* H. B. Harris
8:30	*Armchair Traveler*
8:40	*The Pigeons:* Studio Drama Production
9:00	Feature Film
10:00	*News Roundup:* Don Morrow
10:05	Sign-off[190]

Potter purchased a $94,000 remote unit called the "Golden Telecruiser." The unit telecast wrestling matches from the Dallas Sportatorium, boxing matches, and basketball games; and in the 1949 football season, it assisted in the first network broadcast in the state of Texas, the Southern Methodist University–Notre Dame football game from the Cotton Bowl. During the 1949 State Fair of Texas, KBTV broadcast from studios in the general exhibits building.[191]

The staff of KBTV consisted of Jack I. Potter, president; J. Curtis Sanford, vice-president and general manager; Zach Bettis, advertising and promotion director; Don Morrow, news director; George White, sports director; Frank Norris, staff organist; Pauline Roques, traffic; Earle Marvin, director; Manning Trewitt, staff technician; Larry DuPont, program manager; Bill Sadler, director of continuity; Doug Thompson, film director; Alan Pottasch, director/producer; Bob Stanford, chief announcer; Carl Mann, sports announcer; Del Ramey, commercial manager; Lafe Pfeifer, sales representative; A. Otis Elliott, chief accountant; George Reed, chief auditor; Howard Dickson, accountant; Kay Blossom, secretary; Betty Lee Langston, secretary; Ben January, art director; Morris C. Barton, chief engineer; Mort Zimmerman, transmitter maintenance engineer; George Krutilek, engineer; Douglas Palmquist, engineer; Lee Spooner, engineer; Earl McDonald, audio engineer; Myles M. Bennett, night maintenance; Ralph Ingraham, chief audio engineer; "Bud" Kirksey, assistant chief engineer.[192]

Earl McDonald started working for Channel 8 one week after it began. McDonald had to pass his "First Phone" broadcasting license before he was hired. He took the FCC test in September of 1949 and then started working for Channel 8. "I was the best cameraman in Dallas on those dollies with the two straight wheels on the back and the crazy wheel on the front," said McDonald. "Julie Benell had a cooking show, and she didn't want anybody on camera but me." McDonald did everything:

I did sound. I "shaded" video on those Iconoscope cameras. The electrons floating around on that plate in there. . . . You had to keep inserting saw-tooth waves in it, trapezoidal waves in it, and sine waves in it . . . as the picture changed. You were looking at a video wave-form monitor, and all the wave-form would tilt up on one side, and so you would have to insert some tilt in it so it would tilt back level. You had a horizontal and vertical tilt knob. The picture could be too dark on one side, and so you kept "shading" this thing— and if it got too bright in the middle and too dark around the edges, you had knobs that would take care of that. It would insert a curve in the wave-form and counter-act the problem. There was always something wrong with the picture—there had to be a man sitting there constantly "shading it." The knobs were arranged in an arch, and anytime there was something on that thing you had to keep chasing that thing. It was called "shading."[193]

"The station was losing $1,000 a day," said Ted Potter, "but my Dad was making $10,000 a day from his oil wells. He could have supported the station's losses." In February of 1950, Potter sold the station to the A. H. Belo Corporation. He sold "because my brother kept insisting that owning a television station was wrong." Tom Potter loved owning the station but finally sold on the insistence of his older son. Potter was asked by the Belo Corporation to "stay on" at Channel 8 when the station sold. He declined but stated, "It will always be a matter of pride to me that I was able to pioneer television for Dallas, and also to bring that wonderful Channel 8 to my city."[194]

Channel 4 in Dallas began operations on December 3, 1949. KRLD-TV was formally opened by Tom C. Gooch, president and chairman of the board of the *Dallas Times Herald*. John W. Runyon, president of KRLD-TV, told the television audience, "No expense has been spared in the purchase of equipment, the training of personnel, nor in program contracts." Clyde W. Rembert, KRLD's managing director, promised viewers the best of CBS shows.

A few minutes later, at 12:25 P.M., KRLD-TV joined what was to be the first television network in Texas. Channel 4, Channel 5, and Channel 8 joined to broadcast the Notre Dame–Southern Methodist University football game from the Cotton Bowl in Dallas. WBAP-TV cameramen and equipment covered the game, feeding it to all three stations. The mobile units of both KRLD-TV and KBTV "stood by" at the stadium. An estimated 20,000 receivers were tuned in. The telecast was sponsored by Humble Oil and Refining of Texas. In the Cotton Bowl 80,000 spectators, including the governor of Texas and comedian Bob Hope, watched the game. The telecast began on KRLD-TV at about 12:25 P.M. Channel 5 and Channel 8 started at 12:30 P.M.[195] Ves Box of KRLD-TV remembered the first network telecast:

> In those days colleges and universities were afraid of television. The only way a college football game could be televised in 1949 would be for it to be a sellout, and no other NCAA team could be playing within a fifty-mile radius. It was a sellout, and Humble had the rights. . . . We had a mobile unit, but it was small. We used it for the control room. We had two cameras, total. We operated the mobile unit by moving the two cameras out of the studio and moving them to the site. Then we could only use film and slides in the studio.[196]

Johnny Smith, engineer for WBAP-TV, participated in this historical event:

> There had been a lot of hullabaloo in the paper that it was the first local television network. Channel 4 and Channel 8 had a couple of guys out there. They put a little parabola up on top of the Cotton Bowl to shoot over the old station on Harry Hines. It was raining and cold—a miserable day. We had several leaks up in the front end of the truck. They had a couple of power supplies up on the dashboard, and distribution amplifiers to feed the other stations. Water kept running down the cables into the equipment. We were trying to keep it dry and keep it on.
>
> We got a phone call an hour or so before the game from Bob Gould [program director of WBAP-TV]. He had gotten a call from the manager of Channel 4. They wanted permission to do a little five-minute introduction before the game. They wanted the camera set up to have their announcer—I think it was Ves Box—to make a little quick introduction and show everybody that we were going to have a three-station coverage of the football game. So we put the camera on him and they went on the air a few minutes before we did; then, at straight up 12:30, we all joined at the same time. The next day, half of the

newspaper in Dallas was dedicated to the fact that Channel 4 had come on with the first network telecast of a sporting event. They didn't have a piece of equipment involved. They had done nothing but get permission from us to get a free signal early. I guess that's the onset of competition.[197]

In September of 1948, James P. Nash of Austin was president of a group wanting to establish a television network in Texas. Another director of the group was Governor Beauford Jester. The Texas Telenet System, Inc., had applied for television licenses in Austin, San Antonio, and Corpus Christi and planned to apply for construction permits in Waco and Fort Worth and have affiliates in seventeen other cities. Telenet planned to operate a microwave relay system among several Texas cities, reaching 60 percent of the state's population.[198]

At the end of the 1940s, television, although primitive and not confident about its future, was established and operating. Even though the professionals did not know if television would ever make any money, other media started suffering. In the late 1940s and 1950s, radio began losing programming and listeners to television. Motion pictures found fewer people in theaters. Movies tried to counter with surrounding sound, Cinerama, and 3-D. Nothing worked.

As the 1940s ended, six television stations were operating in Texas. These six had a tremendous advantage because additional licenses would not be granted until 1952. During the four-year freeze these six stations flourished. They used this period of limited competition to discover and refine themselves and their product. In their markets, these stations would dominate for decades. By the time the freeze ended, television, especially these stations, was in control.

CHAPTER 4

The Expansion of Television and the Coming of Color

1950 to 1960

As television entered the 1950s, a period of strong, sustained growth, several major events were imminent. If you had been watching Texas television during these years you might have heard:

"Well, Good Morning!—Dallas, Fort Worth, Houston, San Antonio, Oklahoma City, Tulsa, and New Orleans," greeted Dave Garroway. "We're in New York. We're real people—just like the ones in your town."[1]

"What did you expect, hair?" questioned Richard Pryor.[2]

During the dedication ceremonies, Porter Randall asked Sid Richardson, the new owner of KFJZ-TV in Fort Worth, "What do you think about the new station?"
Richardson said, "We'll see!"[3]

"Welcome to 'Color Day, USA,' an historical event," announced Arman Jones.

The 1950s was a period of rapid growth and major leaps for television in Texas. In 1952 cable brought live network television to the state with the greeting by Dave Garroway. Now state viewers were able to view historical events, like the 1952 political conventions, live, as they happened, rather than delayed two or three weeks. The freeze in FCC license granting ended in 1952, and construction began on new television stations. The opening of KTBC-TV in Austin, one of the first stations to be issued a construction permit after the television freeze, was rather casual, with a close-up of Richard ("Cactus") Pryor's bald head. Millionaire Sid Richardson was quite restrained at the opening of KFJZ-TV in Fort Worth.

Other important events in Texas broadcasting in the 1950s were the establishment of the first educational television station in the nation, KUHT-TV in Houston; the establishment of the first Spanish-language television station in the nation, KCOR-TV in San Antonio; the Harry Washburn murder trial televised by KWTX-TV in Waco, the first televised trial in broadcasting history; and "Color Day, USA" at WBAP-TV in Forth Worth, the first color television program in Texas and the nation's second local color show. The first full decade of television broadcasting in Texas was active, creative, and energetic.

The Unfreezing of Television

The television allocation "freeze," which, according to FCC Chairman Wayne Coy, would last "possibly six months," lasted from 1948 to 1952. One of the questions being considered was the lack of allottable channels in the twelve presently available.

It had not always been twelve. During the early 1930s, the FCC had reserved four Very High Frequency (VHF) channels for experimental television. Near the end of the decade the FCC did not consider this sufficient and raised the number to nineteen: Channels 1 through 19. In the fall of 1939, the FCC assigned Frequency Modulation (FM) radio 42 to 50 megacycles, the frequencies formally assigned to television's Channel 1. Although Channel 1 had been removed from television, the remaining channels were not renumbered. Consequently, since 1939 there has been no television Channel 1.[4] When the National Television System Committee (NTSC) set standards for television in 1941, the number of channels was lowered to seventeen: Channels 2 through 18. In 1946 the FCC reduced the number of channels to twelve: Channels 2 through 13. On August 14, 1947, Channel 1 was taken from FM and reassigned for land mobile services.

Then, in 1948, the FCC again decided that there were not enough channels and "froze" television allocation in order to "polish" the service already authorized. It could not decide what to do about the increasing demand for the existing twelve channels. The action on September 30, 1948, froze 302 pending applications for television stations. A total of 123 stations were authorized; 37 were actually on the air.

At the end of the freeze in 1952, the FCC had 1,500 applications. As a result of studies during the freeze, the FCC reserved 82 channels for television by added channels 14–83 in the Ultra High Frequency (UHF) band. It then started granting construction permits in both the VHF and UHF bands.[5]

While dozens of applicants in Texas waited for the freeze to be resolved so they could bring television to their areas, Brownsville circumvented the FCC. In September of 1952 that city started importing television from Mexico. XELD-TV,

Channel 7, was located in Matamoros across the Rio Grande from Brownsville; but it was 100 percent American. Its transmitter was located just west of the city. Films, programs, and supplies were taken off airplanes in Brownsville and driven across to the station without having to register at Mexican customs. Channel 7 carried the leading U.S. programs, including their national advertising.[6]

As the FCC was resolving its problems, television in Texas was taking a major step forward. The six Texas "pre-freeze" stations were being connected to the world.

Live Network Programming

"Well, Good Morning!—Dallas, Fort Worth, Houston, San Antonio, Oklahoma City, Tulsa, and New Orleans," greeted Dave Garroway. "We're in New York. We're real people—just like the ones in your town." With this greeting, stations in Texas joined NBC for the first live network program. The date was July 1, 1952, and the show was *Today.*[7]

At KPRC-TV in Houston, Bill Hobby threw a switch connecting Houston with the rest of the United States. Just prior, Hobby made a one-minute speech saying, "From this moment on, KPRC-TV becomes truly 'A Window on the World' through which all of us can view the great historic moments of our time."[8]

The event climaxed months of work by telephone personnel to bring live network television to Texas in time for the Chicago political conventions. The phone company hurriedly installed a complicated system of coaxial cables and microwave relay stations from Jackson, Mississippi. The setup was temporary. Original plans called for a permanent television microwave link from Kansas City to Dallas that was to start operating in late 1952. Since that was after the conventions, the television networks asked the phone company to temporarily equip the Jackson-to-Dallas route.[9]

This temporary arrangement permitted only one program at a time to be fed to stations. The networks agreed to share convention coverage and regular programming time. In Houston, KPRC-TV's convention coverage rotated hour by hour among the three networks. The "switch-overs" were handled by AT&T strictly according to the clock. A speech that began on one network often concluded on another. On one occasion a switch-over occurred midway into a commercial. Viewers saw what appeared to be one commercial extolling the merits of two different brands of refrigerators. Even with these problems, Houston viewers watched an important political process.[10]

"It was a big relief to push that button and have the shows come in," said Bob Gould of WBAP-TV in Fort Worth.[11] "Then we were up-to-date. No more Christmas shows after New Year's." Live networking cleaned up the local television picture. There were few, if any, kinescopes, and it made the stations improve their scheduling of time and commercials. A station could no longer run all the commercials its wished. It had to go to network programs at precisely the correct time.[12]

Now, not only were the programs live, but so were nearly all commercials at WBAP-TV. Sets were placed in the studio for a program and the five or six commercials that aired before, during, and after it. Usually there was a set or area for each commercial. Individual sets were placed down both walls and across one end of the studio. In that maze of commercial sets would be the set for a program. Announcers would show up, do a commercial, and disappear; they knew when commercials were booked. Some sets were very large; sponsors wanted to display as much merchandise as possible in the time they bought. Leonard's Department Store wanted ten items in every commercial. Sponsors would ship props to the station, and the staff would keep them locked in a cage. Production members had scripts, and they went to storage and gathered all items needed for a particular commercial. The station had a back room full of refrigerators, washers, dryers, stoves, televisions, radios; anything needed for commercials. The staff hauled refrigerators in and out of the back room as many as ten times each day. The appliances could not be left in place in the studio because there was no space. When the commercial was finished, the appliance was taken back to storage, the set was struck, and another set was assembled. The staff became good furniture movers.[13]

Frank Mills of WBAP-TV did as many as nine one-minute commercials in one program. He would write them on 3" x 5" cards. There was a hollow place on the back of the table or platform used in spots. Mills would stick cards in there in the order of presentation. After he worked with them, the directors learned to keep the camera on Mills until they sensed he had ad-libbed all he could and needed to go to the script. The director would cut to a close-up of the product, then Mills pulled out his card and read the majority of the script. At the end of the commercial Mills would throw the script card back into the hiding place, the director would cut back to a shot of Mills, and he could finish. Some announcers used a reading device, made in the shop, that lashed over the top of the camera. The announcer would read cards in the device while another staff member read along with him and pulled cards.[14]

Johnny Hay, WBAP-TV staff announcer, did ten or more thirty- or sixty-second commercials a day. "A one-minute commercial is a hell of a long time because you're doing things with your hands, you're trying to coordinate everything," said Hay, "and it has to be right or nobody gets paid. I doubt if anyone in the business now could do it. Yet, we had to do it and didn't think anything about it." Hay did back-to-back live commercials. He would be doing one spot in an area; and when he finished, the director would cut to a slide or fade to black for a moment. Hay would then turn to another camera, the director would come back to him, and he would do a different commercial with a different background and props. "I guess I rehearsed a half dozen commercials in my career," said Hay.[15]

New Television Stations in Texas

As the FCC started granting licenses, stations were being constructed and started operating in large and small communities in both the VHF and the UHF bands. Although the FCC granted licenses in the UHF band, transmitter equipment, networks, advertisers, home receivers, and other necessary equipment were not ready. Not until the middle 1960s were television receivers required by the FCC to be manufactured to receive the UHF band. For the first decade after the freeze, granting a station a UHF license was a permit to fail.

Longview

One of the first UHF allocations in Texas was KTVE-TV, Channel 32, in Longview. A. James Henry was awarded a construction permit and built his small station on Highway 26 between Longview and Kilgore. The station was to serve those communities as well as Tyler and Marshall.

The facilities had a permanent kitchen set in a small studio and a tiny control room housing the transmitter and a 16mm projector. The original staff included Barry Monigold, Hershel McClure, Westle Dean, and cameraman Carl Lay. KTVE-TV had one camera and a scanner for slides. When a studio program needed to show a film, the camera swung around and its lens thrust into a specially constructed hole in the wall. This allowed the camera to pick up the image from the projector in the control room. At the conclusion of the film, the cameraman would pull the camera out of the hole and focus on the talent in the studio. Live programming included organist Lawrence "Sonny" Birdsong,[16] who recalled:

> We were only able to go "black" or to the flying spot camera. . . . We would start off in the afternoon with a feature movie. Then we would have a cooking show. Then we would have *Ranger West* and all his cowboys. Then we would have an interview program. Then we would have another movie.
>
> I would come on and play a piece of music on the organ, and when I finished they would go to the flying spot scanner and put the title of the program, which was *Star Time*. While they were doing that, they were getting the camera from me over to the port hole to put it on the projector to run the film that we had. We had a library of musical acts. They would make these up on a reel, and while that was playing I would sit there. They would say, "It's time to go back to the flying spot scanner" to get the camera focused on me again. . . . One night the projector went out and we did not have enough money to fix it.

The engineer was in the control room. He could control all the switches . . . like a two-bit radio station. He did everything himself.[17]

Another musical show featured Tubby Wallace and the Honey Drippers. *Mortarboard* presented academic competition between local schools. There was *Religion This Week* and *Ranger Round-Up* with Ranger Wes. The station had a small number of ancient movies and syndicated shows on kinescope. *Amos 'n' Andy* was one of the most popular shows on Channel 32.

Henry sought network affiliation. Network officials noted the small audience and broadcast coverage area of this UHF station and decided they were not interested. One fall KTVE-TV tried to telecast the World Series. Channel 32 picked up the signal from a distant network station and rebroadcast it. The network learned of the rebroadcast; KTVE-TV only broadcast one game. Because of stated problems and the fact that Channel 7, KLTV-TV, started broadcasting in Tyler, KTVE-TV "went dark" in 1955. Another UHF station in Tyler, KETX-TV, Channel 19, did not survive.[18]

According to Birdsong, the manager went on the air and said, "We're leaving the air and we hope to come back sometime soon." The engineer faded out, cut the power, and they were off. "That was it. We had killed ourselves for three years trying to make this station go." The local newspaper administrators contributed to Channel 32's demise by telling advertisers, "If you advertise on the television station you won't get any advertising in this paper." Advertisers told the station that they were sorry but they could not do without newspaper advertising.[19]

Waco

Another early UHF station was KANG-TV in Waco. Channel 34 started telecasting in November of 1953. Because it was in the UHF band, KANG-TV transmitted with very low power. It could not attract network affiliation other than DuMont, and at first few television receivers in the Waco area could receive the UHF band.

KCEN-TV, located between Waco and Temple, began telecasting on November 1, 1953. Channel 6 was affiliated with NBC. "KCEN-TV had one of the top three contracts with NBC," said Robert Weathers, KANG-TV salesman. "They were being paid so much money by NBC that they did not have to get out on the streets and sell local advertising." According to Weathers, "They got it because of [Lyndon] Johnson."[20] Channel 6 followed one practice common in the 1950s. At that time nationwide advertisers did not have to advertise on the whole network. They could pick the markets in which they wanted their commercials to be seen, and they could exclude other markets. Many did not buy the Waco-Temple market, especially for daytime programming. KCEN-TV was allowed to carry the programs but not the commercials. Consequently, daytime shows were constantly interrupted. When the network show faded out for a commercial, Channel 6 would "cut away" to a local public service announcement or promo or just "sit" on a slide, sometimes with sound and sometimes without, for sixty seconds or more until the network show resumed. A viewer could watch an entire day of daytime network television on KCEN-TV and never see a national commercial. If viewers traveled to Dallas, whose market had been bought, when watching television, these viewers were delighted to see the commercials.

Radio Station WACO had applied for a television license in 1948. When manager Lee Glasgow went to Washington, D.C., after the freeze to present his case, he took Mary Holliday's diary with him. Holliday had been performing and working at the station since the 1920s. She kept a diary of all the community service programs broadcast by the station. When Glasgow was looking for documentation that WACO broadcast in "the public interest," Holliday said, "I have such a record." Her diary contained the names of whom she interviewed, on what days, and for how long. Holliday's diary was presented at Glasgow's television application hearing. It did little good; WACO was passed over.[21]

Glasgow was so sure WACO would be granted a television license that he purchased the equipment needed to start operations. WACO held an "open house" in 1953 where the people of Waco were invited to "Come and See Television." Visitors walked through one of the radio studios where two working television cameras fed monitors. People were fascinated to see themselves on television. Mothers especially liked seeing images of their young children. Headsets for cameramen were not available, so when one thought he had a nice shot, he would yell, "Let me have it," and the man at the switcher would push a button and put that camera's image on the monitors. The station's antenna was lying on the floor in the corner.[22]

"Glasgow had bought some equipment and had been training people from Baylor—and thought since they were the old line station and had equipment and trained people, that they would get it," recalled Stan Wilson, later manager of WACO. "I think they underestimated LBJ." WACO's equipment was sold to Channel 11 in Galveston.[23]

Robert Weathers, worked at KANG-TV:

I meet Bob Walker, who was the manager of KANG in Waco. He was an old radio announcer from WACO before he went to the television station. Channel 34 had just gone on the air. The station was owned by Clyde Weatherby from Hamilton. . . . He was very close to Senator Johnson. I went to work at Channel 34 in sales, and boy, the only thing we had to sell was a little programming from the DuMont Network. We had a lot of live programs—every country and western band was on our station. We had a lot of sports talk programs. We ran a lot of film. We ran *The Little Rascals* three times a day. We had one live camera for our local productions. The sales department was in a little room about ten by ten. There were twelve people in that room. When you tried to sell time, everybody would look at you and say, "What are you talking about?" It was tough.

The reception was good for fifteen miles. That was enough for Waco. One afternoon between 4:00 and 5:00—in 1955—a real tall man with a white Stetson hat came into the station and with him was a short gray-headed man with a white Stetson hat. The tall man told the receptionist, "I want to see the manager." The receptionist called for Bob Walker. He came out and saw that it was Senator Johnson. They all went into his office. They stayed five or ten minutes. Walker came out and said that we were going to have a staff meeting in about five or ten minutes; get everybody together. The tall man came out. He told us who he was and what he was there for. He said that his wife, "Lady Bird," had just acquired us and that he wanted to be a part of Waco. In doing so, the next morning we would sign on with *Captain Kangaroo* at 7:00 from CBS. At 8:00 we would have the *ABC Breakfast Show*, and we would "flip-flop" CBS and ABC throughout the day.

In three weeks' time we were completely sold out. When we went on the air with CBS and ABC, we had to fight the people off of us. KANG-TV had more Ford Motor advertising on its station than any other television station in America because Senator Johnson would get on the telephone, call Benson Ford and say, "Benson, my wife, Lady Bird, has just acquired a little television station down in Waco, Texas, and I need your help. What can you do for me?" Man, we were running Ford Motor Company, Lincoln, Mercury, Ford Tractor; everything that Ford was involved in. We had an aluminum company from Baltimore, Maryland, running with us. We had an insurance company from Philadelphia, Pennsylvania, running with us.[24]

For a short period, Jim Nabors, who was in the army at Fort Hood in Killeen, would come to Waco and do the weather on Channel 34.

A few months later, the staff of KANG-TV was told that in a few days they would be out of a job. Within six months of acquiring Channel 34, Johnson had traded that facility and all its debt for 29.3 percent of KWTX-TV, Channel 10. That was a new station just starting operations. The staff of KANG-TV was invited to apply at KWTX-TV, but no one was hired. Weathers subsequently learned:

The reason KWTX-TV was delayed in getting on the air—WACO was owned by TSN [Texas State Network], which was owned by a group including Sid

Richardson. They were trying to get Channel 10. WACO had bought their television cameras and equipment; the contest was on. [John] Connally was the legal advisor to Sid Richardson and TSN.

They worked out a deal where KWTX paid WACO for all their expenses incurred; WACO bowed out. KWTX got Channel 10. When Senator Johnson took over Channel 34, he traded nothing for 29.3 percent of KWTX Broadcasting. That was the reason we went out of business. Johnson gave the license back to the FCC. Later on, Lee Glasgow got Channel 34 and a construction permit, and he kept it for many years, but nothing was ever done.[25]

THE WASHBURN TRIAL

"To the best of my knowledge, this will be the first time for live telecasting of a murder trial anywhere," stated Bill Stinson, news director of KWTX-TV. The location was the 54th District Court in Waco. KWTX-TV placed one RCA TK-11 in the balcony of District Judge D. W. Bartlett's courtroom on December 5, 1955. Channel 10 broadcast the entire murder trial of Harry Washburn, who was charged with slaying his former mother-in-law, Helen Harris Weaver, in San Angelo on January 19, 1955. It was *the first televised trial in broadcast history.*[26]

Judge Bartlett granted permission after conferring with defense and prosecuting attorneys. The judge said he felt that telecasting "is the coming thing and television should be allowed in courtrooms provided it does not distract from court proceedings." Bartlett called it "a very good thing for the viewing public to see." M. N. (Buddy) Bostick, station manager, stated, "Several schools are using it as a classroom project for civic classes since it's the first time the students have been able to look at an important trial while in class."

Stinson did not allow the camera to view the jury of ten men and two women. "We didn't want people recognizing them on the street later and maybe badgering them about the verdict." The camera was sixty feet away on the balcony behind the jury. Cameramen Hillary McDonald and Bob Hecht used three or four different focus-length lenses, changing them while "on the air." "We want to be as inconspicuous as possible," said Bostick, "so no special lighting was used. All we did was substitute 100-watt for the 50-watt bulbs in the courtroom; but we got excellent results. It looks like a studio production." Three microphones were stationed inconspicuously at the witness booth, judge's bench, and prosecution's table.[27]

KWTX-TV canceled all commercials and programming during the proceedings. Even night programming was canceled on Wednesday when the trial didn't recess until 9 P.M. The telecast which cost Channel 10 approximately $10,000, was offered to other Texas stations, but none accepted.[28]

• • •

On December 5, 1955, KWTX-TV placed one RCA TK-11 in the balcony of Judge Bartlett's courtroom and televised the murder trial of Harry Washburn. It was the first televised trial in broadcasting history. Courtesy KWTX-TV, Waco, Texas

El Paso

As the freeze ended, two radio stations in El Paso competed to bring television to that area. Ted Bender of KTSM remembers the contest:

CBS rode with KROD; NBC rode with KTSM. There was no doubt that these two strong lines were going to clash. With the knowledge that Rodrick [KROD] had bought part of the mountain and was putting a road up the mountain to put his transmitter on, Wyler went ahead with his side of the business. We were strapped for the great wealth that the other side had. Wyler decided to go with a tower through the El Paso Electric Company. They were able to put the tower down there at the electric company on the south side.

There was a mad race to see who would get on the air first. KROD got on the air first, but you could not see it. They ran a bootleg movie which was our property: *Stagecoach* with John Wayne. But nobody could see it or hear it, the picture was so bad. They tried to get on the air in a hurry. I saw this with my own eyes. I climbed the mountain on Christmas Day, 1953. They were literally using coat hangers—bent, and so forth for pieces of equipment—for wiring. Herbie Ran was the chief engineer.

Wyler then said, "Let's lay back now. We can't be first anymore, but let's be best."

The thing which kept us from being first was something called "hens eggs." They are about the size of a coke can, and they fitted in the transmission line that goes up the tower. These damn things were shipped to someplace in Iowa. That kept us from being first.

We went on the air January 4, 1953 . . . with all those good NBC shows at the time, and we had a good picture. Cable was a long time in getting here. "Kines" and films, and we were always running out to the airport and getting them off American Airlines.[29]

According to one opening-day telephone caller, Bender and KTSM-TV did not have as clear a picture as they believed.

"I understand that you people are on the air with television."

The answer from the station was, "Yes, and it's beautiful." "Well, I've been watching my loudspeaker all day, and I haven't seen a damn thing."[30]

Austin

Television in Austin, like radio, became part of the Johnson media empire. It began in the organization of Dr. James G. Ulmer, who started broadcasting in 1930 with a radio station in Tyler. Throughout the decade he acquired an interest in or built numerous stations around the state, including KTBC in Austin. Near the end of the decade he was in financial difficulties. As the FCC investigated Ulmer for "hidden ownership" in many stations, Ulmer sold KTBC to Claudia Alta (Lady Bird) Johnson on December 21, 1942. The station changed ownership for a reported "$15,000 in notes against it."[31]

Just after World War II, Dave Naugle worked for Johnson's station in Austin. Naugle started dreaming of being an announcer by taking his grandmother's "ear trumpet"—"this thing you stick in your ear, and it stuck out kind of like a microphone . . . and I had a lamp stand with no lamp on it—just the pole—I would stick that 'ear trumpet' in the lamp stand, and I would sit there and read copy. . . . I wrote the copy myself or I would read the newspaper."

Naugle was astonished at a critique the station's employees received. Johnson's mother was an employee, although she never came to the station. She listened and did a critique of the station and its staff: hour by hour, day by day. She wrote it up and sent it in every week to be typed. Every Monday morning the staff would receive Mrs. Johnson's critique of the preceding week's programming. She would say things like "Cactus Pryor, 6:10 A.M., sounds like he's got mush in his mouth" and "Bill Pellet, whoever told him he was an announcer?"

"It was pretty silly," said Naugle. "All it was was a way to get her some income."[32]

The television station in Austin could have been a cooperative effort of all three local radio stations. Wendell Mayes, Sr., owner of KNOW, was approached by Johnson:

> At one point Lady Bird owned a station, my dad owned a station here, and a man named Bill Deason owned a station here; it was KVET. Senator Johnson asked Bill Deason and my father to meet with him at the ranch. There was an allocation of one television channel in Austin. Johnson had all these financial projections made and asked Deason and my father to join in some kind of joint venture and apply for and operate the television station. The three radio stations would support the television station until it got to making money. Deason and my father did not have enough money to do it. They had to turn it down. It was anticipated that this television station would lose money for some time. My father decided that his radio station could not make enough money to support television for as long as it took.[33]

Nevertheless, Johnson built KTBC-TV, which was licensed to Mrs. Johnson. It started broadcasting on November 27, 1952. Richard (Cactus) Pryor, staff announcer for the radio station, joined the television side:

> The opening picture was of a bald head. The opening line of broadcasting was "What did you expect, hair?" I didn't wear a hairpiece then. I'm very bald. It was Thanksgiving Day, 1952. We went on about an hour before the Texas–Texas A&M game.
>
> Then I took them on a tour of the transmitter and the studio. The studio was a "glassed-in" closet. It was a square about ten by ten feet. We started on a shoestring. The camera was on the outside shooting through the plate-glass window. The studio was within the confines of the transmitter building on top of Mount Larson.
>
> We started with twin [news] anchors: Paul Bolton and Lymon Jones. The announcer, in order to deliver the commercial, had to get under the table. When it was time for the commercial he would pop up and deliver it. When the director said, "Go to black," we would literally put a black card in front of the lens. . . . We probably had just one camera. We lit it very poorly. The men's rest room was behind the camera, and if the door should open to the rest room with the light on, it would reflect off the plate-glass window.
>
> Later I did a show with Pat O'Brien and Zsa Zsa Gabor sitting outside with

the town of Austin and Lake Austin in the background. When we went down-town to the Driskill Hotel, everything was live. We had two cameras, and because they would make mistakes, we gave personalities to the cameras. They were called "Ralph" and "Fabby Lou." We painted eyes on them . . . and they had the nose, which was the lens. We put a hat on "Fabby Lou."[34]

Possibly Pryor's worst experience in broadcasting was at a station in Alice:

In 1946 I went to Alice, Texas, to become program director of KVKI. That's controversial country—that's George Parr country—the Duke of Duval—Box 13 that put LBJ into the Senate. Parr told the Mexicans how to vote . . . even after they had been dead for a number of years, he still told them how to vote. I was program director and not aware of the politics down there that could get me killed.

My news editor came to me one day and said, "The sheriff here is doing a lot of illegal stuff—importing softball pitchers for the city tournament—keeping them in the jail at taxpayers' expense—bootlegging going on—prostitution going on." He said, "I want to put it on the air."

I said, "Can you prove it?"

He said, "Yeah."

So he put it on the air, and it created quite a sensation. The wire services picked it up.

Mike and I were playing golf one Saturday, and here comes Deputy Sheriff [Smithwick] across the fairways—six foot and 275 pounds—pearl handled pistols.

He said, "Are you those two guys who put that story out?"

We said, "Yeah."

He said, "You've got to sundown to get out of town."

Literally said it. So we went to the station owner, Ed Lloyd, a lawyer, and laughingly told him the story. He said, "Boys, take my advice and don't wait till sundown."

I had been offered a job in Corpus Christi, so I took it. I was gone by three o'clock. My successor was Bill Masion, who exposed the corruption in the sheriff's department.[35]

Smithwick saw Masion on the streets of Alice one day. Smithwick called Masion over to his patrol car. Masion walked over, and when he arrived, Smithwick pulled out his gun and killed him. Later, Smithwick allegedly committed suicide in the Belton jail.[36]

• • •

San Antonio

WOAI-TV and KEYL-TV (KENS-TV) in San Antonio started broadcasting during the "freeze." During this period, W. W. Lechner, a Dallas oil executive, and Alamo Television Company applied for Channel 35. Lechner also applied for television licenses in Dallas and Houston.[37]

KCOR

Raul Cortez came to San Antonio from Mexico in the 1940s. He started KCOR-AM in 1946, *the first Hispanic-owned and operated Spanish-language radio station in the nation.* In January of 1955, he directed the establishment of KCOR-TV, Channel 41, *the first Spanish-speaking television station in the United States.* Programming was 50 percent live variety and entertainment shows from the studios of the radio station and simulcast on radio and television.

Although Channel 41's programming was very popular, the station was not supported by the advertising community. According to Emilio Nicolas, general manager, "advertisers did not acknowledge this market and failed to use it extensively for commercial promotions. During those early years, Hispanic viewers were not accounted for in the standard ratings services. One reason for this was that in the 1940s and 1950s, Mexican-Americans were cautious in either acknowledging their heritage or exposure to Spanish-language media for fear of blatant discriminatory practices." Thus, in a few years Cortez was forced to sell. He kept the call letters for the radio station. Don Emilio Azcarraga Vidaurreta purchased the station in 1961 and established *the first Spanish-language television network in the nation.*[38]

KONO-TV in San Antonio started broadcasting on January 21, 1957. Its first program was the inauguration of President Dwight D. Eisenhower over the ABC network. KONO-TV was owned and operated by the Mission Telecasting Corporation. Eugene J. Roth, who had founded KGRC and KONO in the 1920s, and his sons Bob and Jack, were the major stockholders.[39] They first applied for a license for Channel 12 in 1948. At the comparative hearings, according to George Ing, director of engineering at KONO, the other applicant made a mistake: "We proposed two cameras on a bus for remotes and two or three cameras in the studio. One of the ways we beat the opposition was, they said they were going to have one camera. They were going to have two studios on two different floors and showed 'back-to-back' programs with that one camera. That did not impress the FCC."[40]

The station had a 573-foot antenna with studios across from Central Catholic High School on North St. Mary Street. Key Herbert was named news chief, George Ing became director of engineering, Justin Duncan was operations manager, and Katie Ferguson was program coordinator.[41]

. . .

Houston

In Houston the FCC assigned five television channels in addition to Channel 2, KPRC-TV. The added allotments were Channels 8, 13, 23, 29, and 39. Channel 11 was assigned to Galveston.

KGUL-TV in Galveston began broadcasting on March 22, 1953. The station's transmitter was situated at Camp Wallace and delivered a very poor signal into Houston. "The station could not move its tower closer to Houston," explained Jack McGrew, manager of KPRC-TV, "because that was as close as it could get to Fort Worth, which was also assigned Channel 11."[42]

KUHT-TV

Channel 8 was reserved for educational programming. When the FCC lifted the freeze, it reserved 242 television channels for noncommercial educational broadcasting. Channel 8 was granted to the University of Houston. KUHT-TV was *the first educational television station in the United States.* The station cost $250,000 and ran its first test on May 12, 1953. In the first years, according to Dr. John C. Schwarzwalder, station manager, "KUHT-TV did more television teaching than any other station in the entire U.S." Forty different college courses were televised.[43] Programming ranged from psychology to "Electricity in the Home."

The station helped its own financial situation and gave experience to the students by having music students perform music, art students work on sets, photographic students operate cameras, and so on. The university was assisted in the financing of the station by a grant from the Ford Foundation Fund for Adult Education, which offered one dollar in matching funds for every two dollars the station could raise.[44]

Channel 13 in Houston had four applicants: KTRH Broadcasting Company; W. W. Lechner of Dallas; South Texas Television Company, composed of John Paul Goodwin, Howard Tellepsen, and C. P. Simpson; and Houston Area Television Company, composed of Dillon Anderson, W. A. Kirkland, George Bruce, Dudley Sharp, George Kirksey, and other Houston businesspersons. Channel 13 was granted to KTRH. The station started broadcasting November 20, 1954.

The FCC also awarded construction permits to KNUZ to operate on Channel 39 and Max Jacobs of UHF Television Company of Dallas for Channel 23. Three Texas independent oil operators were additional owners of UHF Television Company. They were W. L. Pickens of Dallas, R. L. Wheelock of Corsicana, and H. H. Coffield of Rockdale.[45]

KNUZ-TV, Channel 39, was Houston's first UHF station. It was situated in the Texas Television Center on Cullen Boulevard near Wheeler. David H. Morris was vice-president and general manager. Channel 39 was affiliated with the

DuMont network. Local women's programming featured Wilma Rutherford on *What's Cooking* and Mitzi Wayne on *Window Shopping*. The station broadcast eight hours a day from 3:00 P.M. to 11 P.M. Studio equipment featured four DuMont cameras and a flying spot scanner film camera. Total cost to construct the station was $500,000.[46]

The first applicant for Channel 29 was Glenn McCarthy, president of Shamrock Broadcasting Company, operator of KXYZ. Shamrock had been an applicant in February, 1948, for Channel 13 but had withdrawn. McCarthy made the decision to seek Channel 29 "in order to bring a second commercial television station to the Houston area at the earliest possible date," stated McCarthy. "The staff of KXYZ has been making television plans for some four years and at this moment the station is ready and waiting to provide television service to Houston should the application for Channel 29 be approved."[47] The other applicant for Channel 29 was T. Hill, operator of a station in Tulsa, Oklahoma.

Dallas–Fort Worth

In the Dallas–Fort Worth area, Channel 10 had three applicants: the Fort Worth Television Company, formed by F. Kirk Johnson, Arch Rowan, O. P. Newberry, R. O. Shaffer, and Sterling C. Holloway; KFJZ; and W. W. Lechner of Eagle Mountain Lake just outside Fort Worth. There was an application for Channel 20 from "automotive people," according to Harold Hough of WBAP-TV. Mr. Kellam and Mr. Lightfoot of Texas Motor in Fort Worth had applied, but "they are merely doing it for protection in the future," stated Hough. "They don't expect to build."[48]

WRR, the City of Dallas radio station, considered applying for Channel 10. The idea was to employ television to inform the public on traffic control problems and operations of the police, fire, water, and health departments. According to Durward Tucker, chief engineer, "Television could go even farther in bringing visual education into the homes of Dallasites." Pictures were to be taken with movie cameras by employees of the city and then shown later on television. "Video programs could bridge a gap between the city government and the people on the activities of just about every department," stated Tucker. In December, 1952, the Dallas City Council voted six to three against pursuing a station.[49] Channel 10 was not allotted to the Dallas–Fort Worth area. It was granted to KWTX-TV in Waco. KFJZ was granted Channel 11 and began broadcasting on September 11, 1955, after the Fort Worth Television Company withdrew. Pete Teddlie heard how the owners of KFJZ financed the station:

Gene Cagle and Charlie Jordon pooled all their collateral to put a television station together. It was very expensive. They pooled everything they had and came up $500,000 short. Gene Cagle knew Sid Richardson. He and Charlie went to see Sid, told him their plan, and told him how much stock they would give if he would loan them the money. So he pulled out his checkbook, sat down, wrote out a check for $500,000, and handed it to Cagle.

They sent it into Washington, and T. J. Slawery, the secretary who was handling it, saw it and he fell over; it floored him. He picked up the phone, called the bank in Fort Worth on which the check was written, and talked to the president. "Look here, I've got a check from a man named Sid Richardson for half a million dollars. It's not a certified check; it's just a plain check. It's for the operation and opening of a new television station."

"What do you want to know?" asked the bank president.

Slawery asked, "Is it good?"

The president said, "I don't know. I haven't looked today. The last time I looked he had 85 million. He might have spent a dollar last night. I'll go check."[50]

Johnny Smith, engineer staff, remembered Gene Cagle's attitude toward television:

Cagle didn't really want this thing. I remember him saying, "The only good thing is that we don't go on the air until three o'clock." Sid Richardson wasn't really interested. I think we got it because we didn't want anyone else to get it. It did not change our radio at all.

We went on the air while the construction people were still working. We put the whole thing together in a warehouse. We had a big old vacant warehouse with a concrete floor. We taped the floor—designed the floor where all the racks were going to set, the production equipment, the projectors, and studio—cut all the cable, wired up all the racks, and plugged in the stuff. Built it right there; laid it all out. Then, when the building got finished enough to start moving in there, unplugged it all, carried it all out there, set it where it was supposed to set, and plugged it in. We hired just about anybody who could solder. I became the projectionist the first day because I know something about projectors. But I didn't know anything about that Telop: the dog.

We had an opening ceremony on Sunday afternoon. Porter Randall did a little thing about the station going on the air, and he asked Sid Richardson, "What do you think about this?"

Richardson said, "We'll see!" That's all he said. This was on the air, live![51]

When KFJZ-TV first went on the air, Randall, one of the most popular radio news personalities in Texas, did the television newscast. He only lasted a year. Randall was not a television person; he could not grab his ear. It frustrated him.

Channel 11 hired Bill Johns from California. Johns was a small person who wore elevator shoes and memorized his entire script. While presenting the story he would dramatize major points with hand gestures. If the story told of an airplane hitting water, Johns would illustrated it by skipping his hand across the counter in front of him.[52]

Dave Naugle remembered how he prepared for television:

I had been working down in radio in the old building, and the new guy who was going to run the station, Buck Long, came down one night when I was doing the ten o'clock news. There was nobody in the place but me and the engineer across a couple of studios. I was in the little announcer's booth, and I had the door open to the hall. Nobody's there—no noise—and he told somebody, "That guy will never work on my television station. Why anybody cares so little about his work as to leave the door open when he is reading the news has no place on my air." But he told Gene Cagle not that I left the door open but that I could not work out on television because my ears were too big and they could not fit them in on the screen properly.

Cagle said, "Well, we'll see about that."

They owned a station in Abilene. So Cagle had them drive me out to Abilene. I didn't know why they drove me out to Abilene and put me in front of a camera. I thought they were going to see if I could do television. I tried and tried and memorized a Coke spot they were having me do. All they wanted to do was see if my ears would fit on the television screen. I worked on that commercial for thirty or forty minutes, and I got out there and forgot the darn thing. It didn't make any difference because that was not what they wanted to find out. They never said a word about how good I was or how bad I was.

We got back and Buck Long said, "Yes, we were right. His ears are too big. We can't get him on the screen. He does not have any place in our organization."

Cagle said, "Well, we'll see about that." Cagle called me into the office and said, "How would you like to have your ears pinned back?" I thought he meant to stick some gum or something. I said that my wife would be delighted. Cagle said, "We've arranged for you to check into Harris Hospital at five o'clock this afternoon and have your ears pinned back—permanently—because you'll look better on television if your ears are not sticking out." They were going to pay for all of it.

When the station signed on the air I had bandages all over my ears and my head. Man, they were so sore. They were trying to see if I was going to be well enough in time for the sign-on date. Stan Wilson was going to be the television manager.

Cagle said, "Well, I guess we can't use Naugle on the opening day."

Wilson said, "I think we can. He's going to be sports director. What we'll do is get a football helmet and put it on him, and that will hide the bandages."

Cagle said, "Well Stan, you're a good broadcasting man but that is the dumbest idea I have ever heard."

When the station went on the air, I was home watching. It was two weeks later before I got on the air.[53]

KFJZ built its new studios for radio and television in the 4800 block of the East-West Freeway in Fort Worth.[54] Naugle and the staff started in an unfinished building:

Television was on the air, and the building was not finished yet. In fact, they had boards down the hallways. You walked on big 2" x 12" boards; worked on dirt floors. The only rooms really finished were the studio and the film room. We operated with dirt floors for a month or six weeks. They wanted to get on the air on September 11; Channel 11 wanted to start on the eleventh. I would sit on a barrel and set my portable typewriter on another barrel—writing my sports program—out there in the lobby with a dirt floor.[55]

Network Remotes

Cable, which allowed Texas to receive programming from networks, also allowed Texas stations to transmit programming to the rest of the country or participate in network shows. The exchange of programming added a new dimension to local and national schedules. Texans could see the world, and the world could see Texas.

The telephone company completed arrangements by January 1, 1953, allowing NBC to telecast the New Year's Day Cotton Bowl Game from Dallas. It also allowed, for the first time, WBAP-TV to telecast a rodeo to a nationwide audience. The Southwestern Exposition and Fat Stock Show Rodeo aired at 2:00 P.M. on January 31, 1953.[56]

"The relations with the networks were terrible," recalled Rupert Bogan, WBAP-TV engineer. "You could have fifteen cameras, and NBC always wanted two more. The NBC people would come in—they were from the big city and they were supposed to know more than these country hicks down here in Fort Worth." Bogan had a temper, and they irritated him. His attitude toward network personnel was "If they didn't like what the hell I had to offer, well get the hell out and go back to New York. I'm doing the best I can and this is it."[57]

With the coming of live network programming, remote trucks from Texas stations were used by networks for live feeds to shows like *Wide Wide World* with Dave Garroway. In the mid-1950s that program devoted an entire episode to the

Lone Star State. It was called *Texas, USA.* For that show KPRC-TV put a crew on location at the San Jacinto Battleground with instructions to cover both the monument and Battleship Texas. The station's remote crew rigged a camera and remote transmission dish in a helicopter for a view of the Houston Ship Channel. On other programs the crew covered Tabasco sauce being made on Avery Island, Louisiana, or transmitted pictures from a shrimp boat off Galveston by placing a receiving antenna on a balcony of the Galvez Hotel and hanging a white bed sheet off the railing to serve as a visual target for the microwave dish operator on board the boat.[58]

WBAP-TV's mobile unit covered many locations for *Wide Wide World,* such as the Carlsbad Caverns in New Mexico. That setup took one week. Cameras covered the Rock of Ages, the Queen's Place, and the entrance. The staff completely gutted the remote truck, hauled all equipment down the elevators into the caverns, and then reassembled it. They brought one whole truckload of lighting equipment and all the cables they could find at the station. The unit from WFAA-TV in Dallas covered the caverns' entrance.[59]

The next Sunday WBAP-TV's remote unit was on top of Christo Del Ray in El Paso, where cameramen had to be tied to camera platforms to keep them from falling off the mountain. On another program, the remote truck covered a Texas ranch where a herd of buffalo were trucked in just for the show. The crew did a rainy segment at the Gainsville Community Circus with a stubborn donkey that refused to take cues from a "I'm-a-big-TV-director" from New York City. During *Texas, USA,* Channel 5 covered the State Fair of Texas with all twelve cameras from its as well as WFAA-TV's and KRLD-TV's remote units.[60]

The Beginning of Color Television

The idea of color television had existed for almost as long as the idea of television. The Columbia Broadcasting System worked on a mechanical system of color before World War II. During the same period, the National Broadcasting Company experimented with "all-electronic" color television. David Sarnoff, president of the National Broadcasting Company, told a Hollywood meeting in 1930 that a workable means of transmitting color pictures through the air was on the way. "They laughed at me," stated Sarnoff. Eleven years later, on February 20, 1941, NBC/RCA transmitted the first color television picture from the Empire State Building.[61]

Amon Carter and officials of Carter Publications were invited in April of 1946 to New York City for a demonstration of CBS's "Ultra-High Definition, Full-Color Television." That year CBS petitioned the FCC for commercialization of its system. After lengthy hearings the FCC denied the request on the grounds that the state of the art was not far enough along and it required too much space in the broadcast spectrum. The FCC "froze" the granting of television licenses on September 30, 1948. One reason was the unanswered question of what standards were going to be used for color. On October 11, 1950, the FCC issued its "Second Report," adopting the CBS "Color Wheel" as the standard, effective November 20, 1950.[62]

On June 25, 1951, CBS broadcast its first commercial color television program. Soon the National Television System Committee recommended the adoption of standards requiring color television to be compatible with black and white and utilize the same frequency band width. The FCC rescinded its "Second Report." On December 17, 1953, the commission approved the NTSC compatible specifications. The CBS color system was not compatible; the NBC/RCA system was all electronic and compatible.[63]

Color in Texas Television

Amon Carter and Carter Publications signed a contract with RCA on September 23, 1949, to purchase new color transmitting equipment, to be delivered when ready. This was four years before the RCA color system was approved. Carter was not the first; WKY-TV in Oklahoma City placed its order days earlier.[64]

At WBAP-TV, when someone watched a television and a certain type of scene appeared, somebody might say, "I wish we could see this in color." Working for Channel 5, the staff knew that Carter was going to have the first, the biggest, the best. Johnny Smith, engineer, knew that when color was ready, Channel 5 would have it first. The staff was convinced that this was the way things were done. Carter was not going to be second to anybody, especially Dallas.[65]

Rupert Bogan and Phil Wygant went to New York City in 1953 to visit the Colonial Theater where NBC had its principal color production facilities. They observed productions and determined what problems might exist if Channel 5 started telecasting color. Bogan found color amazing even though the picture was "noisy." Wygant stayed two months observing color lighting and buying lighting equipment. He watched NBC colorcast *The Hit Parade*. On March 19, 1954, NBC transmitted its first network color feed. WBAP-TV personnel watched *The Sailboat and the Bathing Girls,* which tested new microwave equipment between Omaha, Nebraska, and the station. The first network color broadcast was *Ding Dong School* at 9:00 A.M. on April 9, 1954. On May 3, 1954, NBC "colorcast" *The Voice of Firestone*. KPRC-TV in Houston broadcast the program even though there were no color receivers on the market. Channel 2 invited civic and business leaders to the station to view the program on its color monitors. The impact was tremendous.[66]

• • •

Color Day: WBAP-TV

On May 7, 1954, a letter invited guests to the Keystone Room of the Hotel Texas to hear David Sarnoff speak and witness *the Lone Star State's first color program. Color Day, USA* was Saturday, May 15, 1954. The program was billed as a color demonstration staged through the cooperation of Fort Worth merchants.[67]

WBAP-TV's move into color was going to be simple. Harold Hough, vice president of broadcasting, phoned Bob Gould, director of production, two or three weeks before *Color Day.* "Son, we're going into color. We've got the equipment ordered, and it'll be here soon. We should have a very simple demonstration." Hough wanted something colorful, like Native Americans with their headdresses, but he wanted it simple. Gould started thinking of an opening-day program. As *Color Day* approached, Hough would telephone, "Now, we need to add Stripling's Department Store; they want to show some fashions. They'll pick colorful clothes. Koslow's needs its furs on the show. Get Bobby Peters and his band, his fourteen-piece band, and a couple of singers and dancers." Something was added every day to Gould's "simple demonstration" until the *Color Day* program ran three hours and fifteen minutes.[68]

WBAP-TV's staff had to completely change all the lighting. The station bought Fresnels and scoops. Black and white television used Par 38 and Par 40 spotlights and fluorescent, but fluorescent lighting could not be used with color. The lighting man had to control the color temperature. If engineers aligned color cameras with 3200° K light and the lighting changed to 2700° K, the picture turned orange.[69]

Rupert Bogan knew in late 1953 that the cameras and film chain were coming. The flying spot film camera arrived the first of April, 1954, and was immediately installed. A few days later Channel 5 signed on with a color test pattern to beat WKY-TV in Oklahoma City, which started color broadcasting on April 8, 1954. Channel 5 broadcast the first local color signal in the nation.

The flying spot camera was a failure. It produced little color, and engineers could not keep it balanced. The camera might have worked better, but there were no quality color films for 35mm slides. Channel 5's two RCA, Model TK-40A color studio cameras arrived on April 23, 1954.[70]

The production crew heard about *Color Day* two weeks earlier. Participating merchants were frantically trying to get color commercial cards made and delivered to the station. *Color Day* for the production staff started when they finished the news the night before. They struck the entire studio of all sets and equipment and then painted the floor rose. This was *color* television.

The staff hung a new cyclorama and changed all lighting equipment. Instead of having the program sets at the far end of the studio, the show used the entire studio. In fact, there was not sufficient room in the studio for all the sets for this program. The staff worked all night, went home the next morning, showered and shaved, changed clothes, and went back to work. When they returned, truckloads of props, supplies, and equipment from merchants were unloaded. The 7-11 Stores brought a large rack completely filled with products. Safeway Stores had another large display with the most colorful items available. Koslow's brought ten models to show their furs. The models had a set and dressing area. Most large local advertisers had some segment in the program, and the staff had to strike and assemble sets during the entire program.[71]

WBAP-TV could not accept the idea of broadcasting color that was not "pretty." An NBC set designer strung roses up the backside of the studio and spent all morning getting the lighting perfect. One area had a red velvet chair, and engineers constantly adjusted the color to be sure it looked like red velvet. The first color camera used dichroic mirrors, which had a tremendous loss of light. In order to bring up blues, the controls had to "knock down" the reds about 75 percent.[72] Cameras had a large number of tubes and were very erratic. Engineers would set a white or black level, and twenty minutes later, every color had changed. Cameras were pointed at chip charts running from black to white through the gray scale. The engineers tried to make every voltage and color response identical to the other. They were constantly raising one reading and lowering another. Two cameras shooting the same object might look identical on red and blue, but green might look green on one camera and cyan on the other.

Black-and-white cameras had advanced so that engineers turned them on forty-five minutes before a show, and five minutes before the cameras were needed, the engineer looked at registration and made a slight adjustment. Color cameras needed constant attention, before and during the program. The color cameras were the last equipment to arrive. On the Friday before *Color Day,* the cameras were in the studio, but cables were missing. They arrived twenty-four hours before the show. That was the first time Channel 5 turned on its cameras. The cameras were heavy. To take a camera off or put it on the dolly, the staff devised a special lift. Four men could not safely lift a camera and put it in place.[73]

Paul Huhndorff, KPRC-TV engineer, saw Rupert Bogan's reaction to that new RCA color camera months earlier at the National Association of Broadcasters convention. "RCA had come out with that monstrous color camera," said Huhndorff. "Looked like a coffin. I remember Rupert standing there in the booth saying, 'You know, that son of a bitch ain't big enough. You can't get enough people around it to pick it up.'"[74]

Bogan worked all night to get the equipment ready. They checked everything possible and then left the equipment on. "Color cameras needed one thousand foot-candles of light," said Bogan. "That would absolutely bake you. We could never get those camera chains to match as far as color balance." The existing

The cameras that helped establish television: WBAP-TV's RCA TK-10A, the predecessor to the TK-11, the workhorse of black-and-white television; and Channel 5's RCA TK-40A, the predecessor to the TK-41, the workhorse of color television. Courtesy KXAS-TV, Fort Worth, Texas

WBAP-TV transmitter had been modified by staff engineers to broadcast color since the new transmitter was not yet installed.[75]

Bob Gould, director of production, received a warning concerning *Color Day:*

> The General [Sarnoff] was there with his entourage and big shots from NBC. They came out to the studio, and we were rehearsing the show without cameras; just a walk through.
>
> This guy comes up to me and said, "Could I give you a piece of advice?"
>
> I said, "Sure, I'm wide open."
>
> He said, "Don't try to do this tomorrow. You're going to fall flat on your face. No color camera has ever worked for three consecutive hours."
>
> I said, "I wish you hadn't told me that, because I'm stupid, we're all stupid, we don't know any better, and so we're going to go ahead with this thing."
>
> He said, "Okay, but don't say that I didn't warn you."[76]

Barry Wood from NBC also warned the staff that the program could not be done; they needed rehearsals. Channel 5 hit the show "cold"; that was the everyday mode of operation. Bob Grammer, director, was accustomed to unrehearsed shows.[77]

At noon on Color Day, three hundred civic leaders, and advertising and media executives from Texas gathered in the Hotel Texas. Amon Carter and Harold Hough accompanied David Sarnoff; Sylvester "Pat" Weaver, Jr., president of NBC; Robert W. Sarnoff, executive vice-president of NBC; Harry Bannister, vice-president of NBC; and Sheldon B. Hickox, director of station relations for NBC. At 3:00 P.M., the luncheon guests adjourned to the Longhorn Room to view the telecast on color receivers.[78] Frank Mills, announcing staff, remembered one crisis:

> About two or three hours before going on the air, one of the cameras went out. Our guys were used to things like this. They didn't get too damn upset about it. NBC personnel like to have had a fit and fell in it. They were running around like crazy. In the first place, they thought we were nuts. We had a three-hour continuous color presentation planned.
>
> "Hell, you can't do that. We only do an hour at a time," the NBC people stated.
>
> Nobody ever told us we couldn't do anything. We would think of something to do, and we did it. These guys were pretty uptight about the idea of being on this long, most of an afternoon. One camera goes out. These NBC guys were running around trying to trouble-shoot this camera; couldn't get it going. Finally, some of our engineers got to work on it, very calmly and deliberately, uncovered the problem, fixed it, and in another fifteen minutes we were on the air. This didn't upset anybody but the NBC representatives. The rest of us; just a matter of course.[79]

Just before 3:00 P.M., Amon Carter and David Sarnoff threw a switch in the Channel 5 studios and initiated color television in Texas. Approximately 125 color sets in the Fort Worth–Dallas area received the program. Most were located at the *Fort Worth Star-Telegram's* Home Show in the Will Rogers Memorial Coliseum and stores participating in the broadcast.[80]

The color program was a series of musical and commercial events. The program had no formal commercials; most of the show was one long commercial. Arman Jones, staff announcer, opened the show, calling it "an historical event." Several times Mel and Katy Dacus sang, giving the staff a chance to change sets. Talent and the master of ceremonies bridged different segments of the program. The production crew stayed on one camera for long periods. Sometimes the director would take a slide while the cameras moved.[81] Bobbie Wygant, production staff, recalled that the staff created techniques as the need arose:

> At one point, one camera just went out. The crew needed to get the working camera from one end of the studio all the way down to the other end. There

was no way to do it without anything to show as you're moving this camera. I told the director, "you've got to get that camera to the other end of the studio—like now."

He said, "I can't move it with the other camera out."

The audio man said, "All you do is blur it, swing it around, get down there, and then have the cameraman pull focus."

It was really a neat trick. It's what we call in the business a "rack focus." Now, "rack focus" is very artistic. We weren't trying to be artistic. It was a means to an end.[82]

Thirty minutes into the show, another camera stopped working. Color cameras would get hot and "jump" registration. It was wheeled over to the side and the engineers worked on it, finally got it repaired, and back into service. As the show progressed, the cameras worked better and better. The staff later discovered that NBC had never had a camera run for three continuous hours because they would run them for short periods and cut them off; when the cameras were turned on later, they would not work.[83]

The *Color Day* program showcased Channel 5's local talent, as listed in *TV Preview*:

Familiar WBAP-TV personalities will be on hand to spice the program with special acts and comments. Margaret McDonald, WBAP home economist; popular announcer Frank Mills; kiddie favorite Bobby Peters; Jimmy Livingston and The Imperial Quartet; newsman Lillard Hill; Farm Editor "Doc" Ruhmann; weatherman Bob Denny—all will make their first color appearance. Dancers Beverly Thompson and Dwane Martin have created special routines just for *Color Day*, and they'll be backed by the show's twelve-piece orchestra. Production numbers range from a "Gay Nineties" opener to a full modern teen-age review.[84]

While a show with, at times, only one camera did not thrill the NBC people, it thrilled the Channel 5 staff because they accomplished what they had planned. The show was continuous for three hours and fifteen minutes, with no glaring errors. All this was done with one walk-through without cameras. The colorcast was like productions had been when the station had first begun broadcasting. Nobody knew what they were doing, so how could they do it wrong?

After the show, NBC personnel were friendly and highly complimentary. They bragged that their cameras had set a new record. The color from the equipment was good, and the network personnel did not criticize the show's content. Channel 5's production crew was not yet finished for the day. They had to get the studio ready for black-and-white operations that evening. *Color Day* had been *the longest continuous color program ever broadcast.*[85]

Over the next year, Channel 5 added more and more color programming. The October, 1955, issue of *Color TV News* proclaimed WBAP-TV "the local color leader." Channel 5 was averaging ten hours of color programming each week. By comparison, WBAL-TV in Baltimore colorcast a half-hour movie each Sunday. WWJ-TV in Detroit broadcast all NBC color programs. In 1954 Channel 5 broadcast 154 hours of local color; 427 in 1955. At times, WBAP-TV broadcast more hours of color programming per week than NBC. On May 7, 1955, Channel 5 broadcast one full day of color.[86]

Network Sharing

Network sharing between WBAP and WFAA in Dallas, which began with radio, carried over into television. The arrangement provided that a television station would get NBC television programming during the times its sister radio station was on 820 kilocycles, the NBC radio network. When the radio station was on 570 kilocycles, the ABC radio network, its television station broadcast ABC pro-

The original studio of WBAP-TV, the first facilities in the nation especially built for television, shown in the 1950s with black-and-white and color cameras in use. Courtesy KXAS-TV, Fort Worth, Texas

WBAP-TV color studio production with announcer Frank Mills standing under the microphone. Courtesy KXAS-TV, Fort Worth, Texas

gramming. Trouble developed when a program started on WBAP-TV's time and ran into WFAA-TV's time, or vice versa. One major conflict was over *The Mickey Mouse Club* on ABC. Whether a station would have or not have a popular television show depended on what time it started.[87] This arrangement was inconvenient for both stations. According to Johnny Smith, WBAP-TV engineer, the decision to end it was made by NBC:

> In 1957 WFAA-TV decided to take NBC away from WBAP-TV. Channel 8 approached the big advertising agencies throughout the country and tried to convince them that the Dallas market was the big money; NBC should be exclusively Dallas, and Fort Worth should be dropped. WFAA-TV personnel approached NBC, declaring that if NBC did not drop WBAP-TV and put the network exclusively with WFAA-TV, sponsors would drop their advertising. [Harold] Hough heard of the maneuvering, picked up the phone, and called [David] Sarnoff. "I need to talk to you here in the next couple of days. Why don't you and Ruby come down and spend the weekend with us, and we'll sit around and talk about old times."

Hough, [Amon] Carter, and Sarnoff were on a first-name basis. They knew each other's grandchildren and sent presents every Christmas. During the weekend, Hough told Sarnoff what WFAA-TV was doing, how the two stations had agreed to share, they had been getting along fine, and that Channel 8 had now decided to eliminate Channel 5.[88]

Jack McGrew heard of the decision at KPRC-TV in Houston:

Alex Keese made one really big mistake. In fact, it cost him the affiliation. WFAA and WBAP were sharing time on television and two different radio frequencies. KRLD-TV [CBS] in Dallas was driving them crazy. Alex met with officials of the *Dallas News,* and they decided that they would make an exclusive arrangement with NBC. Alex went to New York City, went by ABC, and explained that they had made this decision. They had looked at the two networks, and they wanted to go with NBC.

The network [ABC] guy said, "OK, Alex, I understand. We wish you well. We enjoyed having you with the network. We understand your situation. You go ahead."

Alex went to NBC and told them, "We're happy to tell you that we have decided to make an exclusive arrangement with NBC."

The man at NBC said, "I'm sorry, Alex. We came to the same conclusion some time ago and we decided that we're going to stay with WBAP."

Alex said, "For heaven sakes, why? We've got the bigger market."

The guy said, "Alex, we've been looking at the record. You have pre-empted more network programming than any network station that we have. WBAP has carried everything we have ever offered."

So Alex had to go back and throw his hat in the door at ABC and say, "Can I come back with you?"[89]

Curly Broyles, who worked in the mail room at WBAP-TV, was Harold Hough's driver. One trip he remembered was to Love Field in Dallas:

I didn't have any idea what the deal was. We were almost to Love Field and Hough said, "What you see today I want you to forget." At that time, WFAA and WBAP were sharing the frequencies on radio, and when they got into television they continued to do that; which was a nightmare.

At Love Field I saw Harry Bannister, vice-president of NBC, getting off the airplane. Harold Hough said, "Harry and I are going up to the Admiral's Club. I don't know how long we will be there. I hate to have you wait, but just wait until we come down."

Harold V. Hough, "dean of American broadcasters."
Courtesy KXAS-TV, Fort Worth, Texas

That was the day Bannister told them, "You are going to have all of NBC."[90]

A letter terminating the affiliation between NBC and WFAA-TV was mailed to the Dallas station on July 10, 1957. The reason stated by Harry Bannister was that the two stations covered the same area, and the broadcasting of the same NBC programs over both stations would not be in the interest of efficient service to the public.[91]

• • •

The Dean of American Broadcasters

Of all the people who contributed to the history and evolution of broadcasting in Texas, one individual from Texas was selected by his peers to receive a special honor. Harold V. Hough started WBAP in 1922 as a 10-watt radio station, one of the first in Texas and the United States; was WBAP's first announcer and radio personality as "The Hired Hand"; was active in the National Association of Broadcasters (NAB) from its inception; started television in Texas by building WBAP-TV, the first television station south of St. Louis and east of Los Angeles; pioneered color television at the local level; and managed, directed, and motivated both radio and television stations since 1922. At the annual convention of the National Association of Broadcasters in 1963, Hough was named "Dean of American Broadcasters."

Notes

Chapter 1. Pre-Regulation Broadcasting:
The Beginnings to 1927

1. "Powerful Plant Is Completed by News and Journal," *Dallas Morning News and Journal,* undated article, 1922, Texas/Dallas History and Archives.
2. Mary Frazer, "A Life in Radio Broadcasting by a Gypsy Fortune Teller," *Houston Press,* Jan. 13, 1948.
3. "A&M 'Hams' Were First to Air Gridiron Battle," *Texas Aggie,* Dec. 22, 1950.
4. Jerry Flemmons, *AMON: The Life of Amon Carter, Sr. of Texas,* pp. 156–57.
5. Newspaper clip note, Louise Kelly Collection.
6. "Radio's Birth 100 Years Ago," *Fort Worth Star-Telegram,* Oct. 30, 1949; Elliot N. Sivowitch, "A Technological Survey of Broadcasting's 'Pre-History,' 1876–1920," *Journal of Broadcasting* 15, no. 1 (Winter, 1970–71): 1–8.
7. Erik Barnouw, *A Tower in Babel,* pp. 19–36.
8. Sivowitch, "Technological Survey," pp. 16–17.
9. Barnouw, *Tower,* pp. 56–111.
10. Ric Jensen, "The History of Campus Radio at Texas A & M," Feb. 29, 1984, Special Collections, Manuscripts & Archives, Sterling C. Evans Library, Texas A&M University, College Station.
11. Cosimo Lucchese, "Watt's Becoming of Us?" *Listen,* Dec., 1978, p. 8; "KUT-FM's," undated article, files of Wendell Mayes.
12. Frazer, "A Life in Radio."
13. Jack McGrew, interview with author, typewritten notes, in author's possession, Marble Falls, Oct. 1, 1994.
14. Frazer, "A Life in Radio."
15. Spencer, John Morgan, "An Intensive History of Broadcast Station KBGO, Waco, Texas" (master's thesis, Michigan State University, 1974), p. 14, citing William Penn Clarke, 1971.
16. Robin Leslie Sacks, "A History of Station WRR: Pioneer in Municipally Owned Radio" (master's thesis, North Texas State University, 1978), pp. 15–20.
17. Department of Commerce, Bureau of Navigation, *Radio Service,* 1922, pp. 135–45. Note: Subsequent references will be listed as DOC.
18. Sacks, "History of Station WRR," pp. 18–20.
19. "WRR Logs," 1925, WRR Collection, Center for American History, University of Texas, Austin.
20. Molly B. Mimms, ed., *The History of Johnson County, Texas,* pp. 190–92.
21. Sacks, "History of Station WRR," pp. 21–24.

22. DOC, 1922, pp. 70–78.
23. Ibid., compiled from *Radio Service* reports for 1922 through 1927.
24. "Daily News Radio Program Is Given from WDAG Station," *Amarillo Daily News,* June 1, 1923; "Powerful Radio Station Is Plan," *Amarillo Daily News,* Sept. 17, 1926; "WDAG Station Becomes New Organization," *Amarillo Daily News,* Jan. 29, 1928.
25. Ray Davis Hollingsworth, taped interview at the Southwest Collection, Texas Tech University, Lubbock, Texas.
26. Stan McKenzie, interview by author, typewritten notes, in author's possession, Seguin, Nov. 15, 1994.
27. Hollingsworth, interview.
28. "UT Radiocasts Started in 1921," *Daily Texas,* Nov. 9, 1958.
29. "KUT-FM's"; "KNOW," undated history, files of Wendell Mayes; "UT Radiocasts."
30. Jay Elson, "How It All Began," *Austin,* Dec., 1956, pp. 4–5; "Broadcast Pro-File (KUT)," p. 1, files of Wendell Mayes.
31. Elson, "How It All Began," pp. 4–5; "Broadcast Pro-File (KUT)," pp. 1–2.
32. "KFDM's First Program 'A Winner,'" *Magpetco,* Oct., 1924, p. 7.
33. "Program Broadcast by Magnolia Band March 1st Was Very Succesful [*sic*]," *Magpetco,* March, 1924, p. 12.
34. Jack McGrew, "Broadcasting the News," p. 2, files of Jack McGrew.
35. "KFDM History," pp. 56–58, Tyrrell Historical Society Library, Beaumont, Texas.
36. McGrew, "Broadcasting the News," p. 2.
37. Ibid.
38. "KFDM Stages Birthday Party," *Magpetco,* Oct. 1925, p. 6.
39. McGrew, interview.
40. F. K. Matejka–K5RS and H. M. Saunders–K40M, "First Broadcast of a Football Game by Radio," p. 1, Special Collections, Manuscripts & Archives, Sterling C. Evans Library, Texas A&M University, College Station; W. A. Tolson, "First College Football Broadcast Texas A&M–University of Texas, November 25, 1920," p. 2, Special Collections, Manuscripts & Archives, Sterling C. Evans Library, Texas A&M University, College Station; Frank Matejka, "The First Football Game Broadcast, Texas A&M vs Texas University. November 24, 1921," Feb., 1980, pp. 1–2, Special Collections, Manuscripts & Archives, Sterling C. Evans Library, Texas A&M University, College Station.
41. Matejka and Saunders, "First Broadcast," pp. 4–5.
42. "A&M 'Hams'"; Matejka and Saunders, "First Broadcast," pp. 6–7; Jensen, "A History of Campus," p. 3; Matejka and Saunders, "First Broadcast," pp. 6–7.
43. "William A. Tolson, Native San Angeloan, Was One of Modern Pioneers Recently Paid Tribute," unpublished history, 1940, Special Collections, Manuscripts & Archives, Sterling C. Evans Library, Texas A&M University, College Station.
44. Weldon K. Jeffus, interview by author, typewritten notes, in author's possession, Dallas, Feb. 22, 1995.
45. "Powerful Plant," p. 11.
46. "Counting Stars and Kilocycles. 25th Anniversary, WFAA, Dallas," 1947, p. 3, Special Collections, Sam Rayburn Library, Texas A&M–Commerce, Commerce, Texas.
47. "Counting Stars," pp. 3–7.
48. Jeffus, interview.
49. "Counting Stars," pp. 5–9.

50. "Station WFAA," schedule for Station WFAA, June 26, 1922, A. H. Belo Corporation Company History and Archives, Dallas, Texas.

51. "Powerful Plant," p. 11; "Wireless Wedding Is Performed by Aid of 3 Stations," *Dallas Morning News and Journal,* June 29, 1922.

52. "Powerful Plant," p. 11.

53. "Counting Stars," pp. 7–24.

54. "Robert Z. Glass—A Radio and Communications Pioneer," April 21, 1993, Special Collections, Manuscripts & Archives, Sterling C. Evans Library, Texas A&M University, College Station, Texas.

55. John Phelan, "Tribute to Karl Otto Wyler," *Password,* Spring, 1987, p. 21; Loretta Overton, "Radio Executive Recalls Early Years," *El Paso Herald-Port,* Aug. 21, 1964.

56. "'Karl the Kowhand' Looks Back on Crystal Set Start of Radio in E. P. 31 Years Ago," *El Paso Herald-Post,* Aug. 22, 1952; Overton, "Radio Executive."

57. "Broadcast Pro-file (KTSM)," files of KTSM, El Paso; "'Karl the Kowhand.'"

58. Overton, "Radio Executive"; Karl Wyler, "KTSM Gossip," *El Paso Herald,* Nov. 30, 1929.

59. "'Heard in Poly'—That was News!" *Fort Worth,* Feb., 1947, p. 14.

60. Ibid.

61. "Remember KFQB—It was a Forerunner of KFJZ," *Fort Worth,* Feb., 1947, p. 22.

62. "'We'll Spend But $300' and WBAP Was Begun; Hoover Named Station," *Fort Worth Star-Telegram,* Oct. 30, 1949.

63. Flemmons, *AMON,* pp. 156–57; Mabey, "History of WBAP-TV," pp. 1–2, files of WBAP; "'We'll Spend But $300.'"

64. Mabey, "History of WBAP-TV," pp. 1–2; "'We'll Spend But $300'"; Abe Herman, interview by author, typewritten notes, in author's possession, Fort Worth, Sept. 14, 1982; "WBAP's 30th Anniversary Birthday Causes Radio, TV Director to Look Back, Chuckle," *Fort Worth Star-Telegram,* undated article, 1952, files of WBAP.

65. Author's remembrance.

66. Roy Bacus, interview by author, typewritten notes, in author's possession, Fort Worth Sept. 2, 1982; G. C. Arnoux, "It's Here! WBAP, the Star-Telegram's New 500 Watt Radio Station," *Fort Worth Star-Telegram,* undated article, 1922, Carter Collection.

67. Winston Sparks, interview by author, typewritten notes, in author's possession, Fort Worth, Dec. 23, 1996.

68. "'We'll Spend But $300.'"

69. Flemmons, *AMON,* pp. 158–59; Mabey, "History of WBAP-TV," p. 2.

70. Chem Terry, interview by author, typewritten notes, in author's possession, Fort Worth, May 25, 1994; "'We'll Spend But $300.'"

71. Bud Sherman, ed., *Baseball Broadcasting,* April, 1951, pp. 1–6.

72. Ibid.

73. J. R. Curtis, interview by author, typewritten notes, in author's possession, Longview, June 23, 1994.

74. "KFJZ Grew Big from War I Baby," *Fort Worth,* Feb., 1947, pp. 9–10.

75. David Naugle, interview by author, typewritten notes, in author's possession, Fort Worth, June 7, 1994.

76. "KFJZ Grew Big," pp. 9–10.

77. W. Walworth Harrison, *History of Greenville and Hunt County, Texas,* pp. 293–94.

78. Leo Hackney, interview by author, typewritten notes, in author's possession, Greenville, June 9, 1994.

79. Jeffus, interview.

80. Ibid.

81. DOC., 1922, pp. 70–78.

82. Frazer, "A Life in Radio"; David Westheimer, "First Performer Tells of Initial Broadcast," *Houston Post,* Feb. 21, 1955.

83. "*Post's* Daily Radio Concert Wins Praise from Many Stations," *Houston Post-Dispatch,* May 20, 1922.

84. "WEAY Is First," p. 1, undated article, 1922, Texas Room, Houston Public Library, Houston.

95. DOC., 1922, pp. 70–78; ibid., 1924, pp. 68–71; "First Radio Station Here Was WCAK," *Houston Press,* May 9, 1961.

86. "Impressive Array of Talent on Hand When Program is Broadcast," *Houston Post-Dispatch,* 1925, undated from the Texas Room.

87. Frazer, "A Life in Radio."

88. "Impressive Array."

89. "From Small Beginnings . . . ," *Houston Post,* March 21, 1972.

90. "Jack McGrew," files of Jack McGrew.

91. "Advertiser's Prizes Night Is Success," *Houston Post-Dispatch,* undated article, 1926, Texas Room, Houston Public Library, Houston; "Write a Radiogram Win a Prize," *Houston Post-Dispatch,* March 9, 1926.

92. Hoxie Mundine, interview by author, typewritten notes, in author's possession, San Antonio, Oct. 5, 1994.

93. "Revised Schedule for Broadcasting," *San Antonio Express,* Sept. 25, 1922.

94. Ibid.

95. Mundine, interview.

96. "Messages Can Be Heard from Atlantic to Pacific Starting at 10:30 This Morning," *San Antonio Express,* Sept. 24, 1922; Carolyn Elliott, "Movies Take Time Out for 'Amos 'n' Andy,'" *San Antonio Light,* June 25, 1978.

97. Mundine, interview.

98. Eugene J. Roth, interview by author, typewritten notes, in author's possession, San Antonio, Oct. 3, 1994.

99. Elliott, "Movies Take Time Out."

100. Roth, interview.

101. George Ing, interview by author, typewritten notes, in author's possession, San Antonio, Oct. 5, 1994.

102. Roth, interview.

103. Mundine, interview.

104. Ibid.

105. "Broadcast Pro-File (KNOW)," files of Wendell Mayes.

106. "Ham Radio Operator Brought First Football, Weather Reports," *Waco Times-Herald,* March 25, 1960; Spencer, "Intensive History," p. 14, citing William Penn Clarke, 1971.

107. Ibid.

108. Bob Darden, "WACO Marks 60 Years on the Air," *Waco Tribune-Herald,* July 25, 1982.

109. Spencer, "Intensive History," pp. 15–16, citing William C. Tinus, 1971.

110. Ibid., "Intensive History," pp. 16–17, citing Elfrieda Jackson; ibid., pp. 38–39, citing Tinus.

111. Jack Holliday, interview by author, typewritten notes, in author's possession, Farmers Branch, May 3, 1994.

112. "Broadcast Pro-File (WACO)," files of Robert Weathers; Spencer, "Intensive History," p. 17.

113. Frazer, "A Life in Radio."

114. Ted Bender, interview by author, typewritten notes, in author's possession, El Paso, Mar. 29, 1997.

115. McGrew, interview.

116. Terry, interview.

117. Mundine, interview.

118. Roger Dickey, interview by author, typewritten notes, in author's possession, Grand Prairie, May 5, 1994.

119. J. R. Cruse, interview by author, typewritten notes, in author's possession, Aledo, June 22, 1994.

120. Claude Goode, interview by author, typewritten notes, in author's possession, Greenville, May 16, 1994.

121. Stan Wilson, interview by author, typewritten notes, in author's possession, Fort Worth, July 6, 1994.

122. Goode, interview.

123. McGrew, interview.

124. Dickey, interview.

125. Ing, interview.

126. Mundine, interview.

127. Dickey, interview; Jack Romey, letter to author.

Chapter 2. Regulations Come to Broadcasting: 1928 to 1939

1. Charles Townsend, *San Antonio Rose,* 1976, p. 68.

2. Ansel Harlan Resler, "The Impact of John R. Brinkley on Broadcasting in the U.S." (Ph.D. diss., Northwestern University, 1958), p. 97.

3. McGrew, interview.

4. Barnouw, *Tower,* pp. 180–97; ibid., p. 190.

5. Ibid., p. 199.

6. "Revised List of Broadcasting Stations," *Report of the Federal Radio Commission,* 1928, pp. 200–214.

7. Ibid.

8. "For the Federal Communications Commission, Frequency and Power Changes 1922 to 1946," undated article, Carter Collection.

9. Jim Byron, interview by author, typewritten notes, in author's possession, Fort Worth, July, 1974.

10. "Time Division Between WBAP, Carter Publications, Inc., and WFAA, Dallas News and Journal," June 28, 1931, and June 30, 1931, Carter Collection.

11. "WRR and WFAA Consolidate under WFAA Management by Order of the City Commission," *Dallas Morning News,* Nov. 21, 1928.

12. Herman, interview; James David Pratt, "A Micro Study of Television News at the Local Level: Television Station, WBAP-TV, Fort Worth-Dallas; Television News Director, James A. Byron; Television Newscast, 'The Texas News'; Each a First in Texas" (Ph.D. diss., University of Texas at Austin, 1981), p. 28; Herman, interview.

13. "City's First Radio Founded in 1926," *Wichita Daily Times,* Sept. 9, 1928; DOC, 1928; "2 Radio Stations Will Exchange Frequencies," *Fort Worth Star-Telegram,* June 20, 1935.

14. Frank Mills, interview by author, typewritten notes, in author's possession, Fort Worth, Oct. 30, 1982.

15. Bob Hicks, interview by author, typewritten notes, in author's possession, Midland, Mar. 28, 1997.

16. Mills, interview.

17. Ibid.

18. Pratt, "A Micro Study," pp. 30–33.

19. Herman, interview.

20. Pratt, "A Micro Study," pp. 32–33.

21. Mills, interview.

22. Byron, interview.

23. Pratt, "A Micro Study," pp. 33–35; list of radio stations carrying the KGKO dedication program, June 13, 1938, from the Carter Collection.

24. Mabey, "History of WBAP-TV," pp. 1–4; Pratt, "Micro Study," pp. 34–35.

25. Terry, interview.

26. Clarence Bruyere, interview by author, typewritten notes, in author's possession, Dallas, Feb. 28, 1995.

27. David Naugle, interview by author, typewritten notes, in author's possession, Fort Worth, June 7, 1994.

28. Alex Burton, interview by author, typewritten notes, in author's possession, Dallas, Feb. 19, 1994.

29. Terry, interview.

30. Denson Walker, material sent to author.

31. Pratt, "Micro Study," pp. 37–38.

32. Edwin L. Glick, "WBAP/WFAA—570/820: Till Money Did Them Part," *Journal of Broadcasting* 21, no. 4 (Fall, 1977): 476–77.

33. Ibid., p. 477.

34. Herman, interview.

35. Glick, "WBAP/WFAA," p. 478.

36. Ibid., pp. 476, 483–84.

37. Frank Parrish, interview by author, typewritten notes, in author's possession, Fort Worth, Apr. 29, 1994.

38. Ibid.

39. Johnny Smith (KFJZ), interview by author, typewritten notes, in author's possession, Fort Worth, July 6, 1994. Two Johnny Smiths were interviewed for this book: Johnny Smith who worked for radio station KFJZ in Fort Worth will be referred to as Smith (KFJZ).

40. Ing, interview.

41. Ibid.

42. Terry, interview.

43. Ing, interview.

44. Cruse, interview.

45. Paul Huhndorff, interview by author, typewritten notes, in author's possession, Houston, Sept. 9, 1994.

46. McKenzie, interview.

47. Cruse, interview.

48. Bill Bradford, interview by author, typewritten notes, in author's possession, Sulphur Springs, Feb. 21, 1994.

49. Cruse, interview.

50. Bradford, interview.

51. Parrish, interview.

52. Ing, interview.

53. McGrew, interview.

54. Bradford, interview.

55. Ing, interview; Bradford, interview; McGrew, interview.

56. Ves Box, interview by author, typewritten notes, in author's possession, Dallas, May 4, 1994.

57. Burton, interview.

58. Mundine, interview.

59. "Station to Have Large Variety of Transcriptions for KPLT Programs," *Paris News,* Dec. 13, 1936.

60. Wendell Mayes, interview by author, typewritten notes, in author's possession, Austin, Oct. 4, 1994.

61. Mundine, interview.

62. Burton, interview.

63. Ing, interview; Cruse, interview; McGrew, interview.

64. Bender, interview.

65. Romey letter.

66. Gene Fowler and Bill Crawford, *Border Radio,* 1987, pp. 104–107; "WEAY," undated article, Texas Room, Houston Public Library, Houston.

67. Fowler and Crawford, *Border Radio,* pp. 107–13.

68. Hicks, interview.

69. J. C. Furnas, "Country Doctor Goes to Town," *Saturday Evening Post,* April 20, 1940, pp. 12, 50; Fowler and Crawford, *Border Radio,* p. 15.

70. Fowler and Crawford, *Border Radio,* p. 16; Furnas, "Country Doctor," pp. 12, 50; Resler, "Impact," p. 97.

71. Fowler and Crawford, *Border Radio,* p. 16.

72. Resler, "Impact," pp. 63, 97; Fowler and Crawford, *Border Radio,* p. 17.

73. Resler, "Impact," p. 65.

74. Ibid., p. 66; Fowler and Crawford, *Border Radio,* pp. 19–21.

75. Resler, "Impact," p. 82.

76. Furnas, "Country Doctor," p. 13; Resler, "Impact," p. 84.

77. Fowler and Crawford, *Border Radio,* pp. 24–29.

78. Darrell Yates, interview by author, typewritten notes, in author's possession, Lufkin, Sept. 6. 1994.

79. Goode, interview.

80. Furnas, "Country Doctor," pp. 12–50.
81. Resler, "Impact," pp. 116, 154–55.
82. Fowler and Crawford, *Border Radio,* pp. 195–98.
83. Ibid., pp. 59–62.
84. Ibid., pp. 62–67, 72.
85. Westbrook Pegler, "It Seems to Me," *Fort Worth Press,* Jan. 3, 1946.
86. McGrew, interview.
87. Fowler and Crawford, *Border Radio,* pp. 79–95; "Norris Turned to Radio to Spread Religion Afar," *Fort Worth Star-Telegram,* Oct. 30, 1949.
88. Fowler and Crawford, *Border Radio,* pp. 93–95.
89. Ibid., pp. 110, 177, 182.
90. Bruyere, interview.
91. Jeffus, interview.
92. Yates, interview.
93. Mayes, interview.
94. Roth, interview.
95. Ing, interview.
96. McGrew, interview.
97. F. Leslie Smith, *Perspectives on Radio and Television,* p. 23.
98. Ibid., pp. 23–24.
99. Ibid., p. 24.
100. Ibid., pp. 24–26.
101. Barnouw, *Tower,* p. 146.
102. "In the Air with KFDM During the Past Magpetco Year," *Magpetco,* April, 1928, pp. 7, 54; "On the Air with KFDM," *Magpetco,* Oct. 1927, p. 9.
103. "In the Air," p. 7.
104. List compiled by the author.
105. "Southwest Network Appoints Chilton," *Broadcasting* 5, no. 6 (Sept. 15, 1933): 8.
106. "Texas Net Formed," *Broadcasting* 7, no. 6 (Sept. 15, 1934), p. 58.
107. "Texas Account Extended," *Broadcasting* 6, no. 2 (Jan. 15, 1934), p. 12.
108. Martin Campbell, interview by author, typewritten notes, in author's possession, Dallas, July, 1974.
109. Townsend, *San Antonio Rose,* p. 68; Fowler and Crawford, *Border Radio,* p. 117; Townsend, *San Antonio Rose,* pp. 68–70.
110. Marvin Montgomery, interview by author, typewritten notes, in author's possession, Dallas, Aug. 16, 1994.
111. Townsend, *San Antonio Rose,* pp. 69–70.
112. Ibid., pp. 72–78.
113. Montgomery, interview.
114. Mundine, interview.
115. Herman, interview.
116. McGrew, interview.
117. "15 Sponsors Signed by Texas Quality," *Broadcasting* 9, no. 7 (Oct. 1, 1935), p. 18.
118. "Dr Pepper Soft-Drink Series on TQN Spread to 17 Stations," *Broadcasting* 10, no. 7 (April 1, 1936), p. 16.
119. Montgomery, interview.

120. Ibid.

121. Ibid.

122. Morrell Ratcliffe, interview by author, typewritten notes, in author's possession, Dallas, July, 1974.

123. Ibid.

124. "Humble Oil Sponsoring Football in Southwest," *Broadcasting* 9, no. 7 (Oct. 1, 1935), p. 26.

125. McKenzie, interview.

126. Box, interview.

127. Ibid.

128. McKenzie, interview.

129. Box, interview.

130. McKenzie, interview.

131. Clyde Melville, interview by author, typewritten notes, in author's possession, Dallas, July, 1974.

132. "New Texas Network," *Broadcasting* 17, no. 1 (July 1, 1939), p. 84.

133. Herman, interview.

134. "KFJZ Purchase Is Authorized," *Fort Worth Star-Telegram,* April 15, 1938; Albert Dean Angel, "'For What It's Worth—Nothing': Study of the Texas State Network" (Masters thesis, North Texas State University, 1970), p. 16.

135. Pete Teddlie, interview by author, typewritten notes, in author's possession, Dallas, Sept. 21, 1994.

136. Angel, "'For What It's Worth,'" p. 17.

137. Ibid., pp. 20–22.

138. Jeffus, interview.

139. "All 31 Texas Stations Carry Roosevelt Words to Texas," *Fort Worth Star-Telegram,* July 11, 1938.

140. Cruse, interview.

141. Helen Wombolt, interview by author, typewritten notes, in author's possession, Dallas, July, 1974.

142. Wilson, interview.

143. Naugle, interview.

144. Wilson, interview.

145. Naugle, interview.

146. Jim Lowe, interview by author, typewritten notes, in author's possession, Dallas, Aug. 3, 1994.

147. Naugle, interview.

148. Wilson, interview.

149. Naugle, interview.

150. Wilson, interview.

151. Terry, interview.

152. Ibid.

153. Publicity release, undated, Pan Handle Museum, Canyon, Tex.; Overton, "Radio Executive."

154. Author's files; McGrew, interview.

155. A. Earl Cullum, interview by author, typewritten notes, in author's possession, Dallas, July, 1974.

156. Bruyere, interview; McGrew, interview.

157. Julian Stag, "The Dallas/Fort Worth Radio Market," *Broadcasting* 34, no. 23 (June 7, 1948), p. 16; Bev E. Brown, interview by author, typewritten notes, in author's possession, Carthage, June 6, 1994.

158. Smith, interview; Naugle, interview; Terry, interview; Mills, interview; Dave Morris, interview by author, typewritten notes, in author's possession, Houston, Sept. 7, 1994; and Teddlie, interview.

159. McGrew, interview.

160. Wilson, interview.

161. Naugle, interview; Mundine, interview.

162. Lucchese, "Watt's Becoming," p. 8.

163. "San Antonio—Life in the Raw," pp. 22–25, undated article, files of George Ing; George Ing, "So You Want to be a Cop," 1978, undated article, files of George Ing.

164. Naugle, interview.

165. "Norris Turned to Radio"; Lowe, interview.

166. Ibid.

167. Smith (KFJZ), interview.

168. Richard Pryor, interview by author, typewritten notes, in author's possession, Austin, Oct. 4, 1994.

169. "Campaign Network Formed in Texas," *Broadcasting* 15, no. 6 (March 15, 1938), p. 20; "Southwest Ford Dealers Use 3-Station Hookup in New Radio Campaign," *Broadcasting* 5, no. 6 (Sept. 15, 1933), p. 13; List of Networks, *Broadcasting* 35, no. 3 (1949 yearbook), p. 319; "Enlarged Southwest Net Issues 1935 Rate Card," *Broadcasting* 8, no. 3 (Feb. 1, 1935), p. 39.

170. "Plans for 43-Station FM Network in Texas Given at Austin Radio Forum," *Broadcasting* 31, no. 9 (Sept. 2, 1946), p. 62; "Collegiate System," *Broadcasting* 38, no. 16 (1950), p. 48; "11 FM Grants," *Broadcasting* 34, no. 20 (May 17, 1948), p. 51.

171. "Concealed Control Cited in Revoking 6 Texas Stations," *Broadcasting* 18, no. 4 (Feb. 15, 1940), p. 12.

172. McGrew, interview.

173. J. Evetts Haley, *A Texan Looks at Lyndon,* p. 65.

174. Brown, interview.

Chapter 3. The War and Television: 1941 to 1950

1. "Southwest's First Television Station, W5AGO, Goes on Air," *Fort Worth Star-Telegram,* March 10, 1934; Mills, interview.

2. Mills, interview.

3. Byron, interview.

4. Naugle, interview.

5. Mills, interview; Anne Lee, "Women in Radio Field Do Fine Job," *Fort Worth Star-Telegram,* Oct. 3, 1943; Earl McDonald, interview by author, typewritten notes, in author's possession, Dallas, July 28, 1995.

6. Box, interview.

7. Bradford, interview.

8. Ibid.

9. Erik Barnouw, *The Golden Web,* pp. 40–42, 129–30, 242–43.

10. Stag, "Dallas/Fort Worth," p. 10.

11. "Times FM Radio Station to Go on Air Monday," *Wichita (Falls, Texas) Daily Times,* Dec. 22, 1946.

12. "El Paso FM Growing," *El Paso Today,* Aug. 1, 1962; Robert Halpern, "KVOF Broadcast Voice of Freedom," *Prospector,* Sept. 2, 1980.

13. "News to 'Print' Paper by Radio," *Fort Worth Star-Telegram,* July 27, 1939.

14. "KVET Founders Recalled," *Austin American Statesman,* Oct. 1, 1966.

15. Wes Wise, interview by author, typewritten notes, in author's possession, Arlington, Mar. 2, 1994.

16. Jack Bell, interview by author, typewritten notes, in author's possession, Center, June 28, 1994.

17. Bell, interview; Brown, interview.

18. McGrew, interview.

19. McKenzie, interview.

20. Ibid.

21. Terry, interview.

22. Hicks, interview.

23. Lowe, interview.

24. Terry, interview; Joe Nick Patoski, "Rock 'N' Roll's Wizard of Oz," *Texas Monthly* 8 (Feb., 1980), p. 103; "McLendon," *Dallas Times-Herald,* Sept. 15, 1986.

25. Edwin L. Glick, "The Life and Death of the Liberty Broadcasting System," *Journal of Broadcasting* 23, no. 2 (Spring, 1979): pp. 117–18; Wise, interview; Glick, "The Life," pp. 117–18.

26. Glick, "The Life," p. 118; Jim Harper, "Gordon McLendon: Pioneer Baseball Broadcaster," *Baseball History* (Spring, 1986), p. 45.

27. "Gordon McLendon," *Radio and Records* (1977), pp. 22–24, Southwest Collection.

28. Wise, interview.

29. Glick, "Life and Death," p. 120; "Gordon McLendon," pp. 22–24.

30. Harper, "Gordon McLendon," p. 47.

31. "Gordon McLendon," pp. 22–24; Glick, "Life and Death," p. 119.

32. Wise, interview.

33. Ibid.

34. "Gordon McLendon," pp. 22–24; Harper, "Gordon McLendon," p. 47.

35. Glick, "Life and Death," pp. 123-124.

36. Harper, "Gordon McLendon," p. 48.

37. "Gordon McLendon," pp. 22–24.

38. Patoski, "Rock 'N' Roll's," p. 104.

39. Ibid., p. 169.

40. Wise, interview.

41. Barnouw, *Tower,* p. 7; Michael Winship, *Television,* p. 4.

42. Winship, *Television,* pp. 4, 6.

43. "Historic Television," *Old-Timer's Bulletin* 26, no. 3 (Dec. 1985), p. 32; Peter Yanczer, "Radio Movies," *Old-Timer's Bulletin* 28, no. 2 (Aug. 1987), pp. 8–9.

44. DOC., 1928, p. 252; Winship, *Television,* p. 4.

45. "Don Lee's KTSL (TV) Marks 18 Years in Television," *Telefiles,* undated article, files of WBAP.

46. "Television Gives Hollywood," 1937, press release from the National Broadcasting Company mailed to network radio affiliates, in the possession of Guy Woodward, mailroom supervisor (retired), WBAP-TV.

47. "Southwest's First."

48. Jack Gordon, "First Television Shown Here 14 Years Ago," *Fort Worth Press,* Sept. 10, 1948; "Southwest's First."

49. Ellen Prestidge, letter to author, July 12, 1993.

50. Gordon, "First Television"; "Southwest's First."

51. Smith (KFJZ), interview.

52. Cruse, interview.

53. Sparks, interview.

54. Gordon, "First Television."

55. Lawrence Birdsong, interview by author, typewritten notes, in author's possession, Longview, Feb. 19, 1996.

56. Ing, interview.

57. McGrew, interview.

58. Rupert Bogan, interview by author, typewritten notes, in author's possession, Pottsboro, Feb. 16, 1983.

59. Herman, interview.

60. Jack Harris, Paul Huhndorff, and Jack McGrew, *The Fault Does Not Lie With Your Set,* 1989, pp. 5–6.

61. Harold Hough, "Growth & Management," 1955, Carter Collection.

62. Herman, interview; Pratt, "Micro Study," p. 56; Herman, interview.

63. Hough, "Growth."

64. Herman, interview.

65. Robert Gould, interview by author, typewritten notes, in author's possession, Fort Worth, Sept. 16, 1982.

66. Pratt, "Micro Study," pp. 56–57.

67. Television application by Interstate Circuit, Inc., from the Interstate Collection, Texas/Dallas History and Archives Division, Dallas Public Library, Dallas, Texas.

68. Wuntch, Philip, "Wilshire Rings Down Curtain on Final Movie," *Dallas Morning News,* April 24, 1978.

69. "Television Withdrawals at 57; Dropouts Cancel Hearings," *Broadcasting,* May 13, 1946, p. 93; Herman, interview.

70. Bruyere, interview.

71. McGrew, interview.

72. "Permit Given for Television Station Here," *Fort Worth Star-Telegram,* June 22, 1946.

73. Hough, "Growth"; Bogan, interview.

74. Pratt, "Micro Study," p. 56.

75. Herman, interview.

76. Hough, "Growth"; Flemmons, *AMON,* p. 160; Herman, interview; Hough, "Growth."

77. Johnny Smith (WBAP), interview by author, typewritten notes, in author's possession, Fort Worth, Oct. 15, 1982.

78. Ibid.

79. "Preview of Television Presented by WBAP-TV," *Fort Worth Star-Telegram,* July 21, 1948.

80. Mills, interview.

81. "Robert Gould, Chief Producer," *Fort Worth Press,* Sept. 28, 1948.

82. Gould, interview.

83. "Video Network's Programs in the Kinescope Process," *Fort Worth Star-Telegram,* Sept. 24, 1948.

84. Bacus, interview; "Three High School Grid Games to Be Televised Each Week," *Fort Worth Star-Telegram,* Sept. 17, 1948.

85. List of Texas television applications, *Broadcasting,* Aug. 16, 1948, p. 68.

86. Jack Rogers, "WBAP-TV's Initial Test Pattern," 1948, files of WBAP.

87. Smith (WBAP), interview.

88. Bogan, interview.

89. McGrew, interview.

90. "'Zoomar' Lens Here Is First in Southwest," *Fort Worth Press,* Sept. 28, 1948.

91. Terry, interview.

92. "Boss Ordered and The Texas News was Formed," *Fort Worth Star-Telegram,* undated article, Sept., 1973, Carter Collection; Lillard Hill, interview by author, typewritten notes, in author's possession, Fort Worth, Oct. 15, 1982.

93. "Channel 5's First Pictures Were of President's Visit," *Fort Worth Star-Telegram,* Sept. 15, 1968.

94. Pratt, "Micro Study," p. 67.

95. Bogan, interview.

96. Herman, interview.

97. Smith (WBAP), interview.

98. Mills, interview.

99. Dickey, interview.

100. "Channel 5's First."

101. Bud Sherman, interview by author, typewritten notes, in author's possession, Fort Worth, Nov. 4, 1982.

102. Gould, interview; Martha Grammer, interview by author, typewritten notes, in author's possession, Fort Worth, Feb. 9, 1983; Phil Wygant, interview by author, typewritten notes, in author's possession, Fort Worth, Feb. 2, 1983; Mills, interview; "WBAP-TV's Debut Recalled by Those That Were There," *Fort Worth Star-Telegram,* undated article, Sept., 1960, files of WBAP.

103. Bogan, interview; Smith (WBAP), interview; Phil Wygant, interview.

104. Dorothy Hodges, "Television's Opening Night Was Success, But It Had Its Traditional Bad Moments," *Star-Telegram Junior,* Oct., 1948, p.2.; Mills, interview.

105. Hodges, "Television's Opening."

106. "Talk—By Amon Carter, September 29, 1948, 7:00 P.M. Opening WBAP-TV, The Star-Telegram Station," 1948, Carter Collection.

107. "WBAP-TV's Debut"; "WBAP-TV Routine Sheet," 1948, p. 1, files of WBAP.

108. Smith (WBAP), interview.

109. George Dolan, "Spectators Enthusiastic about First Telecast," *Fort Worth Star-Telegram,* Sept. 30, 1948.

110. Gould, interview.

111. "WBAP-TV's Debut"; McGrew, interview.

112. "Early Days of WBAP-TV Recalled on Anniversary," *Star-Telegram Junior,* Sept. 1960, p. 6; "WBAP-TV's Debut"; Mills, interview.

113. Hill, interview; Sherman, interview; Hill, interview.

114. Bogan, interview.

115. "WBAP-TV's Debut"; Hill, interview; Mills, interview; "WBAP-TV's Debut."

116. "Program Schedule," 1948, files of WBAP.

117. "Early Days Recalled."

118. Mills, interview.

119. "WBAP 'Where the West Begins,'" *Broadcast News,* Sept.–Oct., 1953, pp. 24–25.

120. Bogan, interview.

121. "TV: The Money Rolls Out," *Fortune,* July, 1949, p. 77; Bogan, interview; "Camera Pierces Dye," *Fort Worth Press,* Sept. 28, 1948.

122. "What Strange Creatures! TV Particular on Rouge," *Fort Worth Press,* Sept. 28, 1948.

123. Bogan, interview; Johnny Hay, interview by author, typewritten notes, in author's possession, Fort Worth, Nov. 6, 1982; Bogan, interview; Smith (WBAP), interview; Bogan, interview.

124. Terry, interview.

125. "WBAP-TV Routine Sheet."

126. Bacus, interview.

127. Ibid.; Grammer, interview.

128. Bacus, interview.

129. Russ Thornton, interview by author, typewritten notes, in author's possession, Fort Worth, Sept. 16, 1982; Luther Atkins, interview by author, typewritten notes, in author's possession, Fort Worth, Feb. 1, 1983; Clint Bourland, interview by author, typewritten notes, in author's possession, Fort Worth, Oct. 14, 1982.

130. Gould, interview.

131. Ibid.; Jim Turner, interview by author, typewritten notes, in author's possession, Fort Worth, Oct. 28, 1982.

132. Bacus, interview; Mills, interview; Turner, interview.

133. Bogan, interview.

134. Turner, interview; Naugle, interview.

135. "More Than 20 WBAP-TV Studio Productions Are 'Regular' Now," *Fort Worth Star-Telegram,* Dec. 4, 1949.

136. Sherman, interview.

137. Ibid.

138. Ibid.

139. Gould, interview.

140. Smith (WBAP), interview.

141. Ibid.

142. "WBAP-TV News Coverage Again Receives Recognition," *Fort Worth Star-Telegram,* Dec. 4, 1953.

143. Thornton, interview; Mills, interview.

144. Bourland, interview.

145. Thornton, interview.

146. Hill, interview; Pratt, "Micro Study," p. 80.

147. Byron, interview.

148. Bourland, interview.

149. Thornton, interview.

150. Bourland, interview.

151. Ibid.; Sherman, interview.

152. Burton, interview.

153. "Nation's 'Outstanding' TV News Service Seen Here," *Fort Worth Star-Telegram,* Nov. 14, 1949; "WBAP-TV News Coverage."

154. Harold Taft, interview by author, typewritten notes, in author's possession, Fort Worth, Nov. 12, 1982.

155. Gould, interview.

156. "Complete Weather Station in Studios Helps WBAP-TV Present 'Weather Telefacts,'" undated article, 1953, files of WBAP.

157. Taft, interview.

158. McGrew, interview; Harris, Huhndorff, and McGrew, *Fault,* pp. 6–7; Huhndorff, interview; Harris, Huhndorff, and McGrew, *Fault,* pp. 6–7.

159. Huhndorff, interview.

160. Ibid.

161. Ibid.

162. "Proves No Bed of Roses," undated article, Texas Room, Houston Public Library, Houston; "'T' Day in Houston, Texas," *Turnover,* April, 1947, pp. 46–47.

163. "KLEE-TV Starts Video Service New Year's Day," *Houston Post,* Dec. 12, 1948; "KLEE-TV Is All Set to Go on Air at 6 P.M. Today," *Houston Post,* Jan. 1, 1949.

164. Huhndorff, interview.

165. Harris, Huhndorff, and McGrew, *Fault,* p. 1.

166. "KLEE-TV Starts Video."

167. KLEE-TV Program Schedule, 1949, files of KPRC-TV.

168. Huhndorff, interview.

169. Harris, Huhndorff, and McGrew, *Fault,* pp. 24–25.

170. Huhndorff, interview.

171. Harris, Huhndorff, and McGrew, *Fault,* p. 7.

172. Ibid., pp. 6–7.

173. McGrew, interview.

174. Ibid.

175. Harris, Huhndorff, and McGrew, *Fault,* pp. 7–8.

176. Ibid., pp. 10–11.

177. Ibid., pp. 11, 12–13.

178. Ibid., pp. 15–16.

179. "T-Day Celebration Planned as Television Arrives in City," *San Antonio Express,* Dec. 11, 1949.

180. "First WOAI-TV Programs Climax of Strenuous Effort," *San Antonio Express,* Dec. 11, 1949.

181. "T-Day Celebration."

182. Ibid.

183. "TV Latest of Many 'Firsts' in Career of G. A. C. Halff," *San Antonio Express,* Dec. 11, 1949.

184. Harold Hough, "About Television," Dec. 17, 1947, pp. 1–3, Carter Collection.

185. "Tom Potter Believed Only Man Owning TV Station by Himself," *Dallas Times-Herald,* Sept. 11, 1949.

186. Ted Potter, interview by author, typewritten notes, in author's possession, Belton, Nov. 14, 1994; "Potter Seeking Site for Dallas TV Tower," *Broadcasting,* June 7, 1948, p. 18; "Two Oil Men to Seek Television Studio for Proposed Hotel Here," *Dallas Times-Herald,* Aug. 3, 1947.

187. "KBTV: Television Album," 1949, files of Ted Potter.

188. Potter, interview.

189. "A History of WFAA," undated article from the files of WFAA.

190. "KBTV: Channel 8," 1950, files of Ted Potter.

191. Ibid.; "World's Biggest State Fair Opens at Dallas," *Houston Chronicle,* Oct. 2, 1949.

192. "KBTV: Television Album."

193. McDonald, interview.

194. Potter, interview; "A History of WFAA."

195. "KRLD-TV Opens," *Broadcasting* 37, no. 33 (Dec. 12, 1949), p. 14.

196. Box, interview.

197. Smith (WBAP), interview.

198. "New Texas Video Network Planned," *Broadcasting* 35, no. 10 (Sept. 6, 1948), p. 30.

Chapter 4. The Expansion of Television and the Coming of Color: 1950 to 1960

1. Marshall Lynam, "Fort Worth Gets Live Network TV, WBAP Joins NBC for New York Show," *Fort Worth* Press, July 1, 1952.

2. Pryor, interview.

3. Smith (KFJZ), interview.

4. Barnouw, *Golden Web,* p. 130.

5. Smith, *Perspectives,* pp. 32, 62, 300; and the files of the author.

6. "Texas Imports U.S. TV," *Business Week,* May 10, 1952, pp. 103–105.

7. Lynam, "Fort Worth."

8. "Advent of TV," undated article, Texas Room, Houston Public Library, Houston.

9. Lynam, "Fort Worth"; "Officials of Bell Telephone Explain How Live TV Will Come to Dallas," *Dallas Times-Herald,* April 13, 1952.

10. Harris, Huhndorff, and McGrew, *Fault,* pp. 19–21.

11. Gould, interview.

12. Phil Wygant, interview.

13. Pat Barnett, interview by author, typewritten notes, in author's possession, Fort Worth, Nov. 12, 1982; Mills, interview; Barnett, interview.

14. Mills, interview.

15. Hay, interview.

16. Gordon Green, "A Television Pioneer: KTVE-TV, Channel 32," pp. 2–3.

17. Birdsong, interview.

18. Green, "A Television Pioneer," pp. 3–7.

19. Birdsong, interview.

20. Robert Weathers, interview by author, typewritten notes, in author's possession, Waco, Sept. 30, 1994.

21. Holliday, interview.

22. Personal recollections of the author.

23. Wilson, interview.

24. Weathers, interview.

25. Ibid.

26. Thomas Turner, "TV Viewers to See Waco Murder Trial," *Dallas Morning News,*
Dec. 6, 1955.

27. "Death Victim's Mate Called in Televised Trial," *Los Angeles Times,* Dec. 7, 1955.

28. "KWTX-TV Covers Murder Trial Live, Sets Precedent in Courtroom Access," *Broad-casting,* Dec. 12, 1955, p. 79.

29. Bender, interview.

30. Ibid.

31. Haley, *A Texan Looks at Lyndon,* pp. 62–65.

32. Naugle, interview.

33. Mayes, interview.

34. Pryor, interview.

35. Ibid.

36. From the files of the author; Pryor, interview.

37. "Television Digest," Dec. 1, 1951, p. 2, Texas Room, Houston Public Library, Houston, Texas.

38. "Hispanic-Oriented Television," *San Antonio Express News,* Sept. 18, 1995.

39. "Four TV Stations Now Serve Alamo City," *San Antonio Light,* Jan. 20, 1957.

40. Ing, interview.

41. "Four TV Stations."

42. McGrew, interview.

43. "KUHT Leads Field in U.S." *Houston Post,* March 29, 1953.

44. "Radio & Television," *Time,* June 22, 1953, p. 66; "TV Can Be Educational, Too," *Life,*
April 20, 1953, p. 34.

45. Norman Baxter, "Houston Gets Two Ultra High TV Stations," *Houston Chronicle,*
Jan. 8, 1953.

46. "KNUZ-TV to Make its Program Debut on Channel 39 Thursday," undated article,
Texas Room, Houston Public Library, Houston.

47. "KXYZ Quits Race For Television Channel 13," undated article, Texas Room.

48. "Third TV Channel 10 Application Is Filed," *Fort Worth Star-Telegram,* Dec. 6, 1952;
"Television Allocations," 1951, Carter Collection.

49. "Municipal Television Planned to Bring Government to People," *Dallas Morning News,* undated article, Texas/Dallas History and Archives Division, Dallas Public Library, Dallas, Texas; "City Rejects Proposal to Operate TV," *Dallas Morning News,*
Dec. 10, 1952.

50. Teddlie, interview.

51. Smith (KFJZ), interview.

52. Naugle, interview.

53. Ibid.

54. "New Television Station to be Discussed by Board," *Fort Worth Star-Telegram,* 1954,
undated article, Carter Collection.

55. Naugle, interview.

56. "Reactions Have Been Mixed," *Fort Worth Star-Telegram,* undated article, files of
WBAP; "The Most Spectacular," *Fort Worth Star-Telegram,* 1953, undated, files of WBAP.

57. Bogan, interview.

58. Harris, Huhndorff, and McGrew, *Fault,* pp. 36–37.

59. Barnett, interview; Smith (WBAP), interview; Barnett, interview.

60. Gould, interview.

61. Jack Douglas, "Gen. Sarnoff to Help Pull Switch Today on Texas' First Live Color TV Show," *Fort Worth Star-Telegram,* May 15, 1954; "Huntley-Brinkley," *Fort Worth Star-Telegram,* p. 2, undated article, 1966, files of WBAP.

62. "Carter Publications Inc.," 1946, Carter Collection; "Color Television: 1941–1953," *Broadcasting* 45, no. 25 (Dec. 21, 1953), p. 31.

63. "Thirst for Color," undated article, files of WBAP.

64. "First Local Color Saturday," *TV Preview,* May 15, 1954; Herman, interview.

65. Smith (WBAP), interview.

66. Wygant, interview; "WBAP 1st to Receive Color in State," *Fort Worth Star-Telegram,* undated article, 1954, files of WBAP; Ira Cain, "First Color Telecast on WBAP-TV," *Fort Worth Star-Telegram,* undated article, 1954, files of WBAP; Harris, Huhndorff and McGrew, *Fault,* p. 29.

67. Bacus, interview.

68. Gould, interview.

69. Turner, interview.

70. Bogan, interview; "WBAP-TV's Experience with Live Color," *Broadcast News,* Dec., 1954, pp. 34–49.

71. Barnett, interview.

72. Smith (WBAP), interview; Wygant, interview.

73. Smith (WBAP), interview; Bogan, interview; Gould, interview; Barnett, interview.

74. Huhndorff, interview.

75. Bogan, interview.

76. Gould, interview.

77. Grammer, interview.

78. Ira Cain, "Gen. Sarnoff RCA Head to Turn on Live Color TV," *Fort Worth Star-Telegram,* May 9, 1954.

79. Mills, interview.

80. Jack Douglas, "WBAP-TV Originates First Texas Colorcast," *Fort Worth Star-Telegram,* May 16, 1954.

81. Barnett, interview.

82. Bobbie Wygant, interview by author, typewritten notes, in author's possession, Fort Worth, Feb. 2, 1983.

83. Gould, interview.

84. "First Local Color Saturday."

85. Gould, interview; Barnett, interview; Gould, interview.

86. "Station Report," *Color TV News,* 1955, files of WBAP; "Total Hours of Local Color," June, 1964, files of WBAP; "25 Years of Leadership, WBAP-TV 1948–1973," *Telescene,* Fall, 1973, pp. 6–7.

87. Gould, interview.

88. Smith (WBAP), interview.

89. McGrew, interview.

90. Curly Broyles, interview with author, Fort Worth, Nov. 17, 1994.

91. "NBC Names WBAP-TV Affiliate," *Fort Worth Star-Telegram,* July 10, 1957; Pratt, "Micro Study," p. 104.

Bibliography

Interviews

Atkins, Luther. Fort Worth, February 1, 1983.

Bacus, Roy. Fort Worth, Sept. 2, 1982.

Barger, John. San Antonio, October 3, 1994.

Barnett, Pat. Fort Worth, November 12, 1982.

Bell, Jack. Center, June 28, 1994.

Bender, Ted. El Paso, March 29, 1997.

Birdsong, Lawrence. Longview, February 19, 1996.

Bogan, Rupert. Pottsboro, February 16, 1983.

Bourland, Clint. Fort Worth, October 14, 1982.

Box, Ves. Dallas, May 4, 1994.

Bradford, Bill. Sulphur Springs, February 21, 1994.

Brown, Bev E. Carthage, June 6, 1994.

Broyles, Curly. Fort Worth, November 17, 1994.

Bruyere, Clarence. Dallas, February 28, 1995.

Burton, Alex. Dallas, February 19, 1994.

Byron, Jim. Fort Worth, July, 1974.

Campbell, Martin. Dallas, July, 1974.

Cruse, J. R. Aledo, June 22, 1994.

Cullum, A. Earl. Dallas, July, 1974.

Curtis, J. R. (Jr.) Longview, June 23, 1994.

Dickey, Roger. Grand Prairie, May 5, 1994.

Francione, Joyce. El Paso, March 29, 1997.

Goode, Claude. Greenville, May 16, 1994.

Gould, Robert. Fort Worth, September 16, 1982.

Grammer, Martha. Fort Worth, February 9, 1983.

Hackney, Leo. Greenville, June 9, 1994.

Hay, Johnny. Fort Worth, November 6, 1982.

Herman, Abe. Fort Worth, July, 1974.

———. Fort Worth, September 14, 1982.

Hicks, Bob. Midland, March 28, 1997.

Hill, Lillard. Fort Worth, October 15, 1982.

Holliday, Jack. Farmers Branch, May 3, 1994.

Huhndorff, Paul. Houston, September 9, 1994.

Ing, George. San Antonio, October 5, 1994.

Jeffus, Weldon K. Dallas, February 22, 1995.

Lowe, Jim. Dallas, August 3, 1994.

Marti, George. Cleburne, May 26, 1994.

Mayes, Wendell. Austin, October 4, 1994.

McDonald, Earl. Dallas, July 28, 1995.

McGrew, Jack. Houston, July, 1974.

——. Marble Falls, October 1, 1994.

McKenzie, Stan. Seguin, November 15, 1994.

Melville, Clyde. Dallas, July, 1974.

Mills, Frank. Fort Worth, October 30, 1982.

——. Fort Worth, April 29, 1994.

Montgomery, Marvin. Dallas, August 16, 1994.

Morris, Dave. Houston, September 7, 1994.

Mundine, Hoxie. San Antonio, October 5, 1994.

Naugle, Dave. Fort Worth, June 7, 1994.

Parrish, Frank. Fort Worth, April 29, 1994.

Potter, Ted. Belton, November 14, 1994.

Pryor, Richard. Austin, October 4, 1994.

Ratcliffe, Morrell. Dallas, July, 1974.

Rembert, Clyde. Dallas, July, 1974.

Roth, Eugene J. San Antonio, October 3, 1994.

Ryan, Bill. Richardson, July 1, 1994.

Sherman, Bud. Fort Worth, November 4, 1982.

Smith, Johnny (KFJZ). Fort Worth, July 6, 1994.

Smith, Johnny (WBAP). Fort Worth, October 15, 1982.

Sparks, Winston. Fort Worth, December 23, 1996.

Taft, Harold. Fort Worth, November 12, 1982.

Teddlie, Pete. Dallas, September 21, 1994.

Terry, Chem. Fort Worth, May 25, 1994.

Thornton, Russ. Fort Worth, September 16, 1982.

Turner, Jim. Fort Worth, October 28, 1982.

Waller, Dudley. Jacksonville, May 17, 1994.

Weathers, Robert. Waco, September 30, 1994.

Wilson, Stan. Fort Worth, July, 1974.

——. Fort Worth, July 6, 1994.

Wise, Wes. Arlington, March 2, 1994.

Wombolt, Helen. Dallas, July, 1974.

Woodward, Guy. Fort Worth, October 21, 1982.

Wygant, Bobbie. Fort Worth, February 2, 1983.

Wygant, Phil. Fort Worth, February 2, 1983.

Yates, Darrell. Lufkin, September 6, 1994.

Archival Materials and Collections

A. H. Belo Corporation Company History and Archives, Dallas.

Carter Collection, Amon Carter Museum, Fort Worth.

Fohn, Horace J. Letter to author, November 8, 1993.

Green, Gordon. "A Television Pioneer: KTVE-TV, Channel 32." Station history sent to author, 1988.

Ing, George. Files.

Interstate Collection, Texas/Dallas History and Archives Division, Dallas Public Library, Dallas.

KPRC-TV files, Houston.

KTSM files, El Paso.

Layland Museum, Cleburne, Texas.

Louise Kelly Collection, Wichita County Archives, Wichita Falls, Texas.

Mayes, Wendell. Files.

McGrew, Jack. Files.

Pan Handle Museum, Canyon, Texas.

Potter, Ted. Files.

Prestidge, (Mrs.) W. C. Letter to author, July 12, 1993.

Romey, Jack. Letter to author, October 25, 1993.

Southwest Collection, Texas Tech University, Lubbock, Texas.

Special Collections Division, University of Texas at Arlington Libraries, Arlington, Texas.

Special Collections, Manuscripts & Archives, Sterling C. Evans Library, Texas A&M University, College Station.

Special Collections, Sam Rayburn Library, Texas A&M University at Commerce.

Teddlie, Pete. Files.

Texas Room, Houston Public Library, Houston.

Texas/Dallas History and Archives Division, Dallas Public Library, Dallas.

Tyrrell Historical Society Library, Beaumont, Texas.

WBAP files at KXAS-TV, Fort Worth.

Weathers, Robert. Files.

WFAA files, Dallas.

Woodward, Guy. Files.

WRR Collection, Center for American History, University of Texas, Austin, Texas.

Books and Articles

"2 Radio Stations Will Exchange Frequencies." *Fort Worth Star-Telegram,* June 20, 1935.

"11 FM Grants." *Broadcasting* 34, no. 20 (May 17, 1948): 51.

"15 Sponsors Signed by Texas Quality." *Broadcasting* 9, no. 7 (October 1, 1935): 18.

"25 Years of Leadership, WBAP-TV 1948–1973." *Telescene,* Fall, 1973.

"A&M 'Hams' Were First To Air Gridiron Battle." *Texas Aggie,* December 22, 1950.

"All 31 Texas Stations Carry Roosevelt's Word to Texans." *Fort Worth Star-Telegram,* July 11, 1938.

Angel, Albert Dean. "'For What It's Worth—Nothing': Study of the Texas State Network." Masters thesis, East Texas State University, 1970.

"Baptist FM." *Broadcasting* 35, no. 24 (December 13, 1948): 70.

"Baptists Plan FM Network in Texas." *Broadcasting* 34, no. 4 (January 26, 1948): 76.

Barnouw, Erik. *The Golden Web,* New York: Oxford University Press, 1968.

———. *A Tower in Babel.* New York: Oxford University Press, 1966.

Baudine, Joseph E., and John M. Kittross. "Broadcasting's Oldest Stations: An Examination of Four Claimants." *Journal of Broadcasting* 21, no. 1 (Winter, 1977): 61–83.

Baxter, Norman. "Houston Gets Two Ultra High TV Stations." *Houston Chronicle,* January 8, 1953.

"Brewster's Baird Television Demonstration." *Old Timer's Bulletin* 27, no. 2 (August, 1986): 8.

Brooks, Elston. "Heart Attack Claims Yodeling Country Boy." *Fort Worth Star-Telegram,* March 29, 1978.

———. "Radio's 'Yodeling Country Boy' Tries Gospel Route for Comeback." *Fort Worth Star-Telegram,* September 1, 1971.

Bumpass, Gita. "Radio Folks Getting Slickered Up for Those Television Commercials." *Fort Worth Star-Telegram,* September 12, 1948.

———. "Trail Blazing Television Event from WBAP-TV Reaches 160 Miles." *Fort Worth Star-Telegram,* September 30, 1948.

Cain, Ira. "Gen. Sarnoff RCA Head to Turn on Live Color TV." *Fort Worth Star-Telegram,* May 9, 1954.

———. "WBAP's 30th Anniversary Birthday Causes Radio, TV Director to Look Back, Chuckle." *Fort Worth Star-Telegram,* May 4, 1952.

"Camera Pierces Dye." *Fort Worth Press,* September 28, 1948.

"Campaign Network Formed In Texas." *Broadcasting* 15, no. 6 (March 15, 1938): 20.

"Channel 5's First Pictures Were of President's Visit." *Fort Worth Star-Telegram,* September 15, 1968.

"City Rejects Proposal to Operate TV." *Dallas Morning News,* December 10, 1952.

"City's First Radio Founded in 1926." *Wichita Daily Times,* September 9, 1928.

"Collegiate System." *Broadcasting* 38, no. 16 (1950): 48.

"Collins-Baylor U. Get 50 kw. Station." *Broadcasting* 24 (July 19, 1943):14.

"Color Television: 1941–1953." *Broadcasting* 45, no. 25 (December 21, 1953): 31.

"Concealed Control Cited in Revoking 6 Texas Stations." *Broadcasting* 18, no. 4 (February 15, 1940): 12.

"Daily News Radio Program Is Given from WDAG Station." *Amarillo Daily News,* June 1, 1923.

"Dallas News Applies For Television Permit." *Fort Worth Star-Telegram,* December 17, 1947.

"Death Victim's Mate Called in Televised Trial." *Los Angeles Times,* December 7, 1955.

Department of Commerce, Bureau of Navigation. *Radio Report.* Washington: U.S. GPO, for the years 1916 and 1919–27.

Dolan, George. "Spectators Enthusiastic about First Telecast." *Fort Worth Star-Telegram,* September 30, 1948.

Douglas, Jack. "Gen. Sarnoff to Help Pull Switch Today on Texas' First Live Color TV Show." *Fort Worth Star-Telegram,* May 15, 1954.

———. "WBAP-TV Originates First Texas Colorcast." *Fort Worth Star-Telegram,* May 16, 1954.

"Dr Pepper Begins Its Fourth Season." *Broadcasting* 15, no. 6 (March 15, 1938): 20.

"Dr Pepper Soft-Drink Series On TQN Spread to 17 Stations." *Broadcasting* 10, no. 7 (April 1, 1936): 16.

"Early Days of WBAP-TV Recalled on Anniversary." *Star-Telegram Junior,* September, 1960.

"El Paso FM Growing." *El Paso Today,* August 1, 1962.

Elliott, Carolyn. "Movies Took Time Out for 'Amos 'n' Andy.'" *San Antonio Light,* June 25, 1978.

Elson, Jay. "How it all Began." *Austin,* December, 1956, p. 4–5.

"Enlarged Southwest Net Issues 1935 Rate Card." *Broadcasting* 8, no. 3 (February 1, 1935): 39.

"FCC Feud Arises in Texas Rulings." *Broadcasting* 19, no. 6 (September 15, 1940):24.

"FCC Recesses Revocation Hearings of Texas Station to Perfect Its Cast." *Broadcasting* 18, no. 6 (March 15, 1940).

Federal Radio Commission. *Annual Report of the Federal Radio Commission,* Washington, D.C.: U.S. GPO, 1928, 1929.

———. *Radio Broadcast Stations in the U.S.* Washington DC: GPO, 1934.

"First Local Color Saturday." *TV Preview,* May 15, 1954.

"First Radio Station Here Was WCAK." *Houston Press,* May 9, 1961.

"First WOAI-TV Programs Climax of Strenuous Effort." *San Antonio Express,* December 11, 1949.

Flemmons, Jerry. *AMON: The Life of Amon Carter, Sr. of Texas.* Austin: Jenkins Publishing Company, 1978.

"Four TV Stations Now Serve Alamo City." *San Antonio Light,* January 20, 1957.

Fowler, Gene, and Bill Crawford. *Border Radio.* Austin: Texas Monthly Press, 1987.

Frazer, Mary. "A Life in Radio by a Gypsy Fortune Teller." *Houston Press,* January 13, 1948.

"Frequencies of 2 Stations Here Will Be Changed." *Fort Worth Star-Telegram,* September 18, 1940.

"From Small Beginnings . . ." *Houston Post,* March 21, 1972.

Furnas, J. C. "The Border Radio Mess." *Saturday Evening Post,* September 25, 1948, pp. 25, 168, 169, 170.

———. "Country Doctor Goes to Town." *Saturday Evening Post,* April 20, 1940, pp. 12, 13, 44, 46, 48, 49, 50.

Glick, Edwin L. "The Life and Death of the Liberty Broadcasting System." *Journal of Broadcasting* 23, no. 2 (Spring, 1979): 117–35.

———. "WBAP/WFAA—570/820: Till Money Did Them Part." *Journal of Broadcasting* 21, no. 4 (Fall, 1977): 473–86.

Gordon, Jack. "First Television Shown Here 14 Years Ago." *Fort Worth Press,* September 10, 1948.

Haley, J. Evetts. *A Texan Looks at Lyndon: A Study in Illegitimate Power.* Canyon, Texas: Palo Duro Press, 1964.

Halpern, Robert. "KVOF Broadcasts Voice of Freedom." *Prospector,* September 2, 1980.

"Ham Radio Operator Brought First Football, Weather Reports," *Waco Times-Herald,* March 25, 1960.

Harper, Jim. "Gordon McLendon: Pioneer Baseball Broadcaster." *Baseball History,* Spring, 1986, pp. 42–51.

Harris, Jack, Paul Huhndorff, and Jack McGrew. *The Fault Does Not Lie with Your Set.* Austin: Eakin Press, 1989.

Harrison, W. Walworth. *History of Greenville and Hunt County, Texas.* Waco: Texian Press, 1976.

"'Heard in Poly'—That Was News!" *Fort Worth,* February, 1947, pp. 14, 40..

"Hispanic-Oriented Television." *San Antonio Express-News,* September 18, 1995.

"Historic Television." *Old Timer's Bulletin* 26, no. 3 (December, 1985): 32.

"History Scene in TV Screen." *Houston,* January, 1956.

Hodges, Dorothy. "Television's Opening Night Was Success, But It Had Its Traditional Bad Moments." *Star-Telegram Junior,* October, 1948.

"Humble Oil Sponsoring Football in Southwest." *Broadcasting* 9, no. 7 (October. 1, 1935): 26.

"In 30 Years, from Crystal Sets to True 'Window on World.'" *Houston Post*, January 30, 1955.

"In the Air with KFDM During the Past Magpetco Year." *Magpetco*, April, 1928.

"'Karl the Kowhand' Looks Back on Crystal Set Start of Radio in E. P. 31 Years Ago." *El Paso Herald-Post*, August 22, 1952.

"KFDM Stages Birthday Party." *Magpetco*, October, 1925.

"KFDM's First Program 'A Winner.'" *Magpetco*, October, 1924.

"KFJZ Grew Big From War I Baby." *Fort Worth*, February, 1947.

"KFJZ Purchase Is Authorized." *Fort Worth Star-Telegram*, April 15, 1938.

"KGUL-TV: Channel 11." *Houston Post*, March 29, 1953.

"KLEE-TV Is All Set To Go On Air At 6 P.M. Today." *Houston Post*, January 1, 1949.

"KLEE-TV Starts Video Service New Year's Day." *Houston Post*, December 12, 1948.

"KLEE-TV Will Become KPRC-TV at 8 P.M. Monday." *Houston Post*, July 2, 1950.

"KRLD-TV Opens." *Broadcasting* 37, no. 33 (December 12, 1949): 14.

"KTSM Formally Goes on Ether," *El Paso Herald*, August 23, 1929.

"KUHT Leads Field in U.S." *Houston Post*, March 29, 1953.

"KVET Founders Recalled." *Austin American-Statesman*, October 1, 1966.

"KWTX-TV Covers Murder Trial Live, Sets Precedent in Courtroom Access." *Broadcasting* (December 12, 1955): 79.

Lee, Anne. "Women in Radio Field Do Fine Job." *Fort Worth Star-Telegram*, October 3, 1943.

List of Networks, *Broadcasting* 35, no. 3 (1949 yearbook): 319–20.

List of Texas Television Applications. *Broadcasting* 27, no. 7 (August 16, 1948): 27.

Lucchese, Cosimo. "Watt's Becoming of Us?" *Listen*, December, 1978, pp. 8–9.

Lynam, Marshall. "Fort Worth Gets Live Network TV, WBAP Joins NBC for New York Show." *Fort Worth Press*, July 1, 1952.

"McLendon." *Dallas Times-Herald*, September 15, 1986.

"Messages Can Be Heard from Atlantic to Pacific Starting at 10:30 This Morning." *San Antonio Express*, September 24, 1922.

Mimms, Molly B., ed. *The History of Johnson County, Texas*. Dallas: Curtis Media Corp., 1985. Layland Museum, Cleburne, Texas.

"More Than 20 WBAP-TV Studio Productions Are 'Regular' Now." *Fort Worth Star-Telegram*, December 4, 1949.

"Nation's 'Outstanding' TV News Service Seen Here." *Fort Worth Star-Telegram*, November 14, 1949.

"NBC Names WBAP-TV Affiliate." *Fort Worth Star-Telegram*, July 10, 1957.

"New Texas Network." *Broadcasting* 17, no. 1 (July 1, 1939): 84.

"New Texas Video Network Planned." *Broadcasting* 35, no. 10 (September 6, 1948): 30.

"News to 'Print' Paper by Radio." *Fort Worth Star-Telegram*, July 27, 1939.

"The Noncommercial First." *Time*, June 22, 1953, p. 66.

"Norris Turned to Radio to Spread Religion Afar." *Fort Worth Star-Telegram*, October 30, 1949.

"Officials of Bell Telephone Explain How Live TV Will Come to Dallas." *Dallas Times-Herald*, April 13, 1952.

"On the Air with KFDM." *Magpetco,* October, 1927.

Overton, Loretta. "Radio Executive Recalls Early Years." *El Paso Herald-Post,* August 21, 1964.

Patoski, Joe Nick. "Rock 'N' Roll's Wizard of Oz." *Texas Monthly,* February, 1980, p. 101.

Pegler, Westbrook. "It Seems to Me." *Fort Worth Press,* January 3, 1946.

"Permit Given for Television Station Here." *Fort Worth Star-Telegram.* June 22, 1946.

Phelan, John. "Tribute to Karl Otto Wyler." *Password,* Spring, 1987, pp. 19–23.

Pickerell, Donna. "A Long Love Affair." *Houston Radio and Television,* May 25, 1969.

Pink, Jack L. "Radio That Caught S. A. by the Ear." *San Antonio Express-News,* May 31, 1987.

"Pioneer Broadcast Recalls Career." *Lubbock Avalanche Journal,* March 3, 1984.

"Pioneering Efforts of Times Herald Brought First TV Station to Dallas." *Daily Times-Herald* (Dallas), April 13, 1952.

"Plans for a 43-Station FM Network in Texas Given at Austin Radio Forum." *Broadcasting* 31, no. 9 (September 2, 1946).

"Post's Daily Radio Concerts Win Praise from Many Stations." *Houston Post-Dispatch,* May 20, 1922.

"Potter Seeking Site for Dallas TV Tower," *Broadcasting,* June 7, 1948, p. 18.

"Powerful Radio Station Is Plan." *Amarillo Daily News,* September 17, 1926.

Pratt, James David. "A Micro Study of Television News at the Local Level: Television Station, WBAP-TV, Fort Worth-Dallas; Television News Director, James A. Byron; Television Newscast, 'The Texas News'; Each a First in Texas." Ph.D. diss., University of Texas at Austin, 1981.

"Preview of Television Presented by WBAP-TV." *Fort Worth Star-Telegram,* July 2, 1948.

"Program Broadcast by Magnolia Band March 1st Was Very Successful." *Magpetco,* March, 1924.

Quinn, Liz. "San Antonio's Oldest Station Remains Unique." *Trinitonian,* February 1, 1985.

"Radio & Television." *Time,* June 22, 1953.

"Radio's Birth 100 Years Ago." *Fort Worth Star-Telegram,* October 30, 1949.

"Remember KFQB—It Was a Forerunner of KFJZ." *Fort Worth,* February, 1947, p. 22.

"Report of the Federal Radio Commission." U.S. GPO, 1928.

Resler, Ansel Harlan. "The Impact of John R. Brinkley on Broadcasting in the U.S." Ph.D. diss., Northwestern University, 1958.

"Revised Schedule For Broadcasting." *San Antonio Express,* September 24, 1922.

Richart, C. L. "Television's First Program Makes Fort Worth History." *Fort Worth Star-Telegram,* September 30, 1948.

"Robert Gould Chief Producer." *Fort Worth Press,* September 28, 1948.

Sacks, Robin Lestie. "A History of Station WRR: Pioneer in Municipally Owned Radio." Master's thesis, North Texas State University, 1978.

Schroeder, Morton Richard. "A History of WBAP—The First Ten Years." Ed.D. diss., East Texas State University, 1983.

Sivowitch, Elliot N. "A Technological Survey of Broadcasting's 'Pre-History,' 1876–1920." *Journal of Broadcasting* 15, no. 1 (Winter, 1970–71): 1–20.

Smith, F. Leslie. *Perspectives on Radio and Television.* New York: Harper & Row, 1985.

"Southwest Ford Dealers Use 3-Station Hookup in New Radio Campaign." *Broadcasting* 5, no. 6 (September 15, 1933): 13.

"Southwest Network Appoints Chilton." *Broadcasting* 5, no. 6 (September 15, 1933): 8.

"Southwest's First Television Station, W5AGO, Goes on Air." *Fort Worth Star-Telegram,* March 10, 1934.

Spencer, John Morgan. "An Intensive History of Broadcasting Station KBGO, Waco, Texas." Master's thesis, Michigan State University, 1974.

Stag, Julian. "The Dallas/Fort Worth Radio Market." *Broadcasting* 34 (June 7, 1948): 3–19.

"Station to Have Large Variety of Transcriptions For KPLT Programs." *Paris News,* December 13, 1936.

"T-Day Celebration Planned as Television Arrives in City." *San Antonio Express,* December 11, 1949.

"'T' Day in Houston, Texas." *Turnover,* April, 1947.

Tatum, Henry. "Growing Up with Big KLIF." *Dallas Morning News,* May 13, 1984.

"Television Withdrawals At 57; Dropouts Cancel Hearings." *Broadcasting,* May 13, 1946, p. 93.

"Texas Account Extended." *Broadcasting* 6, no. 2 (January 15, 1934): 12.

"Texas Imports U.S. TV." *Business Week,* May 10, 1952, p. 103–105.

"Texas Net Formed." *Broadcasting* 7, no. 6 (September 15, 1934): 58.

"Texas Talent Train to Make TV History." *Houston Post,* March 29, 1953.

"Third TV Channel 10 Application Is Filed." *Fort Worth Star-Telegram,* December 6, 1952.

"Three High School Grid Games to Be Televised Each Week." *Fort Worth Star-Telegram,* September 17, 1948.

"Times Radio Station Purposes and Plans Outlined in Dedicatory Event." *Wichita (Falls, Texas) Daily Times,* December 22, 1946.

"Tom Potter Believed Only Man Owning TV Station by Himself." *Dallas Times-Herald,* September 11, 1949.

Townsend, Charles. *San Antonio Rose.* Urbana: University of Illinois Press, 1976.

Turner, Thomas. "TV Viewers to See Waco Murder Trial." *Dallas Morning News,* December 6, 1955.

"TV Can Be Educational, Too." *Life,* April 20, 1953, p. 34.

"TV Latest of Many 'Firsts' in Career of G. A. C. Halff." *San Antonio Express,* December 11, 1949.

"TV: The Money Rolls Out." *Fortune,* July, 1949, p. 77.

"Two More Texas Deletions Advised." *Broadcasting* 18, no. 12 (June 15, 1940): 82.

"Two Oil Men to Seek Television Studio for Proposed Hotel Here." *Dallas Times-Herald,* August 3, 1947.

"UT Radiocasts Started in 1921." *Daily Texan,* November 9, 1958.

"Video Network's Programs in the Kinescope Process." *Fort Worth Star-Telegram,* September 24, 1948.

"WBAP 'Where the West Begins'" *Broadcast News,* September–October 1953, pp. 18–26.

"WBAP's Frances Helm Has Wide National Experience." *Fort Worth,* February, 1947, p. 18.

"WBAP-TV Celebrates 25th Year." *Dallas Morning News,* September 30, 1973.

"WBAP-TV Debut." *Broadcasting* 35, no. 13 (September 27, 1948): 54.

"WBAP-TV News Coverage Again Receives Recognition." *Fort Worth Star-Telegram,* December 4, 1953.

"WBAP-TV's Experience with Live Color." *Broadcast News,* December, 1954, pp. 34–39.

"WBAP . . . Been Broadcasting Forever." *Fort Worth,* February, 1947, 18–44.

"WDAG Station Becomes New Organization." *Amarillo Daily News,* January 29, 1928.

"We Pay Our Respects to—Karl Otto Wyler." *Broadcasting* (January 1, 1941).

"'We'll Spend But $300' and WBAP Was Begun; Hoover Named Station." *Fort Worth Star-Telegram,* October 30, 1949.

Westheimer, David. "First Performer Tells of Initial Broadcast." *Houston Post,* February 21, 1955.

"WFAA Recollects Numerous 'Firsts.'" *Fort Worth Star-Telegram,* May 21, 1950.

"What Strange Creatures! TV Particular on Rouge." *Fort Worth Press,* September 28, 1948.

Winship, Michael. *Television.* New York: Random House, 1988.

"Wireless Wedding Is Performed by Aid of 3 Stations." *Dallas Morning News and Journal,* January 29, 1922.

Wood, Clement. *The Life of a Man.* Kansas City: Goshorn Publishing Company, 1934.

"Word was Received . . ." *Daily Texan,* March 28, 1922.

"World's Biggest State Fair Opens at Dallas." *Houston Chronicle,* October 2, 1949.

"Write a Radiogram, Win a Prize." *Houston Post-Dispatch,* May 9, 1926.

"WRR and WFAA Consolidate under WFAA Management by Order of the City Commission," *Dallas Morning News,* November 21, 1928.

Wuntch, Philip. "Wilshire Rings Down Curtain on Final Movie." *Dallas Morning News,* April 24, 1978.

Wyler, Karl. "KTSM Gossip." *El Paso Herald,* November 30, 1929.

Yanczer, Peter. "Radiomovies." *Old Timer's Bulletin* 28, no. 2 (August, 1987): 8–11.

"'Zoomar' Lens Here Is First in Southwest." *Fort Worth Press,* September 28, 1948.

Index

Note: Pages with illustrations are indicated by italics.